To Gene,

Filer's Files:

Worldwide Reports of UFO Sightings.

By
Major George A. Filer III, US Air Force (ret.)
And
David E. Twichell

Best Wishes

George Filer

Watch the skies!

Copyright © 2005 by George A. Filer III &
David E. Twichell

ISBN 0-7414-2812-1

Published by:

INFIN)ITY
PUBLISHING.COM

1094 New DeHaven Street, Suite 100
West Conshohocken, PA 19428-2713
Info@buybooksontheweb.com
www.buybooksontheweb.com
Toll-free (877) BUY BOOK
Local Phone (610) 941-9999
Fax (610) 941-9959

Printed in the United States of America

Printed on Recycled Paper

Published October 2005

Table of Contents

Acknowledgments

Introduction: By Maj. George Filer   i

Chapter 1: U.S. Daylight Disks   1

Chapter 2: U.S. Nocturnal Disks   19

Chapter 3: Worldwide Daylight Disks   33

Chapter 4: Worldwide Nocturnal Disks   41

Chapter 5: Daylight Triangular-Shaped UFOs   55

Chapter 6: U.S. Nocturnal Triangular-Shaped UFOs   69

Chapter 7: Worldwide Nocturnal Triangular-Shaped UFOs   105

Chapter 8: Cigar-Shaped UFOs   117

Chapter 9: Anomalous Lights   135

Chapter 10: Abductions and Missing Time   149

Chapter 11: U.S. Astronauts and Presidents   167

Chapter 12: UFOs in the News   181

Afterward: By, David E. Twichell   199

Index   203

Acknowledgments

We would like to extend our appreciation to those brave individuals who contributed to this book by reporting their anomalous experiences despite the adversity associated with this controversial subject. Even if they preferred to remain anonymous, the fact that they have come forward has provided immeasurable assistance in helping to solve the riddle that has confounded mankind since the mid 1940s.

Special thanks to Cmdr. Graham Bethune, US Navy (ret.) for the cover art of this book. It is a photograph of an alleged actual UFO taken in Nashville, Tennessee in 1989.

We would also like to thank the following investigators for their contribution to this project and their untiring efforts in the field of UFOlogy:

Linda Moulton Howe: Earthfiles.com, http://www.earthfiles.com
Brian Vike: HBCC UFO Research, http://www.hbccufo.org/index.php
Kim Shaffer: ASD/MUFON, Tennessee, http://www.mufontennessee.org
Tom Ginther: MUFON, Virginia.
John F. Schuessler, MS: MUFON International Director, http://www.mufon.com/
Tom Sheets: ISUR Board, State Director-MUFON, Georgia, http://www.mufonga.org/
Joseph Trainor: UFO Roundup, http://ufoinfo.com/roundup/
Ike Bishop: State Director, MUFON, Idaho.
Roger Sugden: ASD/CFI MUFON, Indiana.
Larry Clark: N.Y. MUFON, www.nymufon.org
Patrick Huyghe: Author of Swamp Gas Times.
Lynn Taylor: AAARC, www.sentinelfiles.com
Jim Hickman: Skywatch International Inc., http://www.skywatch-international.org/
Jeff Rense: http://www.rense.com/
SAUFOR: (South Africa's UFO Resource) http://www.geocities.com/saufor/
Anton A. Anfalov: Ukrainian UFO Research Association (UKUFAS) an@crimea.com
William Chavez: Contacto OVNI Translation (C) 2001. www.epagos.com/contacto-ovni
J-UFO magazine: www.our-j.com
Jerry Farshores: www.100megsfree4.com/farshores/

Steve Walters: AUSTRALIA UFO RESEARCH (NSW), uforesearch@ufor.asn.au

Andrew Griffin: LA MUFON. awg_paperboy@hotmail.com

UFO Wisconsin: http://ufowisconsin.com/

Mark A. Olson: http://www.sonorasightings.com/

Conway Costigan.

Whitley Strieber: http://www.unknowncountry.com/

Barry Taylor: http://home.manyrivers.aunz.com/sting1946/index.htm

Bill Hamilton: Executive Director Skywatch International Inc.

Beverly Trout: State Director, Iowa MUFON.

Jim Aho: W-Files, http://www.w-files.com

Bonnie Meyer: The Lightside, http://www.thelightside.org/

John Novak: webmaster@cazekiel.org

Dave Rosenfeld: http://www.aliendave.com

David Brown: SSD Georgia MUFON.

Cliff Mickelson: http://www.surfingtheapocalypse.com.

Mel Podell: San Diego MUFON.

Vadim Deruzhinsky: Editor-in-Chief of the Secret Researches Analytic Journal.

Toine Trust: UFO Plaza, //www.ufoplaza.nl/

James Allen Tutt Jr.: MUFON Field Investigator.

Scott Corrales: Institute of Hispanic UFOlogy.

Dr. Annamarie Johnstone: Author of "UFO Defense Tactics".

John and Jenny Hoppe: Wisconsin's UFO Reporting Center, http://www.ufowisconsin.com/

Ray Klopchin: New York MUFON. www.nymufon.org

George W. Ritter: Fostoria, Ohio.

Jaime Maussan: Mexican UFOlogist.

Dr. Bruce Maccabee: http://brumac.8k.com/

Stephen Bassett: http://www.paradigmclock.com/

Bill Konkolesky: State Director, Michigan MUFON, http://mimufon.org/

Graham W. Birdsall: Editor of UFO Magazine [UK] http://www.ufomag.co.uk/

Anton Anfalav: Research Specialist for MUFON.

Marilyn Ruben: Alien Abduction Experience and Research. http://www.abduct.com/ritter/ritter.php

W. C. Levengood: Pinelandia Biophysics Laboratory, Grass Lake, Michigan.

Wendell C. Stevens: Lt. Col. USAF (ret.)

Alan Caviness: Carolina Group Research

Jeff Challender: Director Project Prove http://projectprove.com/
Peter Davenport: Director National UFO Reporting Center
http://www.ufocenter.com/
John Thompson: Former Georgia MUFON State director and
Investigator
Dr. Robert Trundl: Author *UFOs: Politics, God and Science*
Bill Bean Investigator: Baltimore, Maryland
Joe Stefula: Investigator and former NJ State MUFON Director
Don Ware: Former Eastern MUFON Director
John Combest: Investigator
Norman Bryden: Mars investigator

Introduction

By Maj. George Filer

I personally became interested in UFOs when I chased one over England when flying for the US Air Force. I've been investigating them ever since. My experience was as an intelligence officer, flier, aerospace science instructor and Vice President of Medcor.

I don't believe that the Earth and its plants and life are here by chance. The complexity of life and the human spirit to me indicates there must have been a creator or designer. I choose to call that creator God. However, God could have sent angles, aliens or meteorites to carry the spark of life and DNA to our planet. The purpose of this book is to provide the reader a small portion of the UFO witness and photo/video evidence that occurs on a daily basis around the world. Many people claim it is impossible for UFOs to visit Earth. I ask you only to keep an open mind and consider the evidence we have accumulated.

I have over 5000 hours flying time and have flown to 62 countries, all of whom have UFO reports. I'm not a scientist; I deal in the analysis of the UFO situation and have a Masters Degree in Business Administration. There is something very strange in our skies with hundreds of reports each month. I personally feel they are here conducting various operations. You may not be a believer, but watch the new evidence collected for over six years and you may change your mind.   Past reports of UFOs can be seen at: www.Georgefiler.com or www.nationalufocenter.com

I've talked to hundreds of people, probably a hundred pilots and astronauts who have seen UFOs, often the size of an aircraft carrier. There is no question in my mind that they exist. I don't know for certain what UFOs are or who is flying them, but something is flying in our skies.   They could be a natural phenomenon not understood. Several times while in Air Force intelligence, I briefed UFOs to numerous general officers.   I attempted to obtain documentation and films of UFOs from the Air Force. I was told the evidence was there, safes full of evidence, but I needed the signature of my four star commanding general to see it.   I have dozens of friends who also know they exist, and have seen various types of evidence. I'm part of the "Disclosure Project" that includes over one hundred military and government personnel ready to testify to Congress about the phenomenon and about three hundred more who would need a formal release from their security restrictions before they would be willing to testify.

When flying for the 420th Air Refueling Squadron from Sculthorpe RAF Base, England in February of 1962, we were in orbit for USAF refueling operations over the North Sea at 30,000 feet in our six engine KB-50 J tanker aircraft.   About 9:00 PM, London Control excitedly notified us that they had an unidentified object hovering between Oxford and Stonehenge at around 1,000 feet altitude.   We were asked if we were willing to investigate.   Our refueling mission was about over, so we quickly agreed to chase their UFO. We were given an intercept heading and started to dive toward the UFO. This was really fun and exciting compared to a standard mission. I never could recall such speed and power as our six engines were advanced to full military power as we dove on the target.

London Control was diverting commercial aircraft to clear our path for the intercept. Then we realized we were above our red lined maximum speed and had trouble slowing our aircraft.   London Control started giving our distance to the hovering UFO. They called out "your 100 miles apart . . . 60, and . . . 40." At about 30 miles, my APS-23 Radar seemed to pick up the hovering UFO directly ahead. It was an exceptionally large radar return, reminding me of a large bridge or a large ship.   This craft was as big as or bigger than anything I had seen in the air before.

The return was sharp and solid, as compared to the fuzziness of a rain cloud. I felt this craft must be made of steel or strong metal. We were doing around 425 mph as we approached to about ten miles, when it apparently realized we were intercepting. It was a dark night; we could only see a series of dim lights directly ahead. Now only five miles separated us. Suddenly the UFO seemed to come alive; the lights brightened and the UFO accelerated in a launch similar to the Space Shuttle at night. We saw much brighter lights and fantastic acceleration almost straight up and suddenly it was gone.

We asked London Control if they had any rocket launches in the area. London Control seemed as disappointed as we were. The controller said, "There are no rocket launches in that area. Thank you for the intercept. You are now cleared to return to your mission." Our mission was no longer a priority and we had to fly the normal routine traffic patterns. It is clear they felt there was a strong return for the 20 to 25 minutes it had taken to reach the UFO. We had been cleared directly through various altitudes, airways and commercial traffic, so they must have considered this mission very important. The incident was recorded in my navigator's log and was mentioned the next day in operations, but no intelligence debriefing was made.

I can still see that huge radar return in my mind's eye and I've been chasing UFOs ever since because I know they are real.

Chapter 1
U.S. Daylight Disks

NEW JERSEY: FAST MOVING OBJECTS.

SUSSEX -- Brian Shaw writes, "On May 6, 2001, at around 7:30 PM, my dad and I drove over a hill and got a good view of strange things in the sky. They were shiny orange dots above the mountains in the Sunset sky.

"We saw two objects. One was either a disk or it was a meteor debris trail. It either went below the horizon or simply disappeared but as some vanished; a few more kept popping up. Some were spots and some were disk-shaped. My Mom saw one towards the end of the event, which was definitely like a meteor. One was moving faster than the others and left a trail behind it. The show ended as they all sank below the horizon or just vanished. We definitely were not imagining seeing these things, because other people were staring up into the Northwest part of the sky just over the Sunset.

"We saw at least ten or twelve objects there may have been more,"

Thanks to Brian Shaw -- <u>rico_suave_911@hotmail.com</u>

(Editor's Note): Last weekend, Earth passed through a trail of dusty debris from distant Comet Halley, triggering the annual eta

Aquarid meteor shower. The nearly full Moon reduced the visibility of this year's shower. It seems unlikely you could have seen these during sunset because of its light. Most of the observations were seen in the south an hour before local sunrise on Saturday and Sunday. It's a good chance you saw some UFOs.

For more information visit http://SpaceWeather.com

* * *

PENNSYLVANIA DISK

GRANTVILLE -- My 12 year old daughter came home from school and said that she had to tell me something and that she thought I would not believe her. She proceeded to tell me that she saw two alien saucers approach our area on August 29, 2001, while waiting for the bus.

She said, "One had a sparkly light that came out the bottom of one of the ships in a tubular shape that went towards the ground and stayed there for about 15 seconds and came back up the ship. Then both ships left the area going away from our house."

My daughter is not the imaginative type and she is afraid that something will happen to her or her family. She prayed that whole day that nothing would happen and she cannot sleep well ever since it happened.

* * *

NEW YORK: SILVER DISK.

BROOKLYN -- The witness states, "I had a recent short sighting on Saturday, January 5, 2002, at 8:40 A.M., while on a bus #46. The bus stopped at Church Avenue and I was looking west out the window when I saw a stationary, silver disk in the sky reflecting the morning sun. It didn't move or wobble at any time but just hovered. It had to be above 10,000 feet because there were passenger jets above it to the southwest and northwest.

"I was watching it for about 15 seconds without looking away and it disappeared. It looked about the size of an air rifle pellet. I have been doing a lot of thinking since I finished reading a Wendell C. Stevens book. People have been having contact with ET's for a long time and yet the information like those in his books goes unreported or unknown to the majority of people.

"I know very well that abductions/contacts continue happening but I think that the world should know of these older reports from the 50's through 70's as a way of promoting interest and investigation in other countries. Why aren't the major organizations enlisting investigators around the world to reinvestigate those older contacts along with the newer contacts?

"I had never reported my sightings until I did with you and I am glad that I did because I can read your Filer's Files and know that others are having sightings and reporting them."

Thanks and God Bless. grodriguez@windelsmarx.com

(Editor's Note): There are a few researchers attempting to spread the word and gather data such as retired Lt. Col. Wendell Stevens. MUFON and most other UFO organizations do not have the funds to support any research. Virtually all investigation is paid for individually by the investigators themselves. Therefore, there is very limited capability. Your corner Pizza Restaurant spends more, so consequently there is little real scientific research that can be done except by volunteers. Real research is very expensive. Those who make large amounts of money in the Entertainment Industry or Business do not appear interested in supporting UFO research. I'm hoping that this will change.

George Filer.

* * *

WASHINGTON: SILVER DISK.

GRANITE FALLS -- The witness reports, "On January 10, 2002, around 3:20 PM, when my mom and I were on our way home when I noticed a bunch of lights and thought I saw a plane hovering above the mountains. The object began to move closer in our direction. When we pulled up to the stop sign it was almost over us and we could see that it was a round silver disk with colored lights all around it. There was a smaller silver disk rotating in the center. We got out of the car and we noticed that it made no noise and headed west towards the water.

* * *

NEW JERSEY: DAYLIGHT DISK SIGHTED.

SOMERSET -- On June 17, 2002, a disk was sighted at 10:00 AM moving in a straight line over Somerset. The witness states, "I was stopped at a red light on Howe Lane and happened to look up and saw a bright silver disk moving across the sky rather slowly that suddenly disappeared when a jet plane came into view.

"What I saw previously bore no resemblance to a plane from any angle. What struck me the most was how the disk was there and then poof, gone! The disk moved slower than any planes that are normally in the area but it was too far away and too bright to see any details even though I was wearing Polaroid Sunglasses. The surface was reflective and about the size of a penny held at arm's length."

Thanks to MUFON HQ and Bruce Cornet.

* * *

COLORADO: DAYLIGHT DISK.

LITTLETON – "The weather changed today on June 3, 2002, from unseasonably hot to cool and windy as the front moved in and storm clouds appeared," an office worker reports. "As I looked out my office window, I noticed a black, circular shape in the sky that remained stationary for 20 or more seconds at 3:03 PM." He states, "My first impression was that the object might be a rather large balloon within a half mile of my position but oddly it remained stationary in the wind.

"I put my caller on hold and looked more closely. After remaining stationary for about 30 seconds, it began to move slightly in almost a fluttering way or jagged way, suddenly dipping to the left and downward and changing shape from circular to more flat. Then it went up again and a little to the right, again becoming more circular but also changing shape so that it was periodically circular and then more ovoid.

"It headed back to the left and would remain somewhat stationary and then dip further down."

* * *

OKLAHOMA DISK CHASED.

BARTLESVILLE -- On July 10, 2002, my wife called me from where she works and asked me to please go outside and crank up the umbrellas she had positioned over her new plants to protect them from the 100 degree heat we had here today.

I was outside cranking up the second umbrella around 1:30 PM and I looked in time to see a fast moving disk-shaped object flying low to the northeast with two low zooming US fighter jets not too far behind it. Right after they passed by, a giant sonic boom occurred that rattled everything so much even the trees quaked.

When I came into the house a couple pictures and a mirror had fallen off the walls. I saw just a few minutes ago a news report saying that a blast was felt as far away as Tyro Kansas -- a good 40 minute drive from here. The news says they don't yet know the cause of the blast, but I can tell you what it was. It was two jets in hot pursuit of something flying dangerously low for a populated area in my opinion.

Thanks to STR---LGTFUT@cableone.net

* * *

ARKANSAS: DAYLIGHT DISKS SEEN.

NORTH LITTLE ROCK -- The observers report seeing a saucer shaped object on July 27, 2002, that was silver chrome like with bright sunlight bouncing off of it. "My adult daughter and I were heading west at 4:00 PM, when we both saw a hovering the disk above the tree line about a mile away. As we drove closer, we could see it more clearly and observed for a couple of minutes that it never moved and just reflected the sun like a mirror would. Neither one of us has ever seen anything like that."

* * *

NEW YORK: SMALL DISK NEAR WESTCHESTER AIRPORT.

WHITE PLAINS -- Two witnesses report seeing a small disk. "My twelve-year old daughter and I were heading home from a visit on August 21, 2002, and I turned left out of the Westchester County Airport entrance at 2:30 PM onto 120A south, and I saw something on my left quickly approaching my car. My daughter saw it too. It looked like a small disk; no more than 12 inches or so in diameter and it was rapidly spinning vertically and moving towards us.

"It was dark brown with a metallic quality, and as it passed the car it made a strange sound. Not a buzz or a motor-like sound. More of an electronic sound that changed pitch as it approached my car then hovered for a second just at the left side of my windshield, very close to the driver's side window and then quickly disappeared.

"We both saw and heard the exact same thing. It lasted only a few short seconds but it remains very clear in both of our minds. We didn't actually see it 'disappear '; it just flew away quickly."

* * *

TEXAS: DAYLIGHT DISK.

COLONY -- The witness reports, "My daughter and I observed a bright disk shaped object flying over on August 24, 2002. I was talking to my 16-year-old daughter in the dining room when she pointed to something in the sky at 4:00 PM. We watched a very bright, white disk-shaped object traversing the sky, about 500-700 feet up, going north at a fairly fast pace. It had a definite disk shape to it.

"We grabbed the binoculars and watched it fly south and noticed it seemed to rotate and began to change from a disk to another shape and this is when I knew it was not a plane for sure. It was descending to the ground at a 25-degree angle. My daughter also saw it maneuver in the sky and no sound was detected. The winds were out of the south at 5-10 mph on a sunny day.

"I have a Masters of Education in counseling psychology and research UFO's."

* * *

CALIFORNIA: TWO DISK UFO's.

PALMDALE -- The witness claims to have seen two UFO's in the sky at 2:00 PM on Thursday, October 3, 2002. He states, "I was painting a patio and I looked up and saw one UFO that looked like a silver saucer. I know it was spinning because the sun was reflecting on it making it flicker while it was spinning around. It moved as fast as lighting. I saw the second one and when one moved the other one followed. They both took off as fast as lightening straight up and were gone."

* * *

VIRGINIA BEACH.

On November 4, 2002, the witness reported, "My wife exclaimed, 'Look! What's that in the sky?' I looked up and saw a strangely lit disk shape with a white or blue light blinking on top and bottom. The UFO was lit in a very peculiar manner. It seemed every inch was perfectly lit, as if the object itself was glowing. I checked my watch. It was 6:45 PM.

"The color was a pale greenish. There seemed to be a ring around the disk that was a darker color, perhaps black, though it still was completely visible against the night sky. The only light source I can imagine was from the UFO itself that hovered.

"The tree line blocked our view, so we lost sight. If the UFO was moving, it was doing so very slowly and in a kind of sliding manner.

"As soon as we got out of the car, we heard jets roaring by from Naval Oceania Air Base. The jets were flying in two pairs away from the direction we saw the craft. The speed and throttling of the jets seemed to be slightly abnormal."

* * *

KANSAS DISKS PHOTOGRAPHED.

WICHITA -- Matt Hitt phoned to tell me he was at the local mall on January 8, 2003, when he noticed a disk-shaped craft flying over the area. He went into the local drug store and purchased a camera and film and started photographing at 5:20 PM.

His taking photos of the sky caused a crowd to form and look at the UFOs flying overhead. An Air Force Captain dressed in uniform was amazed to see the disks. He pointed and said, "That's not a plane!" He claimed he was a pilot and had never seen UFOs or anything like that. There were heavy contrails high in the sky and the UFOs were flying around below the contrails.

Matt called me immediately after the sighting and seemed quite excited.

Thanks to Matt Hitt

* * *

CALIFORNIA DISK.

BUENA PARK -- The witness observed a silvery colored disk hovering in an upward position December 31, 2002, at 1:30 PM. The disk leveled out and moved quickly southeast. There was no sound.

* * *

WISCONSIN DISK.

WEYAUWEGA -- On February 1, 2003, at dusk a father reports, "I was filming my son sledding and he pointed up and we noticed some lights coming in from the southwest, so I just pointed the camera up and took some shots of an object that gave me the impression of a balloon with some lights. They seemed to cycle in all different patterns as the object passed almost directly overhead and then headed south towards the train tracks.

"As the object passed over, I could make out more of a disk shape than a balloon shape. My son asked me over and over what it was and I don't have a clue."

Thanks to UFO Wisconsin. http://www.ufowisconsin.com/

* * *

6

TEXAS

DALLAS -- The witness reports sighting a disk-shaped UFO in the distance on March 30, 2003, at 15:45 PM. The disk hovered in the distance for about five minutes before leaving.

* * *

NEW YORK – DISK.

BROOKLYN -- On Thursday, May 8, 2003, at 6:43 p.m. the eyewitness was walking home from the train station and looked up towards the southeast in Canarsie when he saw a silver disk/saucer at about 10,000 feet with the leading edge pointed slightly upwards and moving east.

"I watched it for about 3-4 seconds as it moved slowly and then there was a blur and it disappeared." He states, "The saucer/disk seemed to be wobbling and it had what seemed to be notches that were evenly spaced around its middle rim as it wobbled and rotated.

"I had my 35 mm camera with me but the sighting was so quick that it was gone before I could get my camera out. It did not reappear."

* * *

Weather Channel Shows Disk.

OUT WEST -- Kim Shaffer writes, "On Tuesday, April 20th, I was glancing at the weather Channel when I saw the end of a video clip of a tanker aircraft dumping retardant on a fire out west somewhere. As the clip was ending, the cameraman panned left and upward to show a large dark disk-shaped object in the sky. The clip ended almost immediately and I have tried several attempts to contact TWC to find out the when, what and where of the video but they will not return an email to me. Perhaps, I do not have the 'credentials' to get a response. Do you think this is a job for you? Do you know anyone with clout enough to get an answer from these clowns? The video was certainly very interesting and no response indicated they wish no involvement in the subject of UFOlogy."

Thanks to Kim Shaffer ASD/MUFON TN.
shaffer56@earthlink.net

* * *

Connecticut – Disk.

WOODBURY – The witness states, "On August 22, we were driving home from my birthday party at 1 PM, when I saw a disk with a slightly domed roof hovering in the sky. The disk was hovering at a very high altitude and looked metallic because the sun gleamed off its surface. I could see enough of the craft to tell it was a disk with a slightly domed roof and I had my Mom look and told her, it's a UFO. She responded 'OK, cool, I believe you' (in a sarcastic tone). I turned to argue; when I looked back it was gone."

* * *

North Carolina: Two Disk-Shaped Objects.

HIGH POINT - - Field Investigator Alan Caviness informed me that he and other investigators have been taking a series of images and video of UFOs in his general area. He has obtained an astounding amount of data indicating a heavy concentration of UFOs in his area. He has provided me with numerous examples of these objects. Many are cylinder or disk-shaped and fly above Davidson County and High Rock Lake, North Carolina.

Thanks to Alan Caviness

* * *

California: Man Shoots UFO.

ANZA -- Jack writes, "In 1956 my parents bought a small piece of desert property near California. At the time the area was a real hot spot for UFO's. I did a lot of hunting for rabbits and other varmints while we owned the property.

"I was going along a riverbed looking for something to shoot with my .22 auto rifle, when I heard a noise. Looking in the direction of the sound, I saw a disk in the Manzanita brush just hovering about a foot off the ground. It scarred the hell out of me at first and I shot at it with my 22 rifle. (Probably not the thing to do.) There was no effect and I fell on my butt trying to get back away from it. When I fell I was only three feet from the disk; so I know what I was looking at.

"I saw no aliens and within a few seconds it rose up to about twenty feet and shot away at tremendous speed. It was only about 8 feet across and 3.5 feet high, kind of small. It was the color of those Ruger guns that they call target gray. I did not see any insignia on the craft.

"I took off back to the cabin and told my parents what had happened. The only reason that they believed my story, I was shaking like a leaf in a windstorm. Later my step father and I went back to the spot and found some small prints about 4 inches in length and a Manzanita branch that was burned on one end. I never went back to that spot again and did not report it to anybody else. I did not want to sound like some of the locals that reported men from Mars. I was 13 at the time and remember it like it was yesterday. It did convince me that UFOs were real."

Thanks to Jack in Reno, Nevada.

* * *

VIRGINIA DISK.

VIRGILINA -- On January 21, 2001, a disk was observed at 2:15 PM by Susann and her friend who were driving back from getting a large roll of hay for their horses. They were driving south on Red Bank Road and saw a silver, disk-shaped UFO moving north. It was approximately 5,000 feet high. At first, they thought it might be a jet, but there were no contrails in the clear blue sky.

8

They saw it moving north for about three seconds, and then it vanished after picking up speed and moving faster than a jet. They said if the sun had shined off of it they would not have seen it.

This report was completed by Tom Ginther, VA MUFON.

* * *

ARKANSAS: AIRSHOW BY EIGHT DISK-SHAPED UFOs.

HOT SPRINGS -- I was at work pulling shopping carts inside on March 23, 2001, as my job requires, when an older gentleman said, "What the HELL!'" Concerned for customer safety, I looked around and saw the gentleman looking into the sky. I looked up also at 7:23 PM.

About 500 feet in the air were eight crafts that appeared to be making high-speed ninety degree (90 degree) turns. The gentleman noticed me watching and asked me if I saw them too. I replied with a, "Yes sir!" and then proceeded to ask him, "What are they?" He replied, "I don't know."

We watched these acrobatic crafts for almost seven minutes before six of them shot off to the North at an astounding rate of speed. The other two craft just sat and hovered for a minute or so and then shot off to the West just as fast as the six to the North did.

I have seen aircraft like F-16's make turns but not as sharp or perfectly cornered, as these craft seemed to be doing.

(Editor's Note): Large mothership cigar-shaped UFOs have been seen more often lately perhaps due to severe solar storms. Smaller disk craft are often seen leaving and entering these motherships.

* * *

NEW JERSEY: FLYING OBJECTS.

SURF CITY - A video was taken on Sunday June 3, 2001, of a strange looking aircraft flying over the Atlantic Ocean at about 4:00 PM. ; A brilliant light was first observed in the sky at 45 degrees above the horizon. The flash of light was most likely caused by a reflection of the sun on a flying object, but it caught my attention.

"Within seconds the brightly lit disk-like object disappeared. A short time later, moving at high speed and faster than normal air traffic, was a white aircraft-traveling north paralleling the New Jersey Coastline. There were no contrails.

"I had been filming beach scenes with a TRV330 Sony video camera, so I attempted to film the craft. A short segment of video was taken revealing an aircraft that looked similar to a C-5 Galaxy aircraft with possibly a small refueling boom hanging down underneath.

"The amazing thing about the craft was that it appeared to have a very large rear-slanting tower on the top of its fuselage. The tower appears to be about 100 feet tall based on the height of a C-5 tail (65 feet).

"It is possible the aircraft is in a turn and the tower is actually part of the wings, although the craft appeared to continue to fly in straight and level flight. Generally four large C-5 jet engines are also easily observed hanging from the wings. These and a horizontal stabilizer are not visible in the video."

The photo can be seen at www.filersfiles.com.

* * *

OHIO: DISK SIGHTING IN 1933.

GIBSONBURG -- John Schuessler reports he received the following report from a 78 year old. The witness states, "In 1933, I was ten years old and returning from school one block from my home at 424 W. Stevenson Street. I heard a whining sound and looked up. Passing from south to north, I saw two disks connected by a thin shaft, moving slowly through the air. I could not guess the height or size of the disks. At the time, I was deeply into the hobby of building model airplanes of the balsam and tissue paper variety with rubber band motors.

"I ran home and told my mother I had seen a different model airplane. She dismissed my story as imagination. I have searched through libraries to see if I could see a picture in books like the disks I had seen to no avail. I am now almost 78 years old and have never forgotten this. I am a retired FBI agent and was not dreaming when I saw what I saw."

Thanks to John Schuessler MUFON HQ Shoot1066.

* * *

CALIFORNIA: DISK OBSERVED.

SACRAMENTO -- ISUR reports that on Friday, July 6, 2001, at about 6:00 PM, the witness stepped outside of her home in Carmichael and noticed a round object hovering over the treetops to the east. The witness indicated that the object was bright and shiny but appeared to be rotating as it changed from shiny to an almost black color.

She observed it for at least 5+ minutes and added that there appeared to be no lights or other structure, just a round object. There was a haze or some sort of aura around it and no sound was detected. She estimated it may have been a few hundred feet above the treetops, perhaps a mile away, and about the size of an aspirin held at arm's length. The object seemed to fade into the clouds after about 5+ minutes of observation.

After this event, the witness contacted the local news station and was advised that no other reports had been received. This witness provided ISUR with a brief but concise and well-written report. She was willing to cooperate in a more in-depth investigation with MUFON of California. Although she had been a skeptic, she knew what she saw!

Thanks to Tom Sheets, ISUR Board, State Director-MUFONGA.

* * *

10

MASSACHUSETTS: FLYING SAUCER.

HANOVER -- The witness reports that on July 11, 2001, at 5:45 PM driving south on Route 3 he noticed "a white flash, as if something popped below the clouds ahead to my right at 2 o'clock. The flash didn't diminish, so it caught my interest. As it got closer, I saw that there were no wings, so it wasn't a helicopter. I also observed a strange aura/trail around it similar to the heat that rises off a hot road. There were no sounds and the craft seemed also to have a slight wobble, maybe caused by the aura, as it seemed to blur the outline.

"The object was silver and seemed to have black on it. The shape seemed to resemble a trashcan or disk. It continued to approach and passed overhead and I lost sight of it. Total time of sighting was less than 7-8 seconds."

* * *

NEW JERSEY: DAYLIGHT DISK SIGHTED.

MANALAPAN -- "On Sunday, August 11, 2002, at approximately 6 PM, my daughter and I went out in the backyard to go on the swing set," witness Dawn G. reported, "The sky was clear, and it was sunny and hot. I was looking up in the sky and I saw, above the highest airplane, a shiny spot. It looked silver or white. It wasn't moving, so I kept watching it. It still didn't move. Then, all of a sudden, more appeared in a formation, almost as if I was looking at the Big Dipper in broad daylight.

"I watched for a few minutes to see if there was any movement. There was none. Then I ran in the house to get my video camera and binoculars real quick and, when I came out, it was gone.

"I brought the camera and binoculars down to the swing set and kept my eyes on the sky. I saw another one (UFO) just above my head. I quickly grabbed the binoculars and tried to focus them. But all I could see was a silverish or whiteish spot with a sort of halo (aura) around it. It sort of looked like a little cloud. Then I grabbed my video camera and, when I looked up, it was gone.

"I told my husband about what I saw. We both couldn't explain it.

"Crop circles were found in a farm field in Coltsneck, which is only a few miles west of where I live. It really gave me the creeps."

(Manalapan is on Route 33 about 20 miles east of Trenton.)

Thanks to UFO Roundup Vol. 7, # 348/23/02, Editor: Joseph Trainor. http://ufoinfo.com/roundup/

(Editor's Note): A "halo" or "aura", similar to the mirage seen over pavement on a very hot day, often surrounds UFOs and show up on photos. Debunkers cite this as an indication that the photo has been hoaxed. However, witnesses assert that this aura was viewed with the unaided eye at the time of the sighting. It is theorized that this is ionized air as a result of the craft's propulsion system.

David Twichell.

NORTH CAROLINA: CLOSE ENCOUNTER.

MARINE'S CHERRY POINT STATION -- John Thompson writes, "Here's a tidbit I gleamed recently from a former North Carolina resident.

"This man said in the late 1950s, while living not far from the home of the 2nd Marine Air Wing, that he had a remarkable close encounter experience. While playing baseball with high school age friends, someone hit the ball over the roof of his house. He chased the ball and saw a round, disk-shaped craft with platform around it just "sitting" in the air.

"The craft was 40 feet in diameter, sat motionless and soundless about a 100 feet away and about 20 feet high. An opening appeared in the UFO and a humanoid in a skintight suit and skullcap stepped out onto the platform. The humanoid, after only a few seconds, spotted him and immediately reentered the UFO. The saucer then zoomed away.

"The humanoid stood about five feet three and wore a gray suit.

"The sighting occurred on a bright, slightly cloudy, Sunday afternoon at about 3 PM. He said the dramatic daylight sighting left such an impression that he can remember what he saw over 40 years ago as if it was only yesterday.

"The unknown object appeared to use colors to mimic its background for camouflage purposes. He says despite being only several miles from the Marine base he never considered the UFO was a man-made craft because of its seamless construction, zero engine noise and great speed displayed.

"The entity, despite its short stature, did have human form. This sounds much like the New Guinea sighting made by a priest many years ago."

Thanks to John Thompson

* * *

WASHINGTON: AIRLINER PACED BY SMALL DISK.

OLYMPIC MOUNTAINS -- We were walking along a dirt road by our place outside of Shelton at 11:30 AM, on February 24, 2003, when I heard a deep roar of a jet engine. I looked up to see what was making the noise and noticed an airliner going very slow, almost ready to stall, with a small silver disk under the aircraft. I told my wife, and kids to look at that in the sky.

We watched the little silver craft pace the larger airliner for ten seconds, then the little disk shot ahead and above, in front, of the airliner and shot off. They were both heading in a northerly direction at that point.

* * *

CALIFORNIA HIGHWAY PATROL SPOTS DISKS.

LAGUAN NIGUEL -- The observers were celebrating Mother's Day on May 11, 2003, at 10:30 AM, by having breakfast outside on a clear, cloudless morning. They had observed vultures and birds soaring earlier when they noticed a distant object overhead inland. A short time later they noticed the object made a reflection from the sun. From a distance it was speculated to be a glider or balloon.

"Curiosity caused us to get a pair of 10 X 25 binoculars, and we then determined it was a disk-like craft 'soaring' in the morning sky, slowly moving toward the ocean in a general northward path.

"We all took turns looking as it slowly drifted over our location. As it swooped and floated much like a bird in a thermal, we could determine the top was a dark, reflective, shiny surface, much like lenses in a reflective pair of sunglasses. As it turned, it was very thin, almost flat, becoming almost invisible from the side. The bottom side looked like turbine blades in a jet engine, but they were moving slow enough to see. The underbelly was either translucent or reflected the light from the ground on the surface beyond the 'turbine-like' blades.

"I was able to get several shots with a digital camera but, at that distance, the quality was less than marginal. We attempted to get a video but the camera had a low battery and by the time we got it charged the object was out of sight.

"It was difficult to determine the size. As a layperson, I felt it could be some unknown kind of domestic unmanned surveillance craft."

* * *

IDAHO: SILVER DISK.

BOISE -- Ike Bishop, MUFON Idaho State Director, writes, "I was observing with binoculars, a small two engine aircraft circling over at approximately 3000 feet, when I noticed a silver disk much higher up. The disk was unmistakable, silver and flying in a south/southwest direction. I was able to keep the disk in sight for six seconds. There was no contrail and the disk appeared to be at an altitude of 20 to 25 thousand feet.

"Time of the sighting was 11:05 AM on Monday, June 9th, 2003. The sky was clear, blue and unobstructed, making the sighting very obvious."

Thanks to Ike Bishop MUFON Idaho State Director.

* * *

GEORGIA: BRIGHT DOMED DISK.

STOCKBRIDGE -- Tom Sheets, MUFONGA's Director, reports an eyewitness observed an unusual event on I-75 North in the Stockbridge area of Henry County on June 16, 2003, at about 4:59 PM. He observed a bright domed disk and it was moving faster than any aircraft with which he was familiar. ASD Mark Ausmus is attempting to investigate.

13

NORTH CAROLINA: US FIGHTER AND DISK IN DOGFIGHT.

SYLVA - A, Ph.D., professor of computer science in a university, called to explain he had a life changing experience on July 9, at 11:30 AM, when his family observed a disk-shaped UFO being chased by an F-14 fighter. The disk looked similar to a garbage can lid and was only a slightly smaller diameter than the fighter aircraft was long. The professor estimated the diameter of the disk at fifty to sixty feet.

He felt our understanding of physics was very wrong after seeing the performance characteristics of this UFO. He stated, "The fighter would dive toward the disk and it would simply move to another spot in the sky. It seemed to jump from place to place. Actually it would dissolve from one spot and appear a mile away."

* * *

Georgia: Finely Polished Silver Disk.

FLOWERY BRANCH - On January 1, 2004, around 3:30 PM a family was driving home and had turned off of I985 onto Spout Springs Road (heading east), when the wife said "what is that?" The husband states, "It appeared to be several hundred feet up and my first thought was that it was a reflective foil-like balloon but the sun's reflection from the object was very bright and the object's surface was like finely polished silver. My wife, daughter age 5 and son, almost 3, got real curious. We got the impression that the object was 4 to 6 feet in diameter. We passed the object by and turned around and came back and parked. From this vantage point we could clearly see the object was moving slowing away from us, flip and roll, sort of like it was tumbling but not consistently in any given direction.

"From this movement we could make out that the object was an almost flat disk. When it would roll to its thin side it looked black and there was no reflection. When it would roll and reveal its flat side it would appear to be silver and the sun's reflection was strong. It looked like polished silver and in the middle of the object was a red circle. My wife said it looked like a big silver button in the sky with a red dot in the middle that did not reflect the sun.

"The object looked solid and tumbled on its axis and changed direction from west to the northeast. My daughter thought it was a floating CD (compact disc). We tried to follow and my wife was looking at it as we were driving. She turned away and, when she turned back, 'It's gone,' she said. I looked all over the sky and it was just gone. This was the most baffling part to us, how quickly it disappeared. Our eyes were off it only for a few seconds."

Thanks to Brian Vike.

* * *

14

WOODSTOCK - March 27, 2004, a 48-year-old male resident of Georgia reports that he had carried his vehicle to a repair shop in town near his home at 4:25 PM, and noticed what appeared to be a dull gray/silver, metallic sphere hovering just above the scattered cumulus clouds to the north. He continued to watch, stating it was difficult to judge true size and distance, but it may have drifted slightly. This object was then covered by a cloud. Witness continued to look and, within about 5-10 minutes, noticed an identical object, but possibly the original, a little east of the first location. An occasional cloud also covered this second observation off and on. Three or four jet aircraft at much higher altitude passed the area during the 30 minutes of observation.

Witness indicated in his WUFOD (worldwide UFO Database) account that the size appeared to be about like an aspirin at arm's length. Also that his only conventional comparison would be to that of a balloon but UNLIKE balloons he had seen. These spheres seemed to have little or no drift.

This Woodstock resident said that he would provide additional information if contacted by our personnel.

* * *

Indiana: Investigating Sighting by Three Police Officers.

HUNTINGTON -- Roger Sugden, who is a MUFON investigator, writes, "I was the first to look into the Huntington UFO affair. I went to Huntington the very next day after the story in the Herald-Press. I had two MUFON investigators with me – Doug Egolf, and Gene White. We talked with the editor of the paper to verify the facts of the story then went to the police station and talked with one of the police officers that were eyewitnesses. We found him to be very credible and perplexed at what he had seen."

The newspaper report stated, "Officer Chip Olinger was warming up his car December 26, 2003, when he reported seeing a circular object in the sky and radioed officers Greg Hedrick and Randy Hoover, who also saw it. All three say they watched as the object moved out of the northwest, drifted toward a church steeple, then shot straight north without a sound in an encounter that lasted less than a minute about 2:30 PM. The trio describes the object as about the size of a hot air balloon or a backyard trampoline. They said it was low enough in the sky that Olinger thought it might crash into the steeple."

"We were not able to talk with the other officers," Sugden said, "or the other eye witness who is a pilot who viewed the object from his car and told the police officer that it was very low, below 1000 feet, and that even in good daylight, he could not identify what it was, also that its size was larger than a Cessna aircraft.

"We talked with another man who claims he saw a hover disc Mylar balloon. However, this has been ruled out due to the difference in the times that the objects were seen.

"The investigation is ongoing."

An interesting note: The land that the church is built on was given to the church by Miami Chief Richardville. Perhaps it was an old sacred site and he knew that it would remain so by giving it to the church.

Thanks to Roger Sugden ASD/CFI MUFON IN grog25@maplenet.net.

* * *

New Jersey: Elongated Disk UFO.

Morestown – Frankie V reports seeing a UFO for over twenty minutes near Route 295 a few miles east of Philadelphia on March 11, 2004. Several aircraft were also seen passing over the UFO that was hovering or moving very slowly as it flew around the area. The craft was a metallic gray color that would change to red and return to gray. The red color may have been caused by the sun reflecting off its surface in the bright sunny sky at 3:40 PM. Frankie V has his radio show and had never seen a UFO before.

The craft hovered and then climbed almost straight up to an estimated 35, 0000 feet. It just stayed in this position looking like a bright star in the sunny sky.

Thanks Frankie V at www.frankievradioshow.com

* * *

Washington: Fishing Vessels Observe Disk.

NEAH BAY -- Four fishing vessels, 50 to 60 miles off the west coast of Neah Bay, watched a disk for half an hour. What appeared to be a discus-shaped, large object with very bright lights was seen at 6:23 PM on March 16, 2004. The object had mostly white lights but there were also red and green lights that seemed to be mimicking the vessels running lights for navigational purposes. The object would move at extreme rates of speed back and forth in a horizontal direction. Then, occasionally, at a high rate of speed it flew straight up into the sky. The object seemed to hover above one of the vessels in particular and then flew straight up into the sky and was gone. I was told this by several of the eyewitnesses.

* * *

Tennessee: Florescent Disk.

JOHNSON COUNTY -- MUFON's Kim Shaffer writes, "On April 3, 2004, I received a call from a gentleman who was very excited about an object he and another witness saw at 17:30 hours a 'florescent light bulb' high in the sky. There were aircraft in the vicinity leaving condensation trails well below the observed object that was stationary and holding horizontally its very high position. As the planes passed, the object turned slowly vertically and ascended higher into the sky and out of sight.

"The witnesses were adamant that this was a solid object. I contacted the local FAA office and inquired as to whether there had been any pilot reported anomalous objects but received no conformation."

* * *

KNOXVILLE -- Kim Shaffer received a call from another truck driver who witnessed a metallic disk on I-40 just east of Knoxville on the afternoon of April 8, 2004. Witness reported that the disk paced his truck and was quite large (relative size was that of a silver dollar at arm's length), reflective and seemed to rock side to side as it moved in a straight path. Witness stated that the object moved behind some trees and he anticipated seeing it again when he and the object passed the trees. But when he got past the trees the disk did not reappear.

Thanks to Kim Shafer MUFONTN State Director

http://www.mufontennessee.org

* * *

Tennessee: Silver Disk.

BRISTOL -- Kim Shaffer MUFON SD reports, "A man and his wife had just arrived home at about 5 PM, on January 17, 2005, when he saw a large silver disk with a flat bottom at about 70 degrees to his east. He described the object as being highly polished with a smaller dome shape upon the main body. The relative size to the witness was that of a basketball at arm's length. He immediately alerted his wife who exited the car to also see the same object moving away eastward and ascending. The entire sighting lasted no longer than 20 seconds."

Thanks to Kim Shaffer MUFON (eastern) SD.

www.mufontennessee.org

* * *

FLORIDA: HUGE DAYLIGHT DISK.

PINELLAS PARK - On January 31, 2003, at 5:45 AM, I had noticed how big Venus appeared to be, and had called my wife outside to show her. She was getting ready for work and she happened to look west and yelled for me to look. I turned just in time to see a bright, round object descending at a steep angle from north to south across the western sky. It appeared to be very large and changed colors from purple to green to red to yellow and finally to white as it disappeared behind the trees.

We live a short distance from the coast and, from my estimation, it landed/crashed into the Gulf of Mexico somewhere west of the Tampa Bay area.

* * *

PENNSYLVANIA: SILVER DISK.

VAN SCIVER LAKE -- Justin Time writes, "I wanted to advise you of a daytime sighting that I had on July 15, 2001, while fishing in a tournament in Tullytown, Pa. Sometime between 11:00 AM and noon,

17

while speaking with my fishing partner, I noticed a small, silver, metallic colored, oval-shaped sphere to the east.

"The sighting lasted only a few seconds. It looked very similar to the object filmed in Gulf Breeze, Florida that I saw on television. The two objects are very similar.

"I kept waiting for the disk to blink out like the one on the video but it never did until it flew behind a cloud. My fishing partner did not see the object but he saw my facial expression change and asked what I was looking at?

"The day was clear with blue skies and broken, white, puffy clouds. The object moved left to right and right to left, in short, staccato like movements. I did not perceive any altitude changes. It was about the size of the head of a pin at arm's length."

Thanks to tsunami1119@hotmail.com

(Editor's Note): Justin is most likely referring to Ed Walters who wrote several books, such as the "Gulf Breeze Sightings" and "UFOs Are Real; Here's The Proof" by co-author Bruce Maccabee, with an introduction by Major George A. Filer.

* * *

LOUISIANA.

BATON ROUGE -- The witness reports, "I pulled into a Burger King at 1:20 PM on November 13, 2002. I was about to get out of my car when I saw a big, black object in my rearview mirror. At first I thought the mirror had something on it, but when I got out of the car and looked at the sky I saw a big black sphere hovering in mid air. Then, after a moment, it just vanished."

Chapter 2

U.S. Nocturnal Disks

NEW YORK: DISK SIGHTED.

ONEIDA, MARCY COUNTY -- Five witnesses observed a disk-shaped craft on Saturday, March 24, 2001. "The craft had red and green flashing lights with some beams of light coming from it and it hardly moved and floated in the East. Aircraft surrounded it. We all watched it for about two hours. The object was a white light but you could still tell it was disk-shaped. It had red lights and green lights on the bottom and looked as if it was tilted and spinning.

"It hovered in the same spot most of the time. It lasted from around 8:00 PM to about 10:00 PM, and when I came back to see if it was still there, it was gone – totally disappeared."

Thanks to Larry Clark. www.nymufon.org
* * *

CALIFORNIA: DISK-SHAPED OBJECT SLOWLY MOVING.

MAMMOTH LAKES -- I was camping out near Mammoth Mountain when the crickets stopped chirping at 3:45 AM on August 7, 2001. From the West, I noticed a dark disk shaped object slowly moving and stopping as it made its way towards my location. I was inside my sleeping bag next to my girlfriend who was asleep. The object got within fifty feet and I was frozen in fear and curiosity. I watched the craft slowly slip by, stopping for a few seconds at a time and continuing. There was a very slight hum. The craft emitted a dull blue beam from the far edge of the disk as though it was searching for someone. The craft was now clearly visible as a shiny disk and came to a complete stop.

I crawled towards it hoping it didn't detect me. I kept thinking that this craft might have infrared or heat sensors to detect any movement outside but there was no deviation from its course/task. At one point, the craft got to about 2 feet from the ground and the humming became louder.

I got back without causing any notice when the craft became enveloped by the surrounding area. It became invisible but with a slight atmospheric distortion. I watched this mirage-like phenomenon float upwards until I could not see it anymore. Five minutes later, the crickets started again and I stayed up all night.

This has changed my life forever and makes me realize we are not alone.

* * *

INDIANA: PHOTOGRAPHED UFO RETURNS.

INDIANAPOLIS -- Angela R. Clark, a former policewoman, photographed a UFO on August 7, 2001. She writes, "When I was 8 or 9 years old, I saw my first UFO. A few days after that sighting my best friend and I were out playing at night when we heard some strange 'music', which sounded like an Ice Cream truck. We looked above the treetops and saw an Ice Cream truck that was flying. I have been terrified of those trucks ever since!

"Last night, I went outside about 12:45 AM and it started to rain with lightening. That's when I heard it. I heard ice cream truck music! My husband, the skeptic, heard it too. I came inside and got in bed as my husband was turning off all the lights. ICE CREAM TRUCK MUSIC was right outside of my 2-story window! It was so clear and distinct; you would think that it was literally outside of the window. My husband looked at me and said, 'Did you hear that?'

"It doesn't make sense an ice cream truck would be out at 1:00 in the morning, during a storm! What the heck is going on?"

Thanks to Angela and Jim Osborne MUFON Investigator.

(Editor's Note): George Hansen has written a new book called, "The Tricksters". Many true UFO stories have this strange trickster or joker aspect.

George Filer.

* * *

NEW YORK: FLYING DISK.

BROOKLYN -- Gil Rodriguez writes; "I was in the kitchen on October 24 or 25, 2000, at about 9:00 p.m. when my 15 year old daughter came running downstairs yelling and crying that she saw something strange and large flying across the sky outside her window. I ran upstairs, looked to the west, and saw this well-lit object moving across the sky. It looked like a huge disk (hamburger-shaped) floating slowly across the sky without any sound.

"My daughter was very scared and still crying. She didn't sleep that night and didn't sleep much for about a week. The object had a flashing or strobe light on the top. Below that there was a row of windows with yellowish light shining out all the way around to the left and right. Below the windows was a row of lights of different colors around the middle that went on and off in sequence very quickly (blue, green, yellow, white but not exactly in this order). The bottom half was sort of dark with no lighting.

"I was in complete awe of this huge object that was bigger than I had ever seen in the sky. It seemed almost as wide as two 747 aircraft. I would guess it was at least 75 to 100 yards wide. I then remembered my loaded cameras, but when I returned to the back yard it had gone out of sight.

"This was the third sighting for my daughter and me. She had seen a similar huge hamburger-shaped craft with her niece in late 1999."
Thanks to grodriguez@windelsmarx.com
* * *

OREGON: FAST MOVING DISK.

ST. HELEN'S --On June 26, 2002, the witness woke up around 3:00 AM, and looked out the bedroom window and saw an object that measured about 1/16th of an inch, eight inches higher than her nine-foot arborvitae hedge, which is ten feet from the house. "The object first caught my eye as a white light, speeding left to right. It stopped and I could see what appeared to be white lights rotating around the disk-like bottom.

"Then, fifteen seconds later, it moved quite rapidly about four inches to the right and stopped. After thirty seconds it moved rapidly right to its original position. This was repeated four times. I watched for fifteen minutes."
* * *

NEW JERSEY DISK LIT UP.

KEARNY -- Patrick Huyghe reports, "My name is Sergey. And on August 31, 2002, my wife Natasha and I saw something, which we could not classify, as an ordinary event. About 11:30 PM, I came to the kitchen to take a coke from refrigerator. The light in the room was off but I did not turn it on because I came only for short time. Since it was dark in the room the light object suddenly appeared in the window and drew my attention. It was a disk-shaped, brightly lighted object flying in the sky. It came out from behind the tree and crossed the part of the sky visible from our window and disappeared behind the building.

"It was about 5 miles away above Newark and heading west or northwest and was moving fast. I cannot judge the object's size but can assume it was the same or larger than a passenger aircraft and flying below the clouds. I observed it for about 10-15 seconds.

"I called my wife, Natasha, who was just in the next room and she also saw it but for less time. We are absolutely sure the object was real and are amazed."
Thanks to Patrick Huyghe author of Swamp Gas Times.
* * *

VIRGINIA: DISK UFO SIGHTING.

POQUOSON -- The witness reports, "I saw a brilliant, bright light streaking across the sky on September 15, 2002, something that I have never witnessed in my life. At about 9:35 PM, I was driving and stopped my van to look as the object traveled across the sky at an extremely high rate of speed and disappeared. I contacted Langley Air Force Base who confirmed that they had no aircraft up tonight. We had cloudy conditions due to a tropical depression. I also contacted the local TV station but they had no other calls."

There have been no meteor reports.

* * *

WASHINGTON: FAST-MOVING DISK SAUCER SHAPED LIGHT.

RENTON -- I saw one UFO moving very fast across the sky on October 12, 2002. I was in the military and I've seen A-10's moving at high speed and low altitude but this was the fastest I've ever seen anything move. What I saw was a little more than a half circle of light, with the brightest section facing the direction of movement, kind of like you would expect a meteor to look as it was coming down through the atmosphere. It appeared about the size of a quarter from my perspective.

* * *

CALIFORNIA: FLYING SAUCERS SEEN BY POLICE.

BURBANK -- The witness was monitoring the 8 PM radio transmissions of Burbank Airport Police units talking to each other on their radios. The various police units in different locations were observing six objects flying over the Burbank Airport on February 16, 2003. They were discussing six flying saucers and contacted the tower. The tower contacted the Burbank police helicopter that began searching for the objects.

"I'm sure all of this radio traffic was recorded by the city of Burbank 911 center. Also, the tower transmissions would be recorded by the FAA. I, personally, did not see the craft and only heard the radio communications."

* * *

CALIFORNIA DISK.

LIVERMORE -- I was driving north on Route 680 near Pleasanton on February 4, 2003, and, as I came down the mountain pass at 11 PM, I saw two shooting stars come down and split directions. I looked out my right hand window and saw the bottom of a circular, dark disk 'float' past with an "eclipse" on the bottom.

I'm highly positive what I saw was a craft of some sort, and I know I saw the shooting stars just before the UFO. It may have been the same thing. There were no lights as it floated by, just the grayness of the bottom of the disk.

* * *

New Mexico – UFO Expands 500 Times its Size.

The January 1 (2004) sighting of the flat disk in Flowery Branch, GA, reminded me of a UFO I saw near Los Alamos, NM, Monday evening of Memorial Weekend, 1983. A friend and I were

22

camping when we saw a round, white light moving slowly on the ground in a zigzag pattern on the side of a hill, several miles to the east. We assumed it was an army tank on maneuvers, as it would go over the hill, disappear and return to our side of the hill. After about fifteen minutes of zigzagging, it suddenly rose into the sky and hovered over the hill for about five minutes. Not really believing in UFOs at that time, I thought it was a Harrier jet as I groped for a "logical explanation."

As the white light hovered over the hill, it suddenly expanded so fast (like a controlled explosion) to about 500 times its original size. It floated obliquely to the south and much nearer to us. My friend and I felt like targets and were terrified. We jumped into our rental car but the car wouldn't start. It was completely dead. Strangely reasoning that "they" wanted the car, we got back out.

The object stopped at 2,500 feet up and about 2000 feet from us. It was shaped like a huge disk with a flat side facing us. I heard a quiet, pulsating, high-pitched hum that almost made my ears hurt. I felt the hair on my head and arms rise, as if static electricity was strong. At arm's length the object would have been a yard in diameter. It began to slowly flip over backwards. As it flipped over, the thin edge of the disk was completely transparent – we could see stars through it. As it flipped over to its other side, it was opaque again and was bright red, like a huge neon sign.

It paused for a second and seemed to "take a deep breath". Then it suddenly zoomed off to the size of a little star and "got lost" among the other stars. Our car started fine after that. It forced me to realize that UFOs are real and that our conventional science does not have the proper tools or paradigms to study this phenomenon.

By Patricia Hoyt, Florida, pathoyt@comcast.net
* * *

California: Disk and Sphere.

VALENCIA -- Looking out my bedroom window, I observed an unusual, hovering object in the distance. The shape was somewhat difficult to see, as it was far away and high in a dark sky. However, three lights in a horizontal row, each light seemingly multicolored (white, pink, green but difficult to tell for sure), maintained the same position until I went to bed about an hour later. Possible blimp? My husband is an astrogeophysicist and said that it was the closest thing to a UFO he has ever seen.
* * *

Indiana: The Cave Road Sighting.

BLOOMINGTON – On October 14, 2004, the witness was driving west on Cave Road between 10:15 to 10:30 PM, when he observed a cloudbank, ahead of him, "light up". Immediately thereafter, an object with three brilliant spotlight-like white lights descended into view. The lights were shining down onto the ground, below and behind

23

the object at a 45-degree angle. The lights emanating from the craft illuminated its underside, revealing a rounded or disk-shaped structure. As the witness's vehicle made the turn onto Gifford Road, the object was continuing its descent, finally leveling out at tree line height.

The object came to a full stop only twenty yards ahead of the witness's vehicle, with the three "spot lights" shining directly downward onto Gifford Road. The object remained stationary for a few seconds, then "blinked off". No additional navigational lights, beacon lights or forward landing lights were observed on the large craft. When asked about the size of the object, the witness reported, simply, that it was "big!"

From inside his vehicle, the witness could not hear any accompanying sounds from the object, nor did he experience or observe any associated physical disturbances. Monroe County Airport is only a couple of miles east of the sighting location but is situated at a right angle to the object's south-to-northwest heading. Finally, I know the witness personally and rate his credibility as very high.

Thanks to Lynn Taylor. skysentinel@sentinelfiles.com AAARC www.sentinelfiles.com

* * *

New Jersey – Miniature UFO.

MOUNT HOLLY – Jane reports, "I was sleeping next to my husband and awakened about 3 AM on December 11, 2004, seeing two, red, basketball-size lights floating in the corner of the bedroom. I watched their movement as they generally floated or hovered in the corner. A third red plasma like disk entered the room and flew towards the bed and hovered over my husband. The red ball with red lights shining down stayed over him for about a minute and then flew outside through the wall. The disk was about one foot in diameter."

On January 6, 2005, two, red, plasma-like basketballs again appeared about 2 AM, and Jane was wide awake. "Then a miniature disk-shaped UFO appeared from the left wall and slowly flew across the room to above my husband's head. The disk hovered and eventually flew through the wall. The disk was gray and white and appeared to have windows around its center and a second set circling the bottom of the craft. It was two feet in diameter and one foot high and was perfect in detail. Once the craft left, the other red balls departed with it. My husband's health remains good except for a cold."

Thanks to Jane for her drawings.

(Editor's Note): We have many similar reports of miniature UFOs. Some reports indicate the UFO's ability to enlarge and miniaturize when needed.

George Filer.

* * *

INDIANA: FLEET OF DISKS.

EVANSVILLE -- It was like seeing a fleet of plates, all gray except for the lights flying through the air on April 13, 2001. We saw the visitors real early in the morning at 2:37 AM. The disks were hovering there for about twenty seconds then they took off toward the north. They had numerous lights on the bottom that were a reddish color and turned green when they left. They had many weird looking fins that were in the shape of a spiral that led into the center, which constantly opened and closed. They were very quiet except when one dropped a few hundred feet and that only sounded like a jet engine far in the distance.

* * *

WISCONSIN DISK DOES 180-DEGREE TURN.

DePERE - The witness reports, "A disk approached from south to north flying over us and then made a hair pin, 180 degree turn above us heading south again on April 11, 2001. The disk passed less than 300 feet above us. We could see it was darker than background night sky. It was outlined with many small red lights. The craft made no sound but we could feel its presence getting stronger as it came closer and diminish as it left."

* * *

New Jersey: "wheel within a wheel".

WEST BERLIN -- Mrs. D'Imperio writes, "At 9:30 PM on September 12, 2000, our family saw a very huge lighted disk up in the sky. My brother in-law shouted for the family to come out on the deck. We all looked up and saw a lighted wheel with what looked like bicycle spokes coming out of it. Another ring was on the outside.

"What amazed me was lights were coming down the spokes going around the outside of the other ring coming back to where they started and coming together, all of them in the center of the ring. They kept repeating this action.

"Then, from another direction of the sky, came a second object that joined going around the circle but making another spoke.

"As we watched for some time, two helicopters came overhead. One was bigger then the other and went straight for what we were watching. They were flying around for a while.

"If I attempted to draw the UFO, it would look like a 'wheel within a wheel' with lights going around and coming together in the middle. I posted this information on the web."

Thanks to Mrs. D'Imperio at alian10094@aol.com

(Note): Compare the description of the unknowns with that of Ezekiel's vision in the Holy Bible.

David Twichell.

* * *

INDIANA: LOW HOVERING DISK.

ZIONSVILLE -- The witnesses report seeing a saucer-shaped craft on September 1, 2001. It had solid white lights at the ends and bottom, flashing white light on the top. "We approached by car at 9:30 PM, and the object appeared to be standing still and not moving. The object hovered low then disappeared completely as we got closer."

* * *

CALIFORNIA DISK.

Last Sunday, November 11, 2001, my mother and I saw a UFO. It was about four minutes after seven when my mother called me out of my room to our back porch. She pointed out an object that, at first, looked like a bright star. Then it started to move very slowly and we began to see more detail. There was an intense red aura type of light not totally surrounding the object, just enough to make out a shape with binoculars.

This thing was far away, at least a thousand feet up and kind of a disk shape with a black mass to it. It appeared then it would disappear for about 4 to 6 seconds. Then a red ball object came out of the lighted end and seemed like it dropped like a flare after you shot in the sky.

I can tell you, I had never been so excited. I finally saw one after all these years of looking in the sky.

Thanks to RT.

* * *

NEW JERSEY: DISK LOW OVER TREES.

HAZLET -- Robert La Marco writes, "My wife and kid's had a sighting of a very bright disk-shaped object over Hazlet on January 22, 2002. I myself did not see it but they were going to basketball practice, south bound on Route 35, when my wife saw a bright disk low over the trees in the direction of Holmdel, NJ.

"She stated to me it just sat there in the sky, not moving. Then, in the blink of the eye, it shot off east at incredible speed towards the Atlantic Ocean. She stated to me, 'IT WAS NO PLANE!' Her and both my boy's saw it very clearly. It was at about 8:00 PM."

Thanks to R. J. La Marco, funnycar1232000@yahoo.com

* * *

NEW YORK: PULSATING OBJECT AND FIVE DISKS.

LOCKPORT -- The witness reports, "I was up at 4:45 AM, Friday on January 10, 2003, working at the computer and opened the window to get a breath of fresh air and saw in the distance a hovering light, that was pulsating colors. It looked like somebody took a flashlight and shut it off and on repeatedly but very quickly.

"I saw white, the main color with different hues of red and yellow. I watched this for about seven minutes and the light did not move at all, it seemed to be perfectly stationary. I would have expected some movement. Near the end of this event, the light became very bright and then dimmed out with a reddish hue and vanished – sort of 'winking' out."

* * *

OKLAHOMA: TWO FLYING DISKS SPOTTED.

RETROP - Jim Hickman reports he was contacted by a radiology technician who spotted two UFOs on June 3, 2003, near Highway 6 at about 10:35 PM just south of town. Retrop is 130 miles west of Oklahoma City.

The witness states, "I slowed down and rolled down the window to see two disk-shaped objects with extremely bright white and red lights that flashed in sequence around the fuselage."

No stars or other aircraft were seen. The objects were seen for about three minutes before vanishing. The weather was good and the objects made no noise.

She contacted two police officers in Elk City when she arrived in town. Jim says, "I have interviewed the witness and she seems very credible." Altus AFB tower reported no air traffic in the area at that time.

Thanks to Jim Hickman, MUFON- Research Specialist for Media Operations, jhickman@gprmc-ok.com

* * *

New Jersey: Large Disk.

SURF CITY – I was notified personally concerning this sighting from a professional who has long denied the possible existence of UFOs. She was talking with a group of friends at 1:00 AM in a gazebo overlooking the Atlantic Ocean, on August 1, 2004. She looked out over the ocean and to the left of the full moon and noticed a large disk-shaped object with three rings of lights, one above the other, running parallel to each other. Each row of lights had about twenty lights similar to a commercial aircraft surrounding what seemed to be a disk.

The craft was flying to the north of her location towards the Barnegat Lighthouse. The disk wobbled as it descended on a maneuvering course towards the lighthouse.

Many similar UFO reports have accumulated through the years and a book was written concerning these sightings. The craft appeared quite large and had multiple parallel lights similar to a three-decked ship. The sighting is notable by this witness since she has always strongly ridiculed the concept of UFOs in the past.

* * *

Oregon: V Formation of Lights.

PORTLAND – The observer was burning small tree limbs when he saw a V formation of nine objects slowly flying north on 19 or 20 of July 2004, at 3:45 AM. The objects were behind a sheer cloud with auras around them. There seemed to be a slight fog around the nine disks, which made the orange a lighter color with a white aura around them.

The observer states, "The V formation sailed through the sky slowly over the house, moving north, taking up a good part of the sky. Since there was a mist around them, I could not make out anything in detail. It was beautiful and I was in awe. There was no noise whatsoever. The lights did not flash and the disks stayed in formation of the 'V'.

"I live ten miles from an airbase but there were no aircraft flying in the area."

Thanks to Brian Vike, Director HBCC UFO Research

* * *

Tennessee.

WASHINGTON COUNTY -- A retired algebra professor, who was driving home on Sunday, September 20, 2004, along Highway 11 around 9 PM, saw a large acorn-shaped object moving low in the sky over Buffalo Mountain. The discernible shape was made by noting the arrangement of lights on the object, which he stated were quite like a "marquis". The object was flying in ever tightening circles. The lights were flashing in random, fast way, exhibiting more than five different colors that reminded him of a Christmas tree. He pulled his car over and watched the bizarre object rise, fall and finally moving up and behind the mountain out of view.

This witness states that, in 1966, he and his late wife, along with hundreds of Johnson City citizens, witnessed a gigantic black disk-shaped object block out all the stars in the sky on a summer night. He also remembered that the giant disk had multiple arrangements of lights on the bottom, which flashed sequentially.

The Johnson City Press did a full-page story on the sighting.

* * *

California: Glowing Object Videotaped.

SONORA -- Between 20:00 and 21:15, at 9:45 PM, on September 9, 2004, fifteen glowing disk or orb-like objects were seen heading in various directions, either together, one behind the other or crossing each other's path.

One glowing object in particular flew no more than 200 yards overhead, heading to the northeast. The object was huge, bright yellow or silver-white in color and moved very slowly at first, as it was directly overhead. Then it accelerated at incredible speed and rapidly disappeared over the tree line and was videotaped by both witnesses, one with a Sony Hi-8 Camcorder on a tripod, the other with a hand-held Sony Digital Camcorder

* * *

North Carolina.

GRANITE FALLS -- The witness was on his way to the local video store about 6:45 PM, on November 7, 2004, when he looked up and saw a disk-shaped object with white lights similar to chasing lights on a Christmas tree going all the way around this object. There was a red light on either side of the object. The witness states, "The disk was moving faster than anything I've ever seen in a straight line across the sky."

On his way back home, he decided to investigate further and, in a rural area with lots of hills and trees, he found a UFO and another not too far from it that was identical to the first. They seemed to be communicating with one another by way of a white light that would come out of the side of one and the other would respond. This went on for about five seconds. One of the objects flew away quickly while the other hovered motionless for just a couple of seconds.

They came back into close proximity once but didn't seem to be communicating and appeared to be level with each other until one of them moved in a straight line vertically a short distance, then just as quickly, returned to a level position with the other one.

Thanks to Brian Vike www.hbccufo.com
* * *

Maryland: UFO Sighting.

WOODLAWN -- Bill Bean reports, "I just wanted to report a major sighting that I had at 9:10 PM, from my home on November 29, 2004. I observed a very large white disk-shaped UFO hovering and tilted downward in the southeast. It was about 5,000 feet in altitude. I watched it for nearly a minute and could not take my eyes off it. This thing was very big and the white part was very bright with black edges.

"I was in awe of this amazing craft and didn't move. I initially thought the object to be the moon, as I could see the light through a thin layer of clouds. But as the clouds passed, I saw the entire shape of the UFO.

"Suddenly, the stationary object swiftly moved away to the south and it seemed to ride on the clouds and was descending. It was like watching a speedboat on the water. I've drawn a rough sketch of it on my site."

Thanks to Bill Bean http://ufoman104.tripod.com
* * *

Pennsylvania: Light and Round Disk.

POTTSVILLE – The witness was looking out his window and saw a round, clear light appear in the sky over a ridge southeast of the city, close to the reservoir, on January 18, 2005. "I thought at first that it was a low flying plane. The object did not move and I heard no sound when it appeared. It stayed stationary and emitted a bright light from 6:44 to 6:47 AM. There was no color and it was round in shape.

"The object stayed in one spot for two minutes. Then, it got dimmer and dimmer and moved to the west. It disappeared and reappeared for a period of one minute then it was gone. The object was faint gray in color and had a round sort of translucent glass barely visible with a faint light. I looked at it through binoculars. I had two good views of the large round light. I, then, noticed a faint dim round disk."

Thanks to Brian Vike www.hbccufo.com
* * *

California: Four, Shiny, Disk-Shaped Objects.

CUCAMONGA – The witness was looking north towards the San Gabriel Mountains and saw four disk-shaped objects heading east on January 22, 2005, at 7 PM. They were shiny and reflective, not unlike polished Aluminum. A small propeller aircraft just south of the mountains started to approach and the four objects disappeared immediately as the aircraft came into view.
* * *

Ohio.

Columbus – A Glowing disk UFO was seen in Columbus on September 20, 2004, at 7:30 PM, that began traveling backwards nearly instantly. "I cannot confirm exactly what it is that I saw. It was flat, however, with no limbs of any sort such as wings found on an airplane. I could slightly tell the shape was reminiscent of a disk or saucer. It began its journey in the near proximity of the moon. As it neared larger cloud formations, I could, at times, see that it was going behind them. The only clouds present in the sky were the high cirrus clouds yet, like I said earlier, I could roughly discern a shape. As it came from behind a cloud, it had lost its glow and then its shape was much more clearly prominent. It was then a dull metallic hue. Moments later it vanished from sight."
* * *

Michigan.

Canton. – The witness writes, "The UFO I saw was back in 1974. It was in Canton, MI along Canton Center rd. north of Ford Road, hovering over a small field. I don't remember the date but I know it was summertime, because my car window was down all the way and it was about 9:30 or 10:00 P.M. Sorry I can't be more accurate with these details. BUT- I can be more accurate with my description of the UFO because I will never forget what I saw:

"It looked like a globe of light hovering about 50 or so feet above the ground. The size of it had to be at least 5-10 feet around. It was very bright but did not have 'rays' streaming off of it like a star. It simply was a round disk of light. The car I was in slowed down for heavy traffic and I saw the thing at first out of the corner of my eye. It caught my attention, so I turned and looked at it. After a few seconds, it stopped hovering and quickly shot straight up into the sky. It stopped at a higher elevation and hovered again for a brief time, then shot up until it was out of sight.

"This all happened in about a two minute time period total – maybe even less. I can't say I saw any great amount of details but I am an avid aviation fan and I know what I saw wasn't anything I knew of in existence – not even today!

"There was no noise at all! The movements were straight lines and incredibly fast. It moved with determination and accuracy. I have witnessed F14's, 15's, 16's, etc. flying and this was by far faster.

"I wish I had seen more of this thing. The only thing I know for certain is that it was a UFO. Nothing else can do what it did. I never wrote this down or made any notations about the date."

Cindy.

Chapter 3

Worldwide Daylight Disks

CHISHOLM – ISUR (International Society for UFO Research), Minnesota.

The witness was out in her yard at 7:00 PM on June 23, 2001, while her 15-year-old son was testing our new digital camera. He was shooting the sky, the river, our 40 acres of land, etc. When we went to download the images to the computer today, two UFO's showed up! He did NOT see them while testing the camera. My husband was near him; he did NOT see or hear anything.

The photos show a disk-shaped, metal object. One is going toward the ground, as though crashing to the ground with FIRE out the back end. It is about 80 feet above our yard. The next picture is another UFO, two minutes earlier, hovering above our swamp, and a foot above the ground. They are identical objects, with metal. They were NOT airplanes; they were very small, about the size of a small car.

We went to the location. We looked at the tree line in the photos but cannot get to the spot, since it is in the swamp.

Thanks to Tom Sheets and ISUR.

* * *

HUNGARY: MILITARY PILOT VIDEOS SAUCER.

BUDAPEST -- Jeff Rense has received a spectacular video of a silver disk-shaped object. On September 29, 2001, the pilot reports that a strange craft was flying to his left side and then moved very fast past him in the clouds as can be seen in the video.

"To my left I saw a bright metal aircraft that was the shape of a perfect disk.

"I was careful to film the object, not to try and chase it since I could not match its speed. As I was flying a reconnaissance aircraft, I got the idea to film it and used our equipment."

The pilot considers the video he made to be his property and not the Hungarian governments as he was flying the plane while not on duty and was transporting it as a favor to save the government money. He has now hired an attorney and wants the video to be released to the public. He hopes the release of a few frames will make this happen.

These spectacular photos can be seen at http://www.rense.com/general15/pilotufo.htm. Thanks to Jeff Rense.

(Editor's Notes): This appears to be a verified disk-shaped UFO of 25 to 30 feet in diameter. These have been filmed by numerous Air Forces of the world and have speeds greater than most jet fighter aircraft.

George Filer.

* * *

SOUTH AFRICA.

PRETORIA -- On June 30, 2002, Chris Barkhuizen spotted a silver disk that approached at a speed five times faster than commercial jets at 4 PM.

Thanks to SAUFOR (South Africa's UFO Resource) http://www.geocities.com/saufor/

* * *

PHILIPPINES: DAYLIGHT DISK.

MINDANAO On June 28, 2002, at 1:30 PM, Eleazar H. Allen and his fellow workers at the Dole Plantation in Polomolok, saw a bright gleam and he reports, "We saw it was coming from the south and was about the size of an A-320 Airbus without wings, approaching at high speed for at least five seconds. Then it abruptly backed away at a speed ten times faster until it was gone." He added that the UFO "was silvery with metal strips along the back, like a wingless jumbo jet. It was approaching at about 150 miles per hour and departing at ten times that speed."

Thanks to UFO Roundup Vol. 7, #28, 7/9/02 Editor: Joseph Trainor. http://ufoinfo.com/roundup/

* * *

CANADA.

HOUSTON, BC -- Brian Vike reports, two local residents stated, "My buddy and I were traveling along Highway #16 just east of town on March 3, 2003, at 7:55 AM, during daylight and just before Perow, we noticed a large object paralleling us along the highway. We were going 50 kilometers an hour and the object was 300 to 400 feet away, so we both had a very close up look at it.

"Sometimes there were trees between the truck and UFO, which hindered our view, but there was no disturbance in the trees. The craft was slightly wobbling, like looking through a heat wave. The UFO looked like an 'Air Stream Trailer' and its size was close to a Greyhound Bus. It was metallic in color and no other features could be seen on it. No lights, windows, nothing! The object stayed straight across from our truck as we drove along!"

The passenger rolled down the window to see if he was able to hear any sound, but none was heard. After almost a kilometer, the craft turned slowly away from the highway, wobbled slightly, sped up, wobbled once again and then shot off out of sight very quickly.

* * *

UKRAINE: CIRCULAR HOVERING DISK.

CRIMEAN PENINSULA -- Anton A. Anfalov writes, "I would like to report a new, remarkable UFO observation on October 7, 2002. My old friend, Mr. Victor A. Zdorov, was on a business trip driving his 'Lada' vagon car, in the Belogorsk District of the Crimean Autonomous Republic between 3 to 5 PM. Suddenly, he noticed a big circular object no less than 50 meters in diameter, hovering stationary for more than one hour over the forest-covered mountains, five kilometers southwest of the village of Zemlyanichnoye.

"The circular UFO had a flat cone-shaped upper part (something like a Vietnamese or Chinese hat), with a small cone on top, and a short vertical antenna. The lower part was like a big deep saucer, with the upper part wider than the lower. It had segmented structure like several vertical and horizontal sectors, marked by slightly visible lines. The color of the entire object was dull-gray metallic.

"Many local residents saw the UFO, but there are frequent sightings, so many do not pay much attention to the regularly observed UFOs. The local press also often refuses to publish UFO reports, since they are so common.

"I personally interrogated the witness in the most detailed way and a picture of the craft was drawn."

Thanks to Anton A. Anfalov, Ukrainian UFO Research Association (UKUFAS) an@crimea.com.

* * *

UFO WAVE OVER CRIMEA, UKRAINE.

UFO HOVERS OVER HIGHWAY -- On Thursday, April 24, 2003, a disk-shaped UFO was seen hovering over Evpatoriyskoye Highway northwest of Simferopol's outskirts, near the Dzerzhinskiy collective farm. An energetic anomaly flew off the craft that may be responsible for an auto accident. Later that day, at the same location, a road accident occurred when two cars collided. All drivers and passengers survived but both cars were destroyed.

Note: the 24th, of every month is very active date for UFOs.

Thanks to Anton A. Anfalov, UKUFAS (Ukrainian

UFO Association) an@crimea.com

* * *

CRIMEA: UFO HOTSPOT.

FOROS -- On Friday, May 15, 2003, two "daylight disks" were seen hovering over a mountainous ridge at the extreme southwest point of the Crimean peninsula between 2:00 and 2:20 PM. The disks were metallic, 10 to 12 meters in diameter and ~6 meters high, with high central domes and smaller, smooth protruding parts underneath.

They approached from the Black Sea and were seen for twenty minutes.

Note: UFOs are very frequent seen over the Bai'darskaya Valley that can be named "Ukrainian UFO Valley" and often, local residents do not even pay attention because they observe UFOs so often – even more frequently than airplanes!

* * *

Canada – Disk.

WHITBY, ONTARIO -- Around 7:50 A.M., the witness was walking to school on June 3, 2004, when he saw a disk that seemed to have two wings on its sides. It flew at a constant speed at only 250 feet altitude in a horizontal direction. It then climbed at about a 40-degree angle and disappeared. The witness states, "I know what a plane looks like but this craft gave me chills."

* * *

RIDING MOUNTAIN, Manitoba -- An object was seen in the sky to the southeast corner of the Riding Mountain National Park on August 11, 2004, at 1 PM. It was moving up and down and back and forth with blue lights around it with a red light on top. We watched it for about an hour and then went to bed. It darted back and forth in a small area for two hours.

Thanks to Brian Vike http://www.hbccufo.com/

* * *

COLOMBIA: THREE UFOs OVER CAPITAL.

BOGOTÁ -- William Chavez reports that on April 23, 2001, at 4:15 p.m., three objects of unknown origin were seen flying over Bogotá where more than 3,000 people in the city's business district witnessed them. The objects were in the vicinity of Cerro El Cable Hill where they remained motionless for four minutes. Radio broadcaster "Radiodifusora Nacional" and Todelar phoned Contacto OVNI, our research organization, to discuss this sighting live and because in recent years this type of phenomenon has become increasingly common.

Last March, a "mothership" was captured on video over Barrio Santa Isabel. When the video was analyzed, it was possible to see a large tubular object at an altitude of 10,000 feet. This object also headed toward Bogotá's Cerro El Cable Hill.

On April 15th, Mr. Oscar Berrio filmed a disk-shaped object in the vicinity of El Dorado Airport and we are investigating this sighting.

Thanks to SHnSASSY1 and Contacto OVNI Translation (C) 2001. William Chavez www.epagos.com/contacto-ovni

* * *

INDIA DISK.

NEW DELHI -- Sunila reports that on August 15, 2001, huge, dark, silver gray, flying saucer-shaped UFO was observed for 7 or 8 minutes. The object was flying low. The witness indicated the color was silver gray. The object looked like two saucers inverted over each other and moved slowly across the sky. There were no known other witnesses in the neighborhood.

Thanks to sunilatandon@hotmail.com (sunila) and Joe Trainor reports@ufoinfo.com

* * *

CANADA DISK.

SURREY, BC -- On June 20, 2002, the witness was out on his apartment balcony at 6:30 PM, using his phone, when he spotted a disk-shaped craft that was silver on top with a darker bottom. He grabbed his field glasses but was unable to detect a cupola on the craft. The sky was clear and he estimated that the UFO was about 3000' from him at an altitude of 500.'

It was hovering and moving slowly S.S.E. when he first saw it. He watched it move behind a house and finally lost it from view when it headed south and disappeared behind some trees. Total viewing time 3 minutes. During the viewing period he had time to phone Terry Tibando, Vancouver Working Group Coordinator for CSETI (Center for the Study of Extraterrestrial Intelligence) in Port Moody describing what he was watching.

Thanks to Life Boat News.

http://www.lifeboatnews.com%20willthomas@telus.net/index.html

* * *

GREECE: ALIENS LAND AND DAMAGE CROPS.

PRINI -- Aliens have landed on farmers' fields and are destroying the crops. A farmer from Koziakas region reports bizarre flying objects that landed in his field last week wreaked havoc with his wheat field.

"A disk-shaped object appeared over my field, it was full of holes!" said Athanassos Tsioukas. The farmer, confused by what he saw, rushed to the local coffee shop. "When we got back to the field the aliens had gone but their machine had left markings in the soil, each as deep as 20 cm. My crops had been cut off."

Farmer Apostolos Patramanis, who owns the next field, is another witness of the landing. "Bright flashes light up the sky and then a huge object appeared and landed on Tsiokas's crops," he claims. "The children said they also saw the sky glistening above the village when the object was landing."

In recent years, growing numbers of UFO sightings have also been reported in Cyprus, Greece.

Thanks to Sirius.

* * *

SAUCER LANDS IN GREECE.

KOZYAKA -- According to the Athens News Agency, Dozens of peasants saw a UFO land in a farm field near Trikala in northern Greece during the morning hours of August 7, 2002. The flying object was disk-shaped and 10 meters [33 feet} in diameter, with hundreds of small portholes on it. The UFO landed and left traces on the field.

The villagers described the flying saucer, which caused enormous light flashes and made unusual maneuvers.

Thanks to Haktan Akdogan of Sirius Space Sciences Research Center of Istanbul.

* * *

DAYLIGHT DISK CAUSES FENDER BENDERS IN SCOTLAND.

KINGSGATE RETAIL PARK -- The appearance of a huge silver UFO caused spooked drivers to bump their cars at around 8:45 AM, last Wednesday, February 12, 2003.

Drivers were so distracted by the bizarre sightings that at least two minor bumps were reported, as the attention of motorists wandered. A local woman contacted the NEWS and said: "My friend saw something hovering, which was silver in appearance and looked like the dishes you see on the side of television transmitters. It was huge, and it was pulsating. Many saw it, as you couldn't have missed it. He thought, 'Good God!' and was really quite shaken by the whole thing. My friend thinks the accidents at Kingsgate were a result of the sighting."

Colleagues in the Cumbernauld had seen a similar object thirty minutes earlier and alerted their South Lanarkshire counterparts that it was heading their way. The sighting has also intrigued East Kilbride UFO Club, whose members were warned in advance that they might be about to spot something strange.

Lee Close, of the Anglo-Scottish UFO Research Agency, has been investigating last week's events in tandem with the local UFO club. He said, "This is the first time I've come across a UFO that caused a car crash, although I'm aware of it having happened in America before."

Thanks to Jeff,
Rense.http://www.rense.com/general35/daylight.htm

* * *

AUSTRALIA – FORMATION OF DISKS OVERHEAD.

MELBOURNE – The witnesses were at a party and decided to go for a walk down the foreshore nature trail on December 1, 2003. "At 4:24 PM, we were about ten minutes into the trip and we were thinking about heading back and turned around when one of my friends yelled out, 'Hey, what the hell is that?'

"There were a few screams from the females, but then we settled down and stood there in amazement as these nimble crafts floated 800 to 900 meters above our heads. They were disk-shaped objects that seemed to be able to move in any direction and flew about in a pattern. They had no reliance on the winds like the planes of today. We were all frightened and we admitted afterwards that it was a terrifying experience."

* * *

Australia: UFO Hovers.

PERTH – A disk-shaped object flew from a nearby hill then overhead in a 'V' formation. It hovered for about three minutes and then flew over our heads in a suburban area in daylight at 12:24 PM on March 14, 2004. It flew at a slow pace then sped off extremely fast.

* * *

Canada.

CALGARY, ALBERTA – Three witnesses reported seeing two disks on March 28, 2004, at 5:10 PM. "I was looking into the sky at the Confederation driving range watching a ball when I saw the first object moving across the sky at a high rate of speed. I was able to point it out to two friends and they tracked it with me. As we watched it move across the sky, we noticed a second one in front of it. They were moving at such an incredible rate of speed that they simply vanished into the distance.

"The two objects were circular in shape and had a silver metallic color to them."

Thanks to HBCC UFO Research, which is following up the report. Brian Vike, Director. http://www.hbccufo.com

* * *

Cuba: Flying Disk Lands.

HAVANA -- In the surroundings of Expocuba, a fairground located in the capital city municipality of Boyeros, several persons witnessed the presence of a UFO on May 18, 2004, according to the Juventud Rebelde newspaper. Residents saw the descent of a UFO on Saturday, May 8, around 10 AM. A small oval-shaped vessel, silver-colored with a metallic tail, landed in an open field encircled by trees on the El Pedregal farm, located near Expocuba southeast of Havana.

Raul Beltran, 17, states, "I was tidying the shelves when a bright light came through the window that was like a glowing ball with a tail in its lower section. I showed it to my mother and quickly ran outside to see where it would fall and watched at the site until the UFO took off once more. It lifted off rather perpendicularly and then left through the palm trees.

"It didn't make any noise nor issue any smoke. The only thing I'm sure of is its size: more or less the size of a pickup truck tire."

Raul's mother, Odalis, states, "When my son showed it to me, I thought it was a kite or a parachutist, since skydivers drop over Expocuba every so often! After, as it came down, I realized that it could be nothing of the sort, since it was smaller and glowed a lot. It looked like a mirror."

Remigio Sanchez, who works as a warehouseman claims having seen a light in the sky almost at the same time as the other spectators. "It was a powerful glow in the sky, but it was far away so I thought it was a flare. Raul's mom told me that a device had landed nearby."

According to witnesses the grass and small plants at the site where the UFO landed are somewhat burned, although it is true that the current drought at the site is causing similar things to happen at other nearby locations.

"It has not been possible to scientifically confirm the presence of any UFO anywhere in the world." According to Oscar Alvarez Pomares, a specialist in the Science Office of the Ministry of Science, Technology and the Environment. "People want to believe that other beings exist in the universe, although I am not saying that what the protagonists of this episode saw was untrue."

Thanks to Prensa Latina May 19, 2004.
* * *
Japan.
Tokyo -- Our-J-UFO Magazine reports a disk was captured on a Pentax MZ-5 Sigma camera on January 21, 2001, over an Urawa, Corso Department Store and observed by over 30 witnesses. Jun-ichi Kato spotted the UFO in the Southern sky and urged staff photographer Nishikawa to photograph the shiny white sphere ten miles north of Tokyo.

Thanks to Our J-UFO magazine. www.our-j.com
* * *
CANADIAN SIGHTINGS CONTINUE.
TORONTO – "My uncle was looking up at a helicopter on August 4, 2002, when he saw a small circle being followed by a larger circle flying in formation. At 5:00 PM, they were stationary for about ten minutes and the smaller one disappeared and a minute later the bigger one split into two and vanished. After a short period of time many more objects started flying across the sky and then vanished. They circled back and continued flying for 35 minutes. They were stationary in different spots in the sky.

"Looking at them with binoculars, they were two crafts close together. My theory is if they were UFOs. They were watching a large gathering of nearly a million people. They moved much faster than the planes approaching or leaving the airport."

Chapter 4

Worldwide Nocturnal Disks

UNITED KINGDOM 23RD UFO SEEN OVER DALES IS GIANT DISK.

DERBYSHIRE, ENGLAND 2001 -- Andy Darlington of the Matlock Mercury Newspaper writes, "The mystery of UFO sightings over the Peaks and Dales shows no signs of abating after the 23rd reported sighting in the last eight months." Since September, locals have spoken of strange lights, flying saucers, and huge triangular craft in the skies. One was even caught on video. Now a 34-year-old Wirksworth man, who asked not to be named, says he saw a giant disk-shaped craft over Idridgehay.

He was driving to market in Derby at 3:00 AM, when he saw the UFO hovering near the road. In addition, he was the first person who'd seen the UFOs to admit feeling afraid by what he saw. "It did frighten me because I couldn't explain what it was," he remarked. "I've never seen anything like this before and logic couldn't explain it. It was shocking. I've never been a believer in UFOs and sightings but I believe in them now."

The man said the craft was hovering above woods and seemed to rotate. It had blue, red, and white lights. The incident follows another sighting of three flying saucers.

Thanks to Gerry @ Farshores.

* * *

UNITED KINGDOM: UFO WAVE.

DERBYSHIRE DALES -- The Matlock Mercury News of July 5, 2001, reports, L. Alison (29) of Lant Lane says, "I was watching Big Brother and nothing usually drags me away from that!" she joked.

Software sales executive Alison watched the UFO for around 30 seconds at 10:35 PM. She described it as disk-shaped and having four, green, flashing lights, arranged in a square. "I'm not a freak!" she insisted. "I'm not mad and I've never ever seen anything like this before. It was huge and must have been 1,000 feet high. It was nothing like an airplane or star. Someone else must have seen it."

The craft made no movement. Alison stepped outside to call her boyfriend from their garage so he could share in the strange close encounter.

Alison's sighting is now the 27th in the Derbyshire Dales since last September. The region is becoming widely known as a UFO hotspot among enthusiasts and features extensively on websites all over the world.

Fox TV in America is filming a documentary about the famous Bonsall sighting in October and Nottingham's Four Sheets Films is shooting another about the wider picture.

* * *

KELOWNA, BC, Canada.

The witness states, "At 11:30 PM, I observed a disk-shaped object hovering silently 500 feet above Dillworth Mountain on August 7, 2001. The disk had a large red and white ball of light in the center. The color of the disk appeared black against the night sky and produced no sound. The object turned down the illumination of the center red and white ball of light like a dimmer switch."

* * *

CANADA – DISK.

VICTORIA, BC -- My wife and I observed a dark brown/black disk shaped object on December 31, 2001. It was moving above a 9 story high-rise at 11:20 PM, and was the size of a two-dollar coin held at arm's length. I was wearing my glasses, which are not a precise prescription and saw a dome on its top and a disk-shaped underside that seemed to dip slightly back and forth while moving generally south. It tipped slightly at a forward angle. At the same time it swooped a few degrees to the left and back before resuming a straight course south.

I called to my wife, Leann, who came quickly. She also saw the dome on the top but she thought it might have been a balloon. A few things seem to militate against it being a balloon:

1)   It was moving very quickly and it was not windy (at least not at ground elevation).

2)   It appeared to slow down, almost hover, and then accelerate.

3)   It moved side-to-side.

4)   It was disk-shaped and dark.

Later, a fellow mentioned that he and some coworkers had seen the object at 11:30 AM. They were working a block to the west near downtown Victoria. His coworkers were looking at it with some degree of excitement, as they also were not certain what it was either but decided it must have been a balloon.

* * *

PRINCE RUPERT TO TERRACE, BC -- At 10:30 PM, a couple driving home 85 kilometers west out of Terrace witnessed a huge object traveling north across the Skein River on February 22, 2003. The disk shaped craft was dark and moved very slowly, but had two, large, almost rectangular lights that could be seen glowing from the bottom.

The husband wanted to pull over to get a better look, but his wife was frightened, crying and "insisted" that he keep going – and quickly.

* * *

UKRAINE: NEWS FLASH OF UFOs OVER CRIMEA

CRIMEA -- Victor Zdorov was walking his dog near the old center of Simferopol on July 24, 2002, at about 9 PM, when he noticed five to six white lights in line in the northeastern sky. At first, he thought they were planes, but there was no sound and the number and configuration of lights was different from any aircraft.

He thought, it might be landing lights for approach to Simferopol but the airport was too far away. While approaching, the lights started blinking periodically, not like the constant blinking of commercial aircraft. Six flashes were in an interval of every second. The shape of the object was not discernible but the lights indicated it was a disk-shaped object with white lights on its rim.

* * *

SIMFEROPOL' -- On Sunday, June 22,2003 at 10 PM, Anton saw a UFO hovering directly in front of the windows of his flat, near the nearby 9-storied building on Prospect Pobedy (Victory highway). The object was about 200 meters above the town, creating three bright, white flashes at an interval of 7 to 10 seconds. This was definitely not an airplane and the intervals between the flashes were long, indicating that the object was almost hovering over the same place.

The exact shape was not visible since it was dark. There was an airplane with a clearly visible red blinking light and auxiliary lights flying behind the UFO.

On June 24, two UFOs were observed over Simferopol', both flying north. The first was at 22:10, and second at 22:15. Both were disk-shaped or "hat-shaped." The first was brightly shining; the second suddenly increased and decreased its brightness, vividly demonstrating itself.

Mrs. Lenura Azizova states, "I clearly saw the shining of the silver hull of this craft that was flying at a very low altitude of about 150-200 meters above me. The dull-gray object was shaped like two deep saucers joined together. It was ten meters in diameter and five meters high. It was like inside a cloud of dust visibly spraying some powder or aerosol around it."

Thanks to Anton A. Anfalov. an@crimea.com

* * *

SIMFEROPOL' -- The same day, at 9:20 PM, a big disk was seen hovering north of the city. It was clearly visible by a light on its side, that was silver-white and brighter than Venus. The disk was flat and about 30 meters in diameter with a small central dome on top. After several seconds, the light was switched off.

Apparently, aliens are interested in observing Simferopol' International airport, the second biggest in Ukraine, as well as nearby Gvardey'skoye military air base that has Russian Su-24 bombers.

On Saturday, May 17, 2003, at 11:25 PM, a remarkable fish-shaped object was observed flying over Simferopol.' It had an oblong, smooth streamlined hull, visible by 3 lights beneath the bottom of the craft. The front was a green light, the middle a red light and a bright amber light in back. It was 50 to 55 meters in length and about 8-10 meters high. The hull, reflected by lights, was dull-gray or dull-brown. After being visible for ~10 seconds, the lights on the craft died and it vanished.

This thing was absolutely soundless, big and definitely not an airplane. The positioning of the lights is quite different from normal aircraft and pilots do not switch off their lights.

On Monday, May 19, 2003, at 9:50 PM, a bright shining UFO was observed over Simferopol' by local residents, flying from southeast to northwest. This was like a white star, very bright, as Sirius. It was moving 2-3 times faster than any satellite.

Mr. Viktor Zdorov, while walking his dog, could see a dim yellow star of a satellite passing nearby the UFO at the very same part of the sky. The satellite was dim and moving much slower.

On Wednesday, May 21, 2003, at 9:20 Anton became a witness to a bright white-yellowish star over South Simferopol' that was hovering and started slowly moving directly to the east. The star was changing brightness and pulsating. This was definitely not a satellite or ISS. This object was moving directly to the east, following the direction of Earth rotation.

The object was observed on May 13, 15, 17, 19 and 21! So that means with a period of every 2 days! Note, also, that many cases are not reported, so, the real number of cases is likely much bigger and almost daily!

* * *

CANADA DISK AND CYLINDER LIGHTS OBSERVED.

VANCOUVER ISLAND, BC -- On September 10, 2002, it displayed a somewhat circular-shaped outline with changing vibrant colors of purple to green to blue then solid blue with red glow on trailing edge. At 10:50 PM, a bright white light came into view changing to a bright color changing disk with neon blue and a red trailing edge. It moved overhead in a westerly direction, slower than a meteorite with stark and bright colors. Then the object disappeared.

* * *

AZERBAIJAN DISK.

NAXCIVAN -- The witness reports, "My friends own the Internet Cafe and I closed up late that night. It had been raining, but the rain stopped as I left the cafe at 3:30 AM, on September 25, 2002. It was a very dark night, and I looked up and saw a big X, like a disk hovering above us. WOW, it was very big. It was so big that it didn't allow the rain to fall on us. I think it was 500 to 600 meters in diameter and it was hovering over the city. I saw one man shoot his pistol about eight times at the object and it started to move away. Then it started to rain again.

"The police came and arrested the man. I'm 100% sure this was a UFO."

* * *

CANADA SPHERES SPOTTED.

BABINE LAKE -- Brian Vike reports, "I had a telephone call from a nice fellow who reported an incident at a logging camp across the lake from Granisle, BC. He and three other coworkers were logging when one of the workers gave out a loud cry, 'Look at that bright light coming up from behind the trees.'

"A large glowing golden/orangish disk-shaped object with a large halo of white around the craft rose up a half kilometer away, stopped and hovered. The object moved away from their location after ten seconds, heading north. They did lose sight of the craft quickly but still could see the bright light for five minutes."

Thanks to Brian Vike - HBCC UFO Research Editor: Canadian Communicator hbccufo@telus.net

* * *

MALAYSIA: HIGH SPEED DISK SHAPE.

SKUDAI -- On January 17, 2003, at 9:30 PM, my dad and I saw an orange colored flying object move from east to west above my Dad's house. This object moved fast and was stable when it was moving. It was going up and not going down. I'm sure this is a disk-shaped flying object.

The UFO slowed a bit as it hovered above us and seems like it noticed us as we looked at them. After a few minutes it continued with a fast and stable speed and disappeared behind the crown.

This is fifth time I've seen UFOs in the last two years. The last time it was closer, bigger and we even saw the "windows" of the UFO.

* * *

AUSTRALIA: BIG DISK-SHAPED OBJECT FLASHING COLORS.

MELBOURNE -- The witness saw three UFOs on May 25, 2003, at 8:00 PM, while sitting outside. The eyewitness states, "It looked like three disk-shaped things bobbing up and down in the air, flashing blue to white to red back to blue etc. If they landed in my backyard, they would have been about 30 feet long and 30 feet wide."

* * *

Canada.

ORILLIA, ONTARIO -- On December 8, 2003, at 6:30 PM, the witness was looking out the window when he noticed a really bright light just above the tree line. It was ten times the brightest star with a big band of black cloud emerging on it. The witness grabbed his binoculars and parked in an open field where the highways merge. The clouds were under it but the light glare was so immense. It lit up the clouds to an orange color.

The witness states, "I watched for about 15 minutes and saw it up close; a disk, perfectly round, with a glowing white aura around it, flying perfectly flat with no spin. It was beautiful and, when it crossed over me, it was huge. It was the size of a dime at arm's length,

"On October 4, 2003, my children, 9 and 7, out on a nature walk, pointed out to me a cigar-shaped UFO high in the sky over Oro Medonte."

* * *

Canada: Sightings Increase.

VANCOUVER, BC. -- On April 24, 2004, at 9 PM, the witness observed a white light moving in an easterly direction across Indian Arm from Seymour Mountain, flying at about 2,500 feet. It was traveling faster than most small planes and he watched the white light blink out. A few seconds later there was a single, red strobe flash and then the white light reappeared, going back the way it came just as fast. There is no way a small plane could have reversed directions that fast.

The witness states, "I grabbed my new Video camera and in the few seconds it took to warm up, the light blinked out again. There was still a little light in the sky but I could see nothing in the area. I checked with my binoculars but found nothing.

"In the beginning of April 2004, the sky was overcast with low thick clouds at 1000 feet and about 5 PM, I noticed two dull yellow disk-shaped objects flying, one behind the other, in a SSE directions. These glowing disks appeared to be either in the clouds or just over them. I would estimate they were over 108 and King George and, from that distance, appeared to be about the size of the full moon. Their speed was 3 to 4 hundred miles an hour. Duration of sighting was about five to ten seconds."

Thanks to Brian Vike, Director.

* * *

Canada: Disk and Lights.

TORONTO – The witness was on his way home from work on April 20, 2004, at 8:36 PM, and driving through a stretch of farm field area, saw a very white light coming from his right side. The observer stated, "The light was so bright that I tried to speed up to go right past it.

46

As I went past the light I saw a fairly large sized disk shaped UFO. Size wise, I would say it was about the size of a fighter plane but disk shaped.

"I slowed down to a stop about 50 feet past the UFO. I turned around and looked back. It seemed to be floating in the air. I wasn't able to make out a color but I could definitely see the shape in the dark. It floated for about a minute and then it sort of swung like a pendulum, side to side, before blasting to its left up towards the sky. It took about 10 -15 seconds for the UFO to vanish into the sky.

"Confused and shocked I drove home."

* * *

Canada: Mighty close encounter.

Bob Holliday, Staff Reporter of the Winnipeg Sun writes, Terry McDonald thought his eyes were playing tricks last week when he saw a bright light following his truck. "The light was behind me. It was so bright, I thought my dome light was shorting out," said McDonald from his home in Crane River, about 320 km northwest of Winnipeg. McDonald did start to worry when his truck intermittently lost power over the course of about a kilometer.

"McDonald's sighting *wasn't* a rare occurrence," said Manitoba's leading UFO researcher, Chris Rutkowski. "It was fairly quiet and now all of a sudden a whole bunch of things are happening," said Rutkowski. "I've had a number of reports in the past two weeks."

Among the sightings was "a whole bunch of disk-like lights hovering on top of a Greyhound bus traveling on Highway 6 between Ericksdale and Ashern last Tuesday," said Rutkowski. As well, he's received reports of lights west of Kenora, Ontario. A Kenora resident, who wished to remain anonymous, claimed he saw a saucer-like object on Monday. The man said the object was hovering about 18 meters (60 feet) above the ground about 10 km west of Keewatin. He observed the saucer for nearly an hour before it moved fairly slowly across the treetops.

The most reported light show is the convergence of the planets Jupiter and Venus, said Rutkowski. "They are very close together and look like an airplane coming into land but not going anywhere," he added. "A landing plane wasn't what was witnessed in Crane River," said McDonald's daughter, Tracey McDonald, who saw something odd in the sky about 1:30 a.m. on Thursday. "It was many green, red and white, flashing lights that were really low. Then, there was a big white flash, as big as a house," she said. McDonald said neighbors have reported seeing small, disk-like lights darting between trees in nearby forests.

Reports of UFOs in Canada have skyrocketed. "The fact we have 700 sightings (in Canada) this year is interesting," Rutkowski said. "We didn't even have 700 total last year."

Thanks to:
http://www.canoe.ca/NewsStand/WinnipegSun/News/2004/11/13/pf-712255.htm l

* * *

ITALY: CROWD WATCHES UFO.

CREMONA -- Corriere della Sera [Evening Courier June 19, 2001, By Sperangelo] Bandera reports that many people, equipped with binoculars and cameras, saw an orange light in the sky on Friday night, June 15th. It was observed to fly very fast towards the east and then return to the same point in the sky. The flying disk was seen near midnight from the area of Stagno [Pond] Lombardo, Martignana Po, to Casalmaggiore and Vicoboneghisio, all communities that border the River Po.

"I thought that it was Sirius," said Claudia, a witness, "I understood that it could not be that star, because it proceeded to zigzag and emanate an orange light. It moved much too fast to be a satellite."

Pier Toscani and his mother Katia also saw the UFO from their shop in Casalmaggiore. "I am skeptical," he said, "but I admit its intermittent light left an impression on me. My mother was frightened. Many people are being organized with cameras, hoping to discover its true nature."

Thanks to Jerry Farshores
* * *

ENGLAND: UFO BACK IN THE DALES.

DERBYSHIRE -- Matlock Mercury reported how a disk-shaped object had been captured on video over Bonsall Moor last October, for six minutes, just hovering quietly in the sky. Some experts have hailed the footage as "the best UFO video ever" and it has been the subject of national and international interest.

On August 27, 2001, Karen Sismey looked out from the Thorn Tree Inn to spy a similar object in the same area. "My husband Phil had been out there at around 10:45 PM when he saw something hovering in the sky for a good 15 minutes. It was showing very vivid colors with red at the bottom and then ranging from emerald and blue colors to a bright lemon yellow."

Other visitors to the Thorn Tree saw the object. "It was not a helicopter or an airplane and I know that it shouldn't normally be there."

Thanks to Jerry Farshores, www.100megsfree4.com/farshores/
* * *

RUSSIA: HUNDREDS WATCH UFO DOGFIGHT OVER AIRBASE.

SEROV -- Vickie York reports, "Hundreds of awestruck eyewitnesses watched in shock and disbelief as 36 UFOs waged a spectacular dogfight above a Russian air base!"

The incredible aerial battle, which took place at about 5,000 feet, was seen by Russian air force officers and two visiting foreign journalists from Poland and Latvia. "For twelve minutes, the sky was ablaze with rays fired from the battling starships," says Polish news reporter Igor Wroclawski, who was there to cover an air show. "Several

48

of the craft that were hit appeared to be damaged by the rays and one of them caught fire and crashed into the mountains."

The dogfight erupted at 2:05 AM on May 11, 2001 at the foothills of the Ural Mountains. Radar first detected two groups of massive objects entering Russian air space and the base was put on full alert.

"When I went outside, some soldiers were pointing up in the sky," says Wroclawski. "I looked up and I could see dozens of saucer-shaped objects, about 90 feet in diameter, circling overhead." Within minutes of the initial radar sightings, the two sets of flying disks opened fire.

"The weapons were as deafening as thunder and they lit up the entire night sky," says Wroclawski. "After twelve minutes, the UFOs took off to the south."

The Russian government emphatically denies the report, claiming there have been no recent sightings of UFOs at any Russian installations. But U.S. intelligence sources aren't buying it. "If a UFO really did crash in the Ural Mountains, you can bet the Russians are going to keep it secret until they have a chance to salvage any alien technology they can," a CIA source observed.

* * *

ITALIAN UFO SPOTTED BY WATCHMAN.

ORBASSANO --The Italian Center for UFO Studies reports, "A clamor was raised all over Italy because of a mysterious object sighted by a night watchman in Turin, in the early hours of September 28, 2002."

The watchman said, "The UFO phenomenon was preceded by control monitors in the surveillance cabin failing and, at the same time, the electronic-controlled gate opened by itself in the truck rest-area at 4:27 A.M." The young man went outside to investigate and felt something akin to a slight breeze, which was accompanied by a whistling noise. He then found himself enshrouded in a beam of light emanating from above. He saw a luminous disk approximately 3 meters in diameter rotating on itself, which streaked out of sight after a few seconds, as if swallowed up by the sky.

The monitor then came back on. The frightened watchman then telephoned the Carabinieri and appeared shaken when the patrol squad arrived.

There were 38 observations in October, for a total of 615 sightings in Italy for the first ten months of this year.

Thanks to UFOTEL, Edoardo Russo,
http://www.proz.com/translator/723

* * *

NEW ZEALAND: DISK WITH COLORED LIGHTS.

GISBORNE CITY -- On Saturday, April 12, 2003, Laurence Fleming reports that around 11: 50 PM, there was occasional cloud cover. "My wife had been outside our home and spotted this object and watched for about 15 minutes. The object displayed a red to green and yellow color pattern, alternating frequently to blue as well.

"The object was very bright in appearance and hovered in one particular part of the sky. My wife called me and I grabbed my new 10 X 50 binoculars, focusing in on this very distinct, multi color light in the sky. I told her, 'That thing's some sort of craft.' A spaceship or whatever was hovering in close proximity at low in altitude with a very distinct shape.

"After several minutes of observing this craft, it suddenly vanished and then, to our amazement, suddenly reappeared further away in the sky in less than a second! I haven't seen anything like that before! There was something rotating on this object. The craft eventually was lost from our vision by cloud cover."

Thanks to Laurence Fleming.

* * *

Malaysia – Disk.

KUALA LUMPUR – The witness reports, "I poked my head through my 5th floor window April 08, 2004, about 7 PM, to invite my friend who lives upstairs to eat dinner with me. Suddenly I noticed a black eagle-like object, which was hovering close by. It was a black disk-shaped UFO. It floated at the same attitude going forward. I pointed it out to my friend and he thought it was the so-called UFO too.

"We looked carefully at it as it slowly hovered, just like helicopters. I estimated it to be about 100 meters from the ground and about the size of a car. It made no sound. The disk flew in a very unique way. It flew like something injured, because it sloped 45 degree to the left then right then left again as it traveled along. If it were flown by humans, they would easily be affected by nausea in such aircraft.

"I noticed a red light flashing at the back of the craft. The atmosphere near it was a little lighter than normal, maybe due to shimmering. It disappeared in the distance."

Thanks to Brian Vike, CANADA HBCC.

* * *

Iran: Flying Saucer Fever.

TEHRAN – Numerous UFO sightings are being reported over Iran. Fanciful cartoons of alien spacecraft have adorned the front pages of newspapers while state television on Wednesday showed a sparkling, white disk it said was filmed over Tehran on Tuesday night. Fox News showed pictures that appeared to be classic disk-shapes moving over a city area. Iran is developing nuclear weapons and UFO's almost always take an interest in these developments.

Many UFOs beaming out green, red, blue and purple rays were seen over the northern cities of Tabriz and Ardebil and in the Caspian Sea. Newspapers and agencies reported people rushing out into the streets in eight towns on Tuesday night to watch a bright extraterrestrial light dipping in and out of the clouds.

Astronomers explained that the public was just seeing the planet Venus, whose light is very bright in the western sky.

* * *

India: Three Disks.

Steve Walters, AUSTRALIA UFO RESEARCH (NSW), received a report from Swati Sharma that on July 5, 2004, at 9:32 p.m., he saw three disk-like objects rotating rapidly and moving forward with a great speed. They were very high and were a dim red-color light.

"I rushed for my camera but they disappeared. I am from Sharanpur, which is a small city in Uttar Pradesh, India. The disk-like objects were probably UFOs. I wanted to share my information as it might be of great help to you."

Thanks to Swati Sharma in India mast_libran2003@yahoo.co.in and Steve Walters, AUSTRALIA UFO RESEARCH (NSW), uforesearch@ufor.asn.au

* * *

Canada.

SOUTHWEST EDMONTON, ALBERTA – On July 28, 2004, a security guard was at work at about 1:30 AM. Walking outside the building and saw an odd disk object in the west sky with violently flashing red and yellow lights. It hovered in the same spot for about ten minutes. Then it would start to move violently left to right up and down and diagonally like it was shaking. This continued on for about another 30 minutes.

The guard went back inside and completed some work and went back out for another look. The guard states, "Now I saw eight disks stretched across the sky doing the exact same thing. I started to get a bit curious and I went to the front of the building for a look. I saw two more but these were a lot closer and lower than the other ones. One started to get really close and was about 5 to 10 km away and roughly 100 feet in the air. It was moving west and getting lower and lower. It went behind a small hill and it looked like it could have landed.

"At this point I was a bit nervous and notified the police. By the time they arrived the sky was getting light and you couldn't see much."

Thanks to Brian Vike www.hbccufo.com

* * *

UK – Disk.

TREHAFOD, SOUTH WALES --When Alison Moore looked into the night sky, she wondered if it was a bird, a plane or even a spaceship hovering above her home. The 26-year-old was amazed when she saw what appeared to be a bright disk floating above her house and grabbed her video camera and began filming the "alien ship" in the sky. But astronomers say the mystery object was probably Venus.

"I thought it was a shooting star at first because it was so bright," she said. "But when it didn't disappear, I thought it might have been a satellite. So I grabbed my video camera for a closer look because I didn't have binoculars and I knew I could zoom in with the camera. It was pretty amazing but I couldn't really see how good it was until the next day when I replayed the tapes.

"I could not believe my eyes when I looked at them again. It was really strange. The object kept zipping across the screen and the color changes were absolutely amazing.

"I've never believed in things like flying saucers before but, after seeing this, I've changed my mind."

Alison showed the tapes to her uncle, Alfie Passey. "I have always thought that these reports of a flying saucer were bull," he said. "I thought that these things that people had seen were most likely a satellite. But after seeing the tapes of what Alison had seen, I am absolutely convinced that it was a flying saucer."

Thanks to BBC.
http://news.bbc.co.uk/1/hi/wales/south_east/3542418.stm

* * *

India – Disk.

YAMUNA NAGAR, HARYANA -- On July 31, 2004, five witnesses saw a large UFO in the shape of a disk moving north to south in a fire-like color at 11:38 PM. The object was making a buzzing sound. Other facts you may wish to include: I feel that the UFOs appear in India in the months from July - September, because last year I saw an unidentified object on July 26, 2003, the report of which was submitted on your website.

This time it was more clear and prominent in the sky because it was close to me. It was a disk-shaped object emitting bright light and buzz sound on intervals. First, it was stationary at one place and suddenly it flew off at a high speed. I was standing at my fuel station along with my five employees. I took a photograph with my NOKIA 6230 Color screen digital mobile phone.

www.ufoindia.org

* * *

Australia - Disk Shaped Craft and Burns on Body.

URANIA, S.A. – One night in April 1975 a friend of mine called me and asked if I wanted to go spotlighting for foxes, I said yes and traveled to his farm 10 miles south of Maitland and arrived there about 21:00. After going inside and chatting for a while with my friend, Brad, his Mum, Pam and another friend, Michael, I said that I was going outside to get things ready to go spotlighting.

As I walked out the back door (facing east), I noticed what I initially thought was a large shooting star coming down from the east and to the southeast. But the shooting star stopped dead at about 20 degrees above the horizon and began traveling across the sky towards the east and flashing blue, red and white lights at 9:15 p.m. I yelled to the others to "Come out here, NOW! Look At This!"

They came running out and we all stood in the back yard watching as the UFO traversed the horizon. I got my rifle out of my car and began watching it through the telescopic sight and was amazed to see it was about 40 meters across and about 20 meters high. It was disk-shaped with windows around the edge of the disk and a flashing dome on top. It had a polished aluminum top and it looked so close that I had to move the scope to see all of it.

Brad went to get his binoculars while Pam, Michael and I took turns watching through the riflescope. After about 5 minutes, Brad came back. He had been watching it through the binoculars and I could see from the porch light that he was as white as a ghost. The UFO was now around 1000 meters away and traveling towards us. I got scared and was going to have a shot at it but was told off by Pam, so I lowered the rifle. As I did, the UFO started to retreat and slowly move off to the north towards Maitland.

We kept watching, as it became just a red flashing light, until it was over the eastern side of Maitland, where it hovered. Four other little red lights seemed to enter the (Mother ship) UFO and then the UFO took off in a slight arc to the east into the sky and disappeared in less that a second.

We were on a dirt road, parallel to the bitumen road, so the craft would have been only about maybe 50 feet off the ground and pacing us. We were doing about 30 mph. Pam, Brad's Mom, said "Oh I've seen them before they'll be back!"

Thanks to Brian Vike and AUFORN (Australian UFO Network)
* * *

Canada.

EDMONTON -- The witness had just gotten out of work on August 3, 2002, and was waiting at a bus stop at midnight. He states, "I heard an odd buzzing noise and looked up to see a small, silver disk floating several feet above me. I could not define the size of the craft, as it appeared to be both near and far away.

"The object jutted back and forth and moved extremely fast in different directions. After doing so, it sort of blinked a blinding blue light and shot straight into the sky."
* * *

CANADA: DAYLIGHT DISK SIGHTINGS.

MILL BAY ON VANCOUVER ISLAND – Two, Alcan Aluminum smelter employees on February 22, 2003, noticed a large disk-shaped object traveling very low and slowly over the Douglas Channel. The disk rose up to clear the mountains to the north. The witnesses stood completely still with their mouths wide open, watching!

They said, "If it moved towards them, they believed they would have been unable to move".

The low flying disk had large, very bright, white lights that shone on the water that lit up a good sized area and made a portion of the object visible. No other lights were visible but, after two minutes, it gradually gained altitude to climb up over the mountain. They both knew for certain that what they were looking at was no normal aircraft due to its size, speed and strange shape.

* * *

BRITAIN: VIDEOTAPES GIANT UFO OUTSIDE HER HOME.

BONSALL -- The June 2, 2001, "Straits Times" article by Alfred Lee claims, a British housewife, captured amazing footage on her camcorder of a gigantic UFO, which hovered near her home for six minutes.

Mrs. Sharon Rowlands, 41, estimates that the UFO was an astonishing 4.8 km wide. The giant disk was pink and white in color, with yellow, orange and blue lights. It had a dark center and beamed pulses of intense light. It hovered about 3.2 km from her home in the tiny village of Bonsall, Derbyshire, 224 km from London, for two minutes before blasting away into the night sky at fantastic speed. Britain's Metereorological Office has confirmed that there were no freak weather conditions in the area at the time.

Experts at NASA, the American space agency, have asked to see the video footage as a matter of urgency. They will use top-secret imaging equipment and computers to try to figure out what the UFO is. They believe it is the same sort of image captured on one of their own cameras during a space shuttle mission.

Mrs. Rowlands said: "I was a complete and utter disbeliever in flying saucers and UFOs. But what I saw has made me think again. I looked outside and saw this huge disk hovering in the sky. I rushed outside and started filming. Through the camera lens, it looked like it was going to hit me. It looked like nothing I have ever seen before."

The video footage was purchased for 20,000 pounds from Mrs. Rowlands. Mr. Paul Hannan, 37, who lives in the nearby village of Bakewell, saw a dome-shaped craft "dancing in the sky". Two weeks later, a man living in Wirksworth, a 10-minute drive away, saw a similar object in the sky.

Thanks to Hans Bruin hbruin@euronet.nl

Chapter 5
Daylight Triangular-Shaped UFOs

The Space Shuttle is no longer flying (at the time of this writing) due to the apparent complexity of the craft and errors in management that have lead to the crash of two shuttles. Conversely, we have received over one hundred UFO reports each week for the last ten years, and can conclude that a very sophisticated and reliable technology is flying in our skies and in space. Many scientists claim UFOs do not exist, yet they have never examined the data, examined the radar tapes, nor even talked to the eyewitnesses. Some of the greatest and most intelligent people on Earth have been eyewitnesses to UFO technology that is far beyond anything known to exist in our technology. A new exciting world is available to those who will examine this evidence.

Common among hundreds of reports are Flying Triangles that hover or fly at extremely low altitude at 100 to 200 feet above highways and buildings. These craft operate well below the minimum flight rules for the safe operation of aircraft and are often reported by police for over twenty years. They also create a road safety hazard. They are described as having rounded wing tips with bright intense lights on each corner, usually with a large red light in the center. They make little or no sounds. They hover and then depart at high speeds. Today, in a terrorist environment, these craft could also present a terrorist threat and should be reported to Homeland Security and NORAD.

George Filer.

* * *

LOUISIANA SIGHTING: MULTIPLE TRIANGLES.

HONEY ISLAND SWAMP -- On January 13, 2002, Joe and Linda Montaldoy were driving in the swamp that includes Stennis NASA Test Site near Pearl River. They entered near sunset and drove in eleven miles and noticed the last of the hunters drive out about 5:45 PM, so they decided to leave.

They wrote, "As we got close to the gate a very bright, circular, strobing light appeared behind the trees to our left in the south. As it came over the tree line we got out of the car to watch it. I judged from the height of the microwave tower I could see, that it was about 1500 feet high. It continued in our direction and passed directly over our car. We could plainly see that it was a triangular-shaped, black object with an amber colored globe in the center, a red light at its front point and a white light at each of its back points. It was about the size of a commercial jet. We only viewed it for a few minutes because the road is narrow and trees line both sides.

"We left the swamp and were headed back to I-59. As we approached the ramp to the interstate, we saw that it had stopped over the swamp and was hovering in place. Because we are involved with MUFON, we called our State Director on our cell phone. The craft now turned back and headed southwest toward Pearl River. I could tell by the way it was headed that it would pass directly over a dead-end road I had been on before, so I drove to the end of this road.

"We got out of the car and spotted it moving very slowly at maybe 800 feet high. We were reporting over the phone. It stopped, turned on its axis and headed back in our direction and passed directly over us as we stood outside our car. There was absolutely no sound except the barking of some dogs in a nearby yard.

"We got back in the car and followed it down the road. It was no more than 500 or 600 feet over us and was moving very slowly. We were driving only about 20 mph and it stayed right in front and over us. At this point it was hard to tell if we were following it or it was staying with us. When we reached the end of the road the object headed south/southeast. We noticed two planes cross right over it at a much higher altitude.

"As we got back to the interstate, the object began to gain altitude and speed. It was headed towards the Pirate Harbor area. We lost sight of it on the interstate, so I decided to get off I-10 and go to Pirates Harbor Road. We drove down this road 5 or 6 miles and came to an open area. On one side of the road are camps and, on the other side, marsh. We could see the craft over the marshes. It appeared to be tipped over on its side. I could see no lights; I believe I was looking at the top of it. It was like a black shape against the stars.

"Before, it had been traveling like a flat triangle shape and we could see only the bottom of it. As I watched, it seemed to flip over on its other side and I could see the bottom of it. Sort of like a car would flip and first you would see the hood and roof, then you would see the underside and tires. Then it righted itself but continued to wobble. It was headed south-southeast toward the Ringlets Pass, which was about three miles from where we were. The Ringlets Pass is a deep-water channel that eventually leads into the Gulf of Mexico. We had to speed up to keep it in sight but it was slowly loosing altitude.

"When we got to the Ringlets Bridge, we could see it had come down into the marsh. We couldn't tell if it was in the water or above the water. Now it was lit up with bright white lights all along the edge of it. We came off the bridge and pulled into the Fort Pike boat launch.

"We got out of our car and called our State Director back on the cell phone. The object was over the water about 100 to 200 yards from us. To the right of us, in the north, a brilliant white light came into view. It was just above tree level, about 300 o 400 feet high and moving very slowly. It would move a little and then come to a complete stop. There was a beam of light coming from under it, making a searching pattern.

"As we watched, it started to move toward where we were standing. The light turned off and it passed directly over us. There was no sound. We could clearly see that it was a triangular shape with a red light in the front, white lights on both back points and an amber light in the middle. It was the same type of craft that was in the water but much smaller.

"As it passed over us, it made a circle toward the west and came back around. Several times it came to a complete stop. When it was back to the spot it had started from, it started to circle again. This time it was lower, maybe 200 to 250 feet, and moving more in the direction of the downed craft. Again very slow movement and several complete stops.

"As we stood watching, we saw another craft light up from the exact spot the first one had started. Craft #2 was moving in the same path and at the same speed and altitude as craft #1. As #2 passed over us we could see that it was another triangular craft with a red light in front, two white lights in back and an amber globe in the middle. Only this craft had two rows of white lights running down the center of its underside. There were six lights in each row and they were either next to the globe or over it.

"A third craft now showed up in the exact spot as the other two. It made the same slow, stopping movements and circled as the other two. As it passed over us we could see it was again a triangular craft with the same lights; red in front, white in back, and amber globe in the middle. The only difference in this one was that it sent out a beam of light from the front point for about 200 feet. The beam tilted downward but not far enough to reach the ground.

"Now the three crafts were moving in an extremely slow circle in the sky. They would stop completely and then move again. We were still on the phone with our State Director and at this time he told us we should get out of there.

"We took a last look and, to the south, an object was coming our way. We could not see the shape of this object. All we could see was a row of very bright lights. There were six lights; three lights, a space and then three more. They were extremely bright and they seemed to be blinking on very, very fast. So fast that you couldn't really tell when one went off the one next to it came on. They were flashing and strobing so quickly, that I couldn't really focus on them.

"Something caught my attention in the corner of my eye, and I turned around and realized that the craft in the water had changed. The white lights around its edge were now red. Then it simply went under the water and disappeared. At the same moment they all just disappeared. One moment there were four crafts in the sky and one in the water and the next there was nothing.

"We got in our car and made a rather speedy departure. Almost as soon as we were on the road, a triangular craft, red light in front, white lights in back, amber in the center, appeared to our left over the trees. At the same time car lights shone right behind us on bright beam.

"As the triangle flew over us the car engine started to cough and felt like it was going out. The lights on the car flickered on and off, the cell phone started to ring, but it said dead cell and went blank. All this happened in an instant. The triangle flew over us at about 100 feet heading east to west and disappeared. The car behind us passed at a very high speed and we saw that the plate said US Government.

"We both got a headache almost immediately. The headache was extremely painful. It felt like an immense pressure in our head and behind our eyes. Our eyes were burning. There was also a feeling of being ill.

"The incident took place between 5:45 and 8:30 PM."

Thanks to Joe and Linda Montaldoy.

* * *

CALIFORNIA SAW A LARGE FLYING TRIANGLE-SHAPED CRAFT.

VISTA -- On August 21, 2001, the witness reports seeing lights on each side of a flying triangle craft at 7:01 PM. "First a bright light came out from behind a cloud like a slow moving plane but it was not a plane because there were no red and green navigation lights on each side. There was no sound. It was just a white dot. Then, a minute later, another bright dot appeared and behind it was a triangle-shaped craft with three lights on each side followed. They all went behind a hill and that was it. I didn't see them leave."

* * *

LOUISIANA: DAYLIGHT SIGHTING.

ALEXANDRIA -- Andrew West Griffin from Louisiana MUFON writes, "A coworker of mine told me today that she was driving down a residential street when she saw a strange triangle-shaped craft slowly going in a northeast direction on October 15, 2001, at 10:30 AM. It was very unusual looking," she said. "It looked like a big flying triangle in a clear sky. I thought at first it might be some new radar plane heading to Barksdale AFB a hundred miles away but it wasn't going that way."

So far, there have been no other reports.
Cordially, Andrew Griffin LA MUFON.
awg_paperboy@hotmail.com

* * *

TENNESSEE: FLYING TRIANGLES.

MEMPHIS -- The witness reports, "I was on my way to work, traveling eastbound on Winchester Road on November 2, 2001, just outside of the Memphis city limits. There was low cloud cover covering the sun at 5:00 AM. I noticed a long, black object traveling south at high speed beneath the clouds. The object was traveling far faster than any flock of geese could fly. There appeared to be a black 'smudge' behind the object. I at first thought this might be a black vapor trail but the smudge seemed to move in tandem with the object but didn't linger in the sky.

"As we got closer, I saw an acute triangular shape with blurred indistinct edges. It moved across the sky at high speed and was out of sight within seconds.

"I'm a professional with two college degrees and sky-watch planes regularly at Memphis International Airport. I've never seen anything to compare with what I saw this morning."

* * *

NEW YORK: LARGE FLYING TRIANGLE GLIDES OVER HIGHWAY.

SCOTCHTOWN -- The witness was traveling westbound on State Highway 17 and saw, in the distance, a group of white lights with a central, blinking, red light moving off in the distance at 6:15 AM. There was heavy traffic in both directions as he drove four miles east of Exit 119 that intersects with State Highway 302, which leads to Pine Bush.

As he approached Exit 119 he was suddenly aware of a very large object (size of 737 at least) with three large, white lights substantially touching each other in a horizontal row. The craft was very low with an altitude of only 300 feet, descending silently as though gliding. Its speed was 60 MPH as it passed over Highway 17 traffic and continued to his right, descending over trees and rooftops and then turned left toward Pine Bush.

The witness says, "It was banking 45 degrees, revealing three large, white, moderately bright, circular lights defining a perfect equilateral triangle and a same size circular red light in the center. None of the lights were blinking. The area between the lights appeared black and triangular, barely distinguishable from the sky, which was still dark and completely overcast.

"The craft passed about 100 feet over and in front of me. The object descended far enough to disappear below my horizon. The terrain to my right at that point is below the elevation of Highway 17, where only treetops and rooftops of buildings are visible.

"I did not pull over to the shoulder because of traffic risk. Within seconds, I saw a road sign saying 'Pine Bush.' I passed same but doubled back onto 17 and then 302 and a side road off 302 in the direction of the apparent landing site, looking for the object but did not see it again. Stewart International Airport is fifteen miles east with C-5 aircraft."

* * *

KANSAS: HUGE FLYING TRIANGLE SEEN.

DESOTO -- The witness reports that on February 4, 2002, "I was going home eastbound on K10 at 6:35 PM and I noticed lots of aircraft. Lights to north were moving in unison but they were not separate aircraft. It was triangular in shape, with a light at each apex. These three lights flashed/blinked red and white at the exact same time. And in the middle of this 'thing' was a row or bank of five lights, which pulsated from right to left. They went from orange, yellowish, red and then white, all down the row.

"I'm sure many others saw this. The damn thing was HUGE! I estimate it at around 800 meters long and 500 meters wide at the base. It was fairly low, flying at about 1000 meters for 6 to 8 minutes."

* * *

TEXAS UFO.

THE SANCTUARY -- James reports that four separate groups at the Sanctuary saw four flying triangles over the Sanctuary and a multitude of other craft during CSETI training. Dr. Steven Greer and 30 guests were witness to the sightings. The triangle was witnessed by all four groups and filmed by three and there is excellent footage.

Steve Mareno with PSI Applications, Dr. Greer's group, Bill, Fern and family and another family were all present. This makes four independent groups, all of which witnessed them – three of which filmed the triangles. The first triangles shut down the cameras. None worked! The last large one allowed three of the groups to film it.

I do not know what it takes to validate the ongoing activity and contacts but to any reasonable mind this should be a clincher.

Thanks to James.

* * *

OREGON.

SPOKANE -- Ed writes, "I want to report a sighting I had on the evening of October 29, at about 5:20 PM, of two triangle-shaped objects flying over my home, 15 miles SE of Spokane. Over the hills to the East, I noticed a very bright light on an object heading WSW. I observed what appeared to be the normal red and green navigation lights on the wing tips and a red and white strobe in the bottom center of the craft. I also heard what sounded like a muted jet aircraft engine. However, what seemed out of place was the extremely bright single headlight on the nose of the craft, not the normal two landing lights.

60

"It was dusk but there was still a band of sunlight and as the craft flew slowly overhead at an estimated height of 1200 feet above me, I could not discern a fuselage or wings. I DID notice dim white lights on the underside, in locations that would correspond to the three corners of a triangle flying with the pointed end forward. I was kind of shocked because I could not see a tail on the aircraft. I watched the object intently as it moved to the band of fading sunlight but I still could discern only a triangle shape with no tail or defined fuselage! Within a minute, I saw a second similar craft with three dim lights in the corners and no discernable fuselage.

"I contacted Fairchild AFB and talked with a Public Affairs officer. I asked whether the B-2 stealth bomber or F-117 stealth fighter were operating in the Spokane area that evening. I saw the B-2 here a couple of months ago. The airman stated that none of their aircraft were operating in our area on the 29th. About 15 minutes later, I got a call from a civilian, apparently working in the Public Affairs office. I explained my observations, and my concern regarding the security concerns which it raised. He advised me that I sounded sincere and said, 'After the Air Force closed the Blue Book investigation, it no longer investigated unidentified Ariel phenomena.' He said that unless an unidentified aircraft appeared on their radar (and I'll use his emphatic words),'We don't care!' He must have said that at least three times during our conversation. The civilian advised that perhaps I should contact the FAA. I stated that I had done that previously.

"I just want to emphasize that the B-2 and the F-117 fighter have a distinctive 'saw-tooth' pattern to the trailing edge of their wings. The craft which I observed appeared to have a perfectly straight trailing edge -- just like a triangle and was at least as large as the B-2."

* * *

WISCONSIN: FLYING TRIANGLE.

EAU CLAIRE -- Larry D. reports, "I am filing this report for my daughter, Amy, who saw a flying triangle on November 25, 2002, directly over our house. The triangle was low on the horizon, 3 blocks southeast of the airport, flying ESE; lower than a normal landing pattern. It was roughly half again as fast as most jets that land over us and its shape was 'stealthy' but an equilateral triangle, not a pointy triangle. It made no noise and was seen for thee seconds and gave my daughter 'the chills' seeing it.

"Its color was a medium gray – not black. I showed her a photo of the F-117 and she felt this was more triangular and flatter on top. I drew several drawings and she chose one that has a small soft bump in the middle of the flat wing section. The speed and location of this plane are totally out of the norm. This is the landing area for the airport and there is no cross low flying traffic allowed for safety, so my only opinion left is a triangular UFO."

Thanks to UFOWisconsin Report.

* * *
CALIFORNIA: FLYING TRIANGLE.

SAN PEDRO -- The witnesses observed 7 to 10 red flashing lights in a triangular shape moving silently and slowly due south at 7:00 PM, on November 13, 2002. Many other small planes in relatively the same area were moving much more quickly than this object.

* * *
GEORGIA MUFON REPORT.

LAGRANGE -- MUFONGA has a source of information from a really sharp, intelligent and observant female resident, whose father is a 33-year veteran airline pilot, and her husband, a veteran Marine. This witness indicated that, shortly after 6 AM on Monday, December 2, 2002, she went onto her porch to feed her cats. She noticed a stationary blinking light above/through the pine trees across her street, where no blinking light should have been. She observed more closely and found it to be similar to a beacon light and she timed the flashes to about every eight seconds. She added that it appeared to be like a light on top of one of the satellite antennas but no such array exists in that area.

She later described it to her husband who told her of his experience during the same time frame. He arrived at his work location about 6:00 AM, which is about ten miles from home. About 6:25 AM that morning, he and a couple of his associates were outside and observed some sort of triangular appearing craft silently "zip" across the sky. It was just beginning to get light outside with only tree outlines visible. The flying triangle had one light in the center and may have been about the size of baseball at arm's length.

Thanks to Tom Sheets, State Director MUFONGA.

* * *
MAINE: BOOMERANG-SHAPED SHIP HOVERS.

OLD TOWN -- Zak Keenan writes, "Last week, Filer's Files reported about a college couple seeing a large flying triangle hovering 200 feet over the Catholic Church at 6:40 PM on January 10, 2003. I am a college student in Old Town and a frequent reader of your reports but I am a little skeptical of that UFO report. I was out at 4:30 AM, on January 20 and I too noticed a triangle shaped craft on the north end of Campus facing the direction of downtown Old Town. I was stunned. It was a ways off in the distance and it was hard to get an estimate as to how far away it was.

"I watched the craft come closer and, seeing how it was triangular shaped, I knew it could very easily be the wings of an airplane. In my view of looking at the object, I saw two towers that I believe are navigating towers for aircraft flying to Bangor International Airport, ten miles to the south.

"The object I was viewing made very little noise but I could faintly hear some noise as it moved closer. As much as I wanted to believe it was a UFO, it made more sense to pass the object off as a C5 cargo transport plane that frequents BIA. With the upcoming war in Iraq it only makes sense that they would be out there at night and flying a little lower trying to get more accustomed to flying in those conditions.

"I appreciate all that you do."

Thanks to Zak Keenan.

(Editor's Note): The witnesses described a silent craft hovering over the church at 200 feet altitude. A C-5 aircraft would make tremendous noise and would stall out of the sky at less than 150 mph.

George Filer.

* * *

NEW YORK: TWO FLYING TRIANGLES.

BOICEVILLE --Last Friday night, March 21, 2003, my mate returned a bit unnerved from her drive passing along a road with a clear view of the Ashokan Reservoir in Olive, NY. She reports that she observed two black flying wedges (triangular) with unusual light configurations. What particularly struck was the silence of their flight and, even more so, the seemingly impossible SLOWNESS of the craft. This was between 8:30 and 9 PM.

It is likely that others also saw the craft. Since this is a distant source of New York City water, the primary road across the reservoir was closed to traffic at the start of the Iraqi invasion.

I don't subscribe to the "aliens" scenario but I hope this was somehow helpful.

Thanks to GA.

* * *

CALIFORNIA: HIGHWAY PATROL SPOTS TRIANGLE.

SAN FRANCISCO - The observers were watching the waves for good surf at Ocean Beach when they noticed a low flying, silent, triangular-shaped object about one mile south of the Cliff House on May 9, 2003, at 1:30 PM.

The witness says, "We first thought it was a Stealth F-117, but I've seen them before and they are quite loud. Still not sure what it was, so I thought I'd report it anyway to see if anyone else had spotted it."

* * *

FLORIDA.

NAPLES -- The witness was traveling south on Interstate 75, eleven miles south of Naples on Friday morning, March 1, 2002, at 6:22 AM, when he noticed an object in the sky to his front left. It had three tiny white lights and came closer at a very slow pace.

The witness says, "I was able to make out the shape very distinctly as a low flying triangle. It was well below the clouds, and its lights were at each apex. The lights did not illuminate any portion of the craft. I pulled over to the side of the road and shut off the engine to listen. It was traveling west and passed by in three minutes. The window was down and the engine off but there was no sound. I turned the ignition to 'Aux' to hear the shuttle launch on the radio but it was not visible due to the clouds. I looked back and the object was gone. I noticed the van's digital clock lost two minutes"

* * *

NAPLES - Edwin R writes, "I have a friend that saw either this same very large black flying triangle craft or one very similar back in 1996, near the Gulf. He was excited and freaked out. He said it was a triangular-shaped craft with either three or five lights on the black, metallic underbelly in a triangular pattern with an array of several smaller lights around the perimeter of the vehicle.

"The most astonishing feature was that it was gliding eight miles per hour, at only 100 yards above the ground and was dead silent. You could probably throw a baseball and hit it.

"We feel sure it was not manufactured on this planet."

Thanks to Edwin R.

* * *

Pennsylvania.

DOUSMAN -- Jeff S. reports, "It was the fourth day of deer hunting for me on November 25, 2003 and I just got out to my stand 6:00 AM, when I heard this low tone noise, like the last low key of a piano. The sun was just starting to show some light on the horizon. On the opposite side, there was a dark blue sky with some stars. So I looked up to see what it was. There were three dim yellow lights in a perfect triangle formation. It was flying too slowly to be an airplane. It came from the south and headed north. I watched this object for about one minute.

"Next, the noise got quieter and quieter until you couldn't hear anything. Then it froze. All three of the lights got close together until it almost looked like one light. Then the front light flashed twice. It flew up for a couple seconds and just vanished.

"Five or ten minutes later an extremely low, jade green airplane came flying from the west and headed north, the same direction of the object/objects. The airplane was flying lower than the object. All the edges of this plane were rounded. I heard the turbulence of this airplane for about seven minutes."

Thanks to Jeff S and UFO Wisconsin.com/

* * *

Utah: Transparent Triangles.

SONORA -- Mark A. Olson was facing east and noticed a bright flash on June 15, 2004, so he grabbed his camcorder and saw something with three lights. "These were not FAA lights! This craft was seen in the DAYTIME! There were three lights in triangular formation but no craft could be seen. A few minutes before I captured an airplane in the same vicinity and I could clearly see its wings, tailfin and even the

64

engines. But the triangular craft could not be seen – just the lights! The three lights were recorded on my camcorder for about four minutes. Video clearly shows these lights flying behind a pine tree and, after the sighting, I became ill."

This is the SIXTH major sighting in Sonora in the past month. Mark has collected a series of UFO shots that are worth seeing.

Thanks to ©2004 Mark A. Olson, D.M. Marks, website: http://www.sonorasightings.com/

* * *

Mississippi: Flying Triangle.

MERIDIAN -- Thursday evening, July 1, 2004, around 6:30 PM, a triangle-shaped object was seen that had three round spheres at each point. The witness states, "The object was flying overhead a 14 story building, three blocks away from Riley Hospital where I work. I went outside to go to my car and I just happened to look up and see an object flying slowly in a straight, level path without making any noise. I observed the object for at least three minutes before it vanished. It was silver in color. The spheres were huge; each one would be three feet in diameter. There were smaller silver objects orbiting around the vessel as it kept flying. These objects had an oval path around the machine."

Thanks to Chris and Brian Vike http://www.hbccufo.com/

* * *

California: Flying Triangle.

MUFON LOS ANGELES reports – On September 10, 2004, many witnesses saw a UFO but were unable to get a video. Luckily it came back September 11th, 2004, and they obtained a very detailed video of the UFO.

They report, "We even saw what appeared to be US Military jets surrounding a bright orange glowing object that seemed to turn into a triangle with various blinking lights. As it was traveling east, we could tell the smaller crafts were jets because of the enormous speed they used to catch up to the craft. Everything we could possibly catch and see with the camera is recorded from the top of a neighbor's roof. This all happened over the downtown Los Angeles skyline where the object didn't leave for 30 minutes to an hour before those smaller crafts got there. There were many people who witnessed the event."

http://www.mufonla.com/sightings.htm

* * *

Washington: Long Narrow Triangle.

SPOKANE -- Two witnesses (a mother and son) were headed west at 7 PM, on September 7, 2004, as the sun was setting, when they noticed an object, very bright, above the horizon about half the size of the moon. "It looked like a jet with a very short contrail heading north at an odd angle toward the ground."

The Mother and her son kept watching the hovering object. "It was brighter and more colorful than the few clouds lit by the sunset. We watched it for about eight minutes until it was out of sight behind some trees. I wish I had pulled over to observe it at the time. When I saw the story on Rense.com this morning, titled 'Portland Oregon Bright Strobing Object Video', I realized it was the same object we saw!"

Thanks to Brian Vike, Director HBCC.

* * *

UNITED KINGDOM: FLYING TRIANGLE.

NORWICH -- On November 7, 2001, a single fighter aircraft that sounded like a NATO F-15 Eagle was escorting a triangular-shaped craft over Norwich at 6:15 PM. The fighter was about six aircraft lengths behind and four widths to the left hand side of the flying triangle. The fighter could clearly be heard but there was no noise from the other craft. The fighter was displaying full navigation lights, while the only illumination from the triangular craft was three small green lights, one at each point of the triangle.

The shape of the flying triangle craft was clearly visible against the stars as it passed between them and the witness. A close friend also saw the two craft for ten seconds as they headed east and disappeared. The black triangle had three sides of equal length. They were flying at an estimated speed of 250 to 400 knots at an altitude of 1500 feet.

Thanks to Joe Trainor Masinaigan and Mr. Davis, (esoxathome@aol.com)

* * *

CANADA: FLYING TRIANGLE.

DARTMOUTH, NOVA SCOTIA -- This same series of events has occurred three times at twilight. I was driving into Burnside Industrial Park on September 10, 2002, when I looked up and observed a black object that has three white lights in a triangle formation. I looked for the marker lights (e.g. the red flasher on the bottom side of most aircraft) but did not see any on these objects. One time I did notice a faint steady red light in the center of one object. This object was going very slow and it seemed to make the same FLAT left hand turn. Most aircraft, except for helicopters, will bank to make a turn. These do not; they make a flat 45-degree angle left hand turn.

I have seen this three times, always at twilight and it appears to follow the same course.

* * *

AUSTRALIA: FOUR SILVER OVALS AND FLYING TRIANGLE.

ALICE SPRINGS -- Researcher Conway Costigan reports he received a call from three witnesses who observed four silver, oval craft high in the daytime sky that emerged from a cloudbank on November 27, 2002. The craft were traveling in a diamond formation. While they were viewing this they heard a "snap" noise and a white triangular object with rounded corners and dark ovoid highlights on the top surface seemed to appear from nowhere. This craft was suspended under a large parachute. It drifted out of sight of the witnesses. The four silver craft appeared to trail it for a few seconds and faded from sight. The witness, who is in the aeronautics industry, estimates the white triangular craft is roughly the size of a 747 jumbo jet in length.

This was a one-shot and I can't phone this guy back. I did verify that the call originated from Australia, although I don't know how they got my number. They said that they were familiar with my attempts to analyze sightings.

Thanks to Conway Costigan.

* * *

PAKISTAN: TRIANGLE WITH WHITE LIGHTS.

FAISALABAD -- On March 15, 2003, at 1:35 PM, the witness writes, "It was triangle-shaped with white lights at each corner of it and a large red one in the middle. I can't explain it because my English is not so good.

"We had a party at home and had many people on the roof talking to each other. The time was between 1 and 2 hours after midnight. Suddenly my cousin, Maria, shouted! She was the first witness who saw it."

* * *

Canada: Black, Flying Triangle.

CHURCHBRIDGE, Saskatchewan-- My stepson, my wife and I were driving down the grid road, 9 km east of Yorkton, when we saw what looked like an oddly-shaped fighter jet coming at us fairly low to the road at 1:30 PM, on April 20, 2004. We yielded, basically in stunned fashion, when the object seemed so slow, almost to a halt, 20 feet in front of our Suburban. The object was a black triangle with no apparent windows and on the bottom was one large light in each of the three corners. It rotated so a different angle was facing forward and took off in a blur over top of our car. It was as if the object went straight up, once it came to view, and vanished into the sky.

Chapter 6

U.S. Nocturnal Triangular-Shaped UFOs

The majority of triangular-shaped UFOs are witnessed at night around the world. They are often quite low and slow, their lighting configuration is distinctive and they make no sound (except, in some cases, a deep, droning, hum may be heard).

There is evidence to suggest that the United States Air Force (or covert operations within the US) is involved in a flying triangle project. Therefore, it is possible that "*some*" of these craft could well be prototypes of terrestrial origin. However, to assume that "*all*" of them fit this category would present some interesting questions:

Why are secret prototypes being flown over heavily populated, urban areas? Why are the lighting configurations and colors of these craft far from FAA standards? Why are they allowed to interfere with commercial airplane traffic? Why are "chase planes" not accompanying these test flights, as in all test flights of prototype craft? Why would military fighter jets be scrambled to intercept or chase off our own aircraft, as has been observed by witnesses and reported by Air Force personnel? What type of propulsion system could allow these craft to go from hovering silently above treetop level to thousands of miles per hour and leave Earth's atmospheric borders without killing its occupants? And why aren't these technologies being utilized in our present wartime environment?

Considering the capabilities demonstrated by these craft, if they are indeed *all* ours, it would appear that they are well beyond the "prototype" stage.

David Twichell.

ILLINOIS.

GRAYSLAKE -- Rick writes, "On the night of April 8, 2001, I was driving back from my fiancé's house down Route 83. About 11:15 PM, I saw a huge triangle-shaped craft hovering over the landfill along the highway. As I came closer to the object, it moved away from the dump. It didn't loop around like an airplane; it actually moved sideways and hovered over the road about 100 feet high.

"I could tell very easily that it was triangle-shaped with a bright light in the front and two at the rear points. The front light was a bright red and the other lights at the rear points were a strange green color. I was going to stop to look at it but it flew off as I came closer.

"This situation was disturbing because I'm a photographer and this was one of the few times that I did not have my camera with me. The object was the size of a 747 aircraft.

"I just thought I should report this. Now keep in mind I'm not a quack and I'm also a major skeptic about UFO stories. However I'm not a skeptic anymore."

Thanks to Rick and Whitley Strieber.

(Editor's Note): This Flying Triangle was operating less than 25 miles from Chicago's O'Hare Airport, one of the busiest in the world. Additionally it was operating at 100 feet over a well-traveled highway. Other reports indicate these craft cause homes to shake, probably due to their powerful propulsion systems. These craft are regularly picked up on the screens of O'Hare air traffic controllers, forcing pilots to take sudden turns unnecessarily. Last year (2000), Terminal Radar Approach Control Center in Elgin, Illinois ordered pilots to avoid what appeared to be planes on their radar, potentially putting passengers at risk. The Chicago Sun Times called them false radar images but I think they are UFOs.

George Filer.

* * *

ALASKA: FLYING TRIANGLES.

SEWARD -- Michael Harman writes, "If you are interested in seeing Flying Triangles, then Seward, Alaska is the place to be. It is a virtual hotspot for UFO activity. My contact is seeing black triangles flying over his home every night after 2:00 A.M. He views them from his bedroom window using a standard pair of binoculars and can easily see the triangular shape. What are they and where are they coming from?

"If there is anyone from Skywatch or MUFON in the area who could investigate, it would be appreciated. I need more people to observe the ongoing activity."

Thanks to Whitley Strieber & Mike_Harman@rocketmail.com.

* * *

SOUTH CAROLINA SIGHTING.

MYRTLE BEACH – Well, on May 1, 2001, at exactly 10:00 PM, my friend and I were walking on the beach, and we sat down looking towards the Atlantic Ocean. We, at first, saw five lights all in a line, which kind of curved around. The object came half way through the clouds then it started backing up slowly to the right.

A second object with five more lights became visible while the other one was backing up. The one on the left then disappeared, while the one to the right backed up really fast and vanished.

Now these lights to the left were all lined up in the same pattern as the first set we saw. There were three elderly people out there that saw the same thing. We all came to the conclusion that it couldn't have been an airplane, because it was too low to the ocean. It was not fireworks and they didn't make any sound at all! There were no boats out in the ocean either.

Thanks to Barry Taylor -stingray@nor.com.au
* * *

VIRGINIA: UFO SIGHTINGS.

BUENA VISTA -- Mr. Wolfman writes, "In last week's files you told of a huge Flying Triangle over Buena Vista, where I had a similar sighting a month earlier in mid-April of 1998. My wife and I live on the side of a hill, which overlooks Buena Vista in Rockbridge County.

"Shortly after 9:00 PM, I set out to drive to the nearby Hilltop Gas Station on Route 60. As I was getting into my car, I noticed a bright orange light in the sky to the northeast of my home. At first I thought it was a bright star but I noticed that the light was traveling south. I observed the light for about 30 seconds and realized that the "plane" did not have any FAA lights at all. Only a single orange light about the brightness of aircraft landing lights passing in front of me in a straight line at 1500 feet off the ground.

"I drove to the gas station and watched some more. I called the cashier out to see and, even under the bright store lights, we could make out the UFO light, which was moving south in a slow and deliberate manner. The light did not produce any sound.

"Another 45 seconds, the light made "clearing turns" (which I am sure you are familiar) and continued slowly on its original course. The cashier asked me a question and the light was gone.

"I was so stunned that I called the County sheriff's office. I didn't tell them I saw a 'UFO,' I told them I saw a low flying plane running in violation of FAA regulations with no engine noise and possibly in distress. The dispatcher advised me to call Roanoke Airport but I couldn't reach anyone so I contacted Langley Air Force Base, which is on the coast. The dispatcher said they couldn't do anything unless there was a crash and advised calling the base. I reached Langley's Control Tower Sergeant and told him what I saw, keeping to my belief that there was possibly a distressed or downed aircraft in the area. He switched me to a speakerphone, I assume so others could listen. The guy had me run through the whole thing three times and kept asking me 'what did you think it was?'

"I was very concerned that there could be a plane down in the woods, but it sounded like someone in the background was laughing. The Sergeant told me that there were no aircraft in the skies above Rockbridge County and all of his planes were on the ground and that I was seeing things."

Thanks to Wolfman.

* * *

CENTRAL VIRGINIA TRIANGLE.

Matthew Moriarty writes, "At 11:00 PM, May 10, 2001, I was out with the dogs and noticed an out of place triangular pattern of stars near the planet Saturn. To my amazement, the triangular arrangement began to rotate counterclockwise very slowly. My attention was riveted, looking to see if the nearby stars remained fixed and if I could discern some definite object within the triangular star pattern.

"I could not see any actual object but the triangular pattern stopped its rotation and proceeded to slowly move in the southwest direction. I watched it disappear over a tree line and that was it.

"The configuration was huge, spanning the size of my hand at arm's length and it must have been very high."

Thanks to Matthew Moriarty, rommell43@nexet.net

* * *

NEW JERSEY.

MATAWAN -- Jacqueline Williams writes, "A few years ago, I witnessed a large triangular object flying over us while we were sitting in my Jacuzzi spa. The Flying Triangle was as big as a football field and had 3 lights on either side and a light in the middle. As it flew silently over us, the lights and the pump on the Jacuzzi spa suddenly turned off.

"I told many people about this experience and, after much negativity, I decided to keep it to myself.

"Recently I have had the privilege to have custody of a 16-year-old boy whose mother is very ill. Last week (May 20?), he came running into the house, out of breath. He said he'd been sitting on the Jacuzzi lid, looking at the stars, when he saw a huge triangular-shaped object fly overhead. He said it was enormous in size and had 3 lights on each side and one large one in the middle. He said it was silent. Then two more came toward it and they all shot off into the night sky. He drew a picture of the craft that was exactly like the one the three of us had seen.

"We told him our story and he slept with the lights on that night. Now we both go outside at night and glance at the sky, hoping to have another opportunity to see those objects again."

Thanks to Jacqueline Williams JakJr65@aol.com

SOUTH CAROLINA: FLYING TRIANGLE WITH HELICOPTERS.

MYRTLE BEACH -- ISUR reports that on May 6, 2001, at about 11:15 PM, a licensed Security Officer was outside on the back deck, along with a friend, when they noticed several aircraft off to the south about 3 miles away. The aircraft continued to approach their location (N.E.) until they were about 5000 feet distant and at fairly low altitude. The witnesses then identified them as 3 helicopters by engine noise, shape and lighting and noticed that they had formed into a triangular formation.

The witnesses could also make out a dark triangular object WITHIN the triangular formation of escorting helicopters.

The size of the unlit dark triangular craft was estimated as larger than a DC-8, but smaller than a 747 that has a 196-foot wingspan and length of 231 feet. A fourth helicopter was trailing at about 200-500 yards.

The witnesses had a relatively good 5-minute view of this fly-over. The primary witness attempted to get to a camera but was unable to get a photo. He indicated that the Navy/Air Force installations at Charleston, SC are seventy miles south, while Shaw AFB is 80+ miles west.

In the recent past a much smaller triangular object had also been personally observed at a nearby beach with a blue haze below the craft. The primary witness is a graduate of military flight school and the second witness was a USAF dependant. The case was referred to SC MUFON for additional local investigation.

Please note that this is ANOTHER case of a dark triangle seemingly escorted by helicopters and within reasonable distance of an AFB.

Thanks to Tom Sheets, ISUR Board, State Director-MUFON of Georgia.

CALIFORNIA: BLACK TRIANGLES.

William Hamilton wrote, "I just returned from the Hi-Desert of Yucca Valley and Joshua Tree. I stopped in to say hello to an old friend who lives near Goat Mountain to the East and beyond that is the 29 Palms Marine Base. My friends say they have seen a flying black triangle that has a blue glow around it and is hard to see against the night sky. It can do 90-degree turns, had a helicopter escort and seems to be coming from the North Base at Edwards.

"Orange-amber orbs just like the videotaped Phoenix Lights have also been seen 'flying' around. These are not flares. That is also true of the orbs in the Phoenix Lights, as I have said repeatedly. Flares are not round like coins. They are fires and they do flicker and smoke.

Their principal purpose is to illuminate the night. Orbs do not illuminate. The Flying Triangle sometimes carries orbs and makes an excellent 'penetrater' since it is very stealthy.

"Other craft have been seen but they are not ours. They look just like the old scout bell ships that used to be seen out there. I haven't seen one of those since 1957. They are very distinguishable as they always have three hemispherical pods on the undercarriage."

Thanks to Bill Hamilton Executive Director Skywatch International Inc.

* * *

MISSOURI: FLYING TRIANGLE.

COLUMBIA -- Jim Hickman reports that a Flying Triangle was sighted while heading home on June 7, 2001. The witness reports that he noticed lights in the northwest sky that initially looked like a plane. It didn't look quite right. It had two lights in front where normally a plane on approach would have one. There were no flashing lights. It circled and flew off to the southwest.

The next night at 10:39 PM, he saw the "plane" again. "I stopped the truck and saw three whitish lights on three tips and a red light in the center. Then it hit me. It's a triangle! I also saw a few additional lights on the body of the craft, which seem to be recessed and bit yellowish. It took the same path as Thursday. I am sure other people saw this craft."

Later I realized that I had seen the same "headlights" as described by the witnesses I interviewed in 1999 who reported seeing a triangular craft.

Thanks to Jim Hickman and "The Hickman Report."

* * *

ILLINOIS: FLYING RIGHT TRIANGLE.

CHANSON -- The witness was sitting outside with his parents at about 10:30 PM, June 10, 2001, watching the stars, when three stars that had been sitting in the same spot started to move across the sky at a constant pace. They stopped for a few seconds and then they would move higher, stop and move across the sky. This continued for two minutes before the objects were completely out of view.

The witness said, "I cannot really say if it was one big craft or three smaller crafts but they formed a perfect right triangle, moved at the same speed and stopped at the same time the entire length of the event.

"Satellites don't form perfect geometric shapes and stop in random spots across the sky. Now the object or objects never really passed close to the ground. The entire time they maintained a high altitude."

* * *

IOWA: FLYING TRIANGLE INVESTIGATION.

AMES -- Beverly Trout, Iowa MUFON State Director, reports they have investigated a case that occurred on May 17, 2001, when a Ph.D. at Iowa State University, his wife and three children witnessed the sighting of a "huge," silent triangle with bright, blinking, strobing and pulsing white lights. It was first seen at about 50 degrees up from the western horizon and was last seen about 30 degrees up from the eastern horizon.

The craft took three minutes to cross this area at 9:45 PM. A few minutes later the witnesses called Beverly. Subsequent investigation shows cloud ceiling at 9,000 feet. The family estimated the object was at an altitude of 5,000 feet, with closest approach at 85 degrees almost overhead. The Flying Triangle was viewed by the husband and wife through binoculars with 378 feet linear diameter field of view at 1000 yards. Binocular field of view could not contain the entire triangular object. (That is, husband and wife could not see the entire object within the field of view of their binoculars.)

These are very credible witnesses. Investigators having checked law enforcement, Iowa State climatologist and FAA, are convinced that whatever was seen was indeed "HUGE" and, since we cannot easily explain it, it remains in the UFO category.

A neighbor to the above family saw an unexplained aerial object between/beside their adjacent homes on a previous occasion. In addition, the wife witness in the above case had a daytime sighting three years ago near the southwestern part of Ames. Plus, MUFON has been contacted with abduction reports by several individuals in the Ames area. All witnesses thus far check out as highly educated, credible individuals with their psychological feet-on-the-ground, i.e., not wanting to over-conclude but realizing that they've been able to remain conscious, at least part of the time, during encounters involving UFOs.

Perhaps it's worth noting that only seven miles from Ames, in 1996, two crop formations were discovered with plant and soil samples subsequently being submitted to Dr. W. C. Levengood's nonprofit laboratory in Michigan with lab results clearing-showing anomalies associated with the formations.

Thanks to Beverly Trout, Iowa MUFON State Director. btufo@netins.net

* * *

ILLINOIS: HOUSE SHAKES – UFOs NEAR O'HARE AIRPORT.

TAYLORVILLE -- It happened so fast, it made my house shake and I looked out the window and saw a triangular-shaped object with lights on it. On March 22, 2001, at around 10:00 PM, I was in my bedroom on the computer and talking to my friends, having a good time. All of a sudden, I felt a sudden vibrant movement of the house. I quickly darted for the window. I looked out and saw a triangular-shaped object traveling in a straight line at what looked like 150 mph.

This triangular object also had lights on the bottom of it and red lights along the back of it. It wasn't flat – It was three-dimensional. It made a huge roaring noise. Right when I lost sight of it. I could still see it hovering, just sitting in mid-air. All I could see at this time were the lights though. And, all of a sudden, it vanished.

This is definitely no plane, helicopter, military base test flight or anything else normal. It is the weirdest thing I have ever seen in my life and I'm still shocked over it.

We're located 200 miles south of Chicago.

* * *

GALESBURG -- Jane S. Derry writes, "I thought I was imagining things until I read last weeks Filer's Files about the house shaking in Taylorville and the man seeing a Flying Triangle over his home on March 22, 2001. This triangular object also had lights on the bottom of it and red lights along the back of it.

"I was watching TV with my son on March 23rd, and all of a sudden the house sort of shook, ONCE. It was really strange. There was a rather muffled thud and it was gone. I asked if Matt felt that and he looked at me oddly, like how could he not! The dogs looked around worriedly, but didn't move. And then there was nothing. I guess I should have gone outside, but they have been here before! I live in Galesburg about 200 miles WSW of Chicago and 125 miles from Taylorsville."

Thanks to Jane S. Derry, derryj@gallatinriver.net,

* * *

WISCONSIN: FLYING TRIANGLE.

DUNDEE -- Jim Aho writes, "We have a hot new sensational UFO report on July 15, 2001, from over 50 witnesses, photos and even VERY CLEAR video taken by a professional. The object was a Flying Triangular-shaped craft."

The witness, Tim, states, "I observed it through binoculars and I could see that it had three lights at the corners; blue, purple and green and a faint blue outline. At first, the object was stationary but a ball of light approached the triangle from the right and changed both course and appearance. It changed from a ball of light to two lights: one red and one flashing white and could have even been mistaken for an aircraft.

"After about 7 minutes, the triangle craft started moving in a tumbling motion, like it was almost rolling away to the right. It was like a pyramid with three sides and a bottom. When it started moving, I could see that it was three dimensional."

Jim writes, "I have seen a photograph of the craft. It's a little blurred because it was moving but is an outstanding sighting. There were about 17 witnesses who were at Bill Benson's UFO Bar facing south who saw orange lights and a light with a bluish 'cloud' around it. I saw a pyramid shape with three lights across the base that were purple, white and blue. The object moved slowly enough for us to get a good long look."

Heidi Hollis is investigating. Thanks to Jim Aho W-Files http://www.w-files.com

* * *

DUNDEE - CORRECTION -- The Flying Triangle sighting report, carried in July 21, Filer's Files #30, took place on July 15, 2000, rather than 2001 at Benson's Hideaway. A new sighting took place on July 21, 2001, about 9:40 PM, when a group from Benson's Hideaway Restaurant, located on Long Lake, again saw UFOs. Both sightings were observed by a multiple group of UFO buffs. A light then came from the south end of the lake next to Dundee Mountain. It was about the size of a quarter held at arm's length. It looked like it was lower than Dundee Mountain and just a little higher than the trees. The light was a golden color and had golden lights shooting out from the edges. As it moved along the Eastern Shore of the lake it made little jumps almost straight up in the air and then continued on its original path.

The light continued to the north end of the lake where we were. At this point someone yelled, "There's another one!" It came north along the western edge of the lake and it too shot up almost straight in the air a couple of times. This one did something different though. It blew up to a white light, which was much bigger than the golden light – at least four times. It then dropped two lights like the sparkles that drop from sparklers. It moved directly across from us while the first light had moved northwest and disappeared.

Bonnie Meyer reports, "I believe that it left the atmosphere so fast that it only looked as if the light went out.

"A third golden light came from the same area and was coming towards us slowly. When it got about half way down the lake, the second one started to move off and then they stayed about the same distance apart and moved off.

"A few minutes latter another light appeared. It came almost the length of the lake and was either much smaller or it was much higher, because it was smaller. As it got closer to us, it turned west and settled almost stationary in the southwest. It stayed there for a long time. It seemed to become three separate lights – one bluish green, one orange red and the other white. They seemed to be playing tag, running circles around each other and zigzagging with each other.

"Then there was a slight popping sound and two lights dropped from the underside of the center light. One of the lights took off in a northwest direction and was out of sight within a minute or two. The greenish blue light stayed in the area and was still there when I left at about 12:30 A.M.

"When I talked to people the next day, they said the light was still there at 2:00 A.M."

Thanks to Bonnie Meyer of Lightside. www.thelightside.org and Jim Aho.

* * *

WASHINGTON: LARGE TRIANGULAR CRAFT WAS SPOTTED AND FILMED.

TROUT LAKE -- John Novak reports that on July 19, 2001, around 11:00 PM, a large ship flew over the Gilliland Ranch expanding into a brilliant yellow-orange light, and then dimmed out as it left the area. This object and large lights were filmed over Mt. Adams. Several other high flyers displayed incredible speeds and turns, some making complete U turns.

On July 22nd, a guest was taking off from Trout Lake airport in his small plane at 12:30 PM, when a UFO flew directly under his plane. The pilot was in radio contact with the witnesses and circled to try to see the UFO but it stayed directly underneath him. The same pilot saw a UFO the previous night over Mt. Adams. It lit up, sent down a beam, then dropped down into the same beam and took off.

On July 23rd, a massive triangular ship came in from the north and was met by a golden colored, smaller ship. The film shows three distinct lights in an elongated triangle that moved in unison, keeping their exact distance.

Tom Dongo, a well-known UFO investigator, spent two weeks at the ranch and will return to Sedona MUFON with some incredible footage.

Thanks to John Novak webmaster@cazekiel.org

* * *

NEW JERSEY: CARTERET CASE INVESTIGATION CONTINUES.

CARTERET -- A new witness claims to have observed the structure of a large Flying Triangle near Sayerville heading for Carteret. Witnesses, further south along the New Jersey Turnpike, saw aircraft on the normal approach to Newark Airport apparently being diverted because of the presence of UFOs in the early morning hours of July 15, 2001. It is normal FAA procedure to divert aircraft away from potential danger without confirming the presence of UFOs to the aircrews.

Unconfirmed reports indicate that radars in the New York area picked up a series of anomalous targets on the night of July 15, 2001, between 12:25 to 12:55 AM. These targets roughly match the ground witnesses' testimony of seeing lights over the New Jersey Turnpike. Dozens of cars came to a stop on the Turnpike to watch the lights as they passed overhead.

Carteret is a very significant case because it occurred the day after the successful US antimissile test in the Pacific, the so-called son of

Star Wars. We can speculate the multiple UFOs were a response to this test. Russia is strongly opposed to the development of this Missile Defense System and their involvement cannot be ruled out at this time.

Carteret is only ten miles from New York City, the home of most major television networks. Numerous police and fireman were witnesses and took video of the event that was shown on many television broadcasts. New York radar operators indicate that dozens of anomalous targets were racing around the area.

There are wide variations in speed, altitude and size. Anomalous targets are those that are not using transponders that are required for all normal commercial traffic and identify the aircraft. The anomalous radar returns were flying too slow or too fast to be normal aircraft and remain unidentified. So far, to my knowledge, the government has not denied the sighting and no military maneuvers have been acknowledged.

MUFON investigator Bob Durant reports, "In the short time the lights were displayed on screen, it was obvious that they were moving right to left at a slow but deliberate angular velocity. There was no relative movement among the lights. The top of a house or building, and possibly a chimney on a house, is visible beneath the lights and offer a reference for their movement. No stars were visible in the video scene. There were a total of ten lights arranged in three groups. Beginning from the left on the screen, this corresponds with the foremost lights. We see five lights, then a space, then four lights, a much longer space and a single light, which brings up the rear of the moving set.

"There is no obvious symmetry to either the groups of five and four lights or to the entire group of lights. The lights depicted in the video are large, steady and white, though there is some slight but perceivable variation in diameter among them. One of the lights, momentarily, nearly "goes out", diminishing to a tiny point and then resuming its original size."

Thanks to Bob Durant.

* * *

OHIO.

EVANSTON -- On August 7, 2001, I looked up at 10:20 PM, and saw a streak of light and then it slowed down. I couldn't tell the exact distance but I would estimate 200 to 300 yards away. It was traveling very slowly, like it was looking for something. I noticed that there were lights all around the side of the ship. It was kind of like a Flying Triangle with a broad side in the front going to a point in the back. The two front tips seemed to have two brighter lights then the rest. It moved real slow for about 15-20 seconds and then streaked off to the north. All lights on the Triangle were bright hazy white.

* * *

WISCONSIN: LIGHTS KNOCK OUT POWER.

MERCER -- J writes, "On the evening of August 3, 2001, I was traveling to northern Wisconsin with a friend for fishing. We were about 3 miles south of Mercer on US 51 at 12:30 AM, when large, bright, yellow-orange lights appeared in the sky directly a mile ahead of us at 1,500 feet altitude. They were about the size of your thumbnail at arm's length.

"The full moon was up and the lights were just slightly smaller. The lights almost looked like yellow orange fireballs but didn't flicker and the outside edges had a blur or hazy appearance. The lights were 'stacked' directly above each other 100 yards apart. We both saw the lights as if someone switched on a light.

"We drove until we were a half mile away and I stopped to get my camera from the trunk. Then the lights moved straight up and the spacing between them doubled. As we exited the car the lights moved to our left about a half-mile all without changing their formation.

"The sky was clear and, as I took the first flash picture, the lights converged towards the middle light and formed a perfect triangle on a horizontal plane at 200 yards apart. I took 6 pictures in 5 minutes.

"There was no noise. Even my hunting dog was quiet and still, which is very unusual. We drove a mile further down the road and snapped another picture, just as a pickup truck swerved sending gravel flying. I pulled along side the truck and a young driver said, 'what the hell am I looking at? I've been watching those lights for about 10 minutes and when I saw your flash I knew you guys saw them too.'

"The three of us watched the lights rise slowly and then the speed increased until they reached an altitude of about a mile and they disappeared.

"We drove into Mercer and realized the town was blacked out. I contacted the power company and they said the outage was caused by a 'regulator reset.'"

Thanks to Jim Aho W-Files http://www.w-files.com

* * *

NEW JERSEY.

POCONO MOUNTAINS -- Eileen writes that on August 13, 2001, around 1:00 AM, she spotted a Flying Triangle-shaped UFO flying south near Tobyhanna. Eileen states, "I thought it was three lights making a triangle but then, the way it went behind a cloud, we all decided it was one UFO. The other UFOs we saw were going from south to northwest. They were coming from behind a cloud and moving very slowly, so we could follow their path until they were hidden behind trees. No matter what time of year I go up there, I am sure to see them."

Thanks to Wileen at Leenie9850.

* * *

CALIFORNIA: FLYING OBJECTS.

WEED, NORTH OF MT. SHASTA -- On August 20, 2001, Mary C. was driving southbound on I-5, looking out of the sunroof to stargaze at 10:00 PM. She noticed three stars moving in unison, southbound.

"They were positioned to make an uneven triangle (no sides equal in length). Initially I thought it was a satellite, however, the 'stars' were too far apart and moved in perfect unison. I questioned the likelihood that the 'stars' were lights on the points of a craft but the space in between the 'stars' was camouflaged against the night sky.

We observed the lights moving southbound and, one by one, they disappeared as it reached a portion of the nebula. The speed was steady, not fast but not slow. The white lights did not twinkle nor blink. They made a triangle at 30,000 to 60,000 feet, but this was only an estimate."

Thanks to (Mary c.) reports@ufoinfo.com em4carmalt@aol.com.

* * *

CALIFORNIA: THREE FLYING TRIANGLES.

Joshua Tree – On August 24, 2001, there was a terrific meteorite shower show, but nothing compared to the 3 black Triangles, seen at approximately 1:30 AM, zipping around rapidly and dead stopping in midair. Shirley and I missed it but not this man-(dalamjiwa@hotmail.com). This morning over coffee at the Country Kitchen Inn, he excitedly told me all about it. If he wasn't a believer before, he sure is now.

Thanks to Dex dexxa@earthlink.net

* * *

CALIFORNIA: FLYING TRIANGLE SIGHTED AND TAPED.

FLORISTON -- On August 16, 2001, the witness got a short clip on videotape of a very strange craft at about 10:00 PM. "My daughter's boyfriend was out on the front porch and banged on my window to get my attention. I looked out and saw a white, flashing, very bright light. It had several white lights and one bright red strobing light as well.

"It flew over the range to the northeast, stopped, all lights went out for a few seconds, then it lit back up and came straight back over again, without making a banked turn. It stopped, then maybe rotated or pivoted and then came back. I got my video camera and took 20 to 30 seconds of a good-sized object about the size of a 727 (maybe a bit bigger).

"It was almost Delta wing-shaped (maybe more of a sharper triangle). It made no noise, even though it was close by."

Thanks to Joe's UFOs <anomalousnews@yahoo.com>

WISCONSIN: FLYING TRIANGLE.

GREENVILLE -- On September 23, 2001, the witness said, "I was traveling south on US 45 just south of the city of Greenville in Winnebago County. I noticed an aircraft flying south, parallel to me, that had its landing lights on at 10:00 PM. The aircraft made a sharp right turn and headed back to the north. As we approached the aircraft near the intersection of 150 and 45, it appeared the aircraft had stopped moving. As we got closer we could definitely see that it was not moving and that it was hovering at about 400-500 feet high.

"Other vehicles were traveling south on US 45 and were slowing down also because of what they were seeing. It appeared that it was no more than 1/4 mile away on the right side of the road hovering over farm fields.

"The aircraft was shaped like a triangle with three or four bright white lights on two sides and two red blinking lights."

Thanks to UFOWisconsin by Duane W

http://www.ufowisconsin.com/county/reports/r2001_0923_winn ebago.html

* * *

NEW JERSEY: FLYING TRIANGLE.

A friend and I observed a flying triangle in the early morning of October 7, 2001. We were around mile marker 85-90 on the Garden State Parkway, northbound, at 1:15 AM. It was essentially three lights of even brightness, white like stars and in a fairly perfect isosceles triangle.

There was no object visible, just the lights, but their precise arrangement gave the impression of it being one object and motionless. It looked like a triangular constellation of medium brightness white stars in the sky and seemed, for some reason, to be maybe twice as large as a regular airplane. It was about a mile up.

Nearby there was a regular star and, at first, we tried to make sure, these were not stars. These didn't twinkle like stars. They were simply three pinpoints of very white lights, very clear and steady and no other lights could be seen as part of an aircraft, like strobes, red/green markers, etc.

It was probably about 20 degrees up on the horizon, I'm guessing, and I would have guessed it was well south of Newark. It certainly wasn't going very fast.

We were not far from McGuire AFB. When I first pointed it out to Mike in the car with me. He was also clearly struck by how unusual it looked in the sky and said something like, "What is that?"

We probably could see it clearly for about ten seconds before it started to fade, all three lights at the same rate, as if it were entering a cloud or a mist. But the sky was actually very, very clear that night. It dimmed to completely invisible within the next 10-20 seconds. My impression of it was maybe I was seeing the famed "Westchester wing", which I think I might have observed from a car at high altitude once before about 10 years ago.

Thanks to bob Larson. http://boblarson.com

* * *

NEW JERSEY: FLYING TRIANGLE.

LITTLE EGG HARBOR -- Arlene Griffith writes, "On October 7, 2001, Sunday morning, at one AM, I was driving home from Sue's, who lives right down the street, when I noticed something odd in the night sky. I looked up, marveling at the crisp autumn night sky, and noticed three stars close together. My first thought was; 'Gee, I've never seen that constellation before.'

"The three stars formed a triangle in the sky. That's when I also noticed that it was too small to actually be a constellation but too big to be an airplane. There were no blinking lights of any color that differentiates a plane or helicopter from the stars in the sky.

"I stopped in my driveway. It was hovering (from my viewpoint) at the end of my street, just over the tree line. We live in the woods (the Pine Barrens), three hundred feet from the road. I paused, then drove the rest of the way down the driveway and ran into the house to get my brother. A minute later, he joined me out by the street. There was no sign of the three 'stars' that formed neither a triangle nor anything else. Given recent events, air traffic activity in Southern New Jersey has been slow to return, so there were not any signs of any other aircraft.

"We live half an hour from the Atlantic City Airport, the FAA Tech Center and McGuire Air Force Base. So we are well acquainted with the signs of aircraft. The first thing my brother asked me was if I could have mistaken it; maybe it was an airplane. No way. These were three steady lights, bright enough to be mistaken for stars and close enough together and arranged in such a distinct pattern to be shortly mistaken for a constellation. It was big . . . bigger than any airplane I had ever seen.

"Considering the events of September 11th, I wouldn't be surprised if some aliens dropped by to see how things were going down here."

Thanks to L. Arlene Griffith, laurana70@yahoo.com and Lida Griffith/Lenox.

* * *

OHIO: SOARING LIGHTS.

AKRON -- Tami writes, "While visiting my sister last night, October 23, 2001, we were out in her yard looking for 'the strange lights'. It was about 9:03 PM, when we first observed bright star like objects moving up and down in the sky. We observed these lights until the last one disappeared but we were able to get several hours of video. They were gone at 8:00 AM this morning.

"We first noticed these 'lights' while camping on Aug 14, 2001, and we have seen these 'lights' every night since then. The 'lights' are very bright and sometimes they can be seen below the clouds. We can only see an actual image of the lights, when viewed through the video. On tape, some of these lights act as though they are alive. They can be seen on video 'morphing'. Other lights will move quickly and silently across the sky coming from the west. They can also be seen returning to the west in the early morning hours.

"We see a lot of triangle formations of three lights that are not as bright as the others. When seen through binoculars you cannot see through the triangle and there is a red light in the center of the triangle. The height of the UFOs varied throughout the night. When clouds were overhead, you could see flashes of lights through the clouds. Some would shoot straight up in the air and disappear and some would stay just below the clouds."

Thanks to Tami Purpleufo@aol.com and Joe Trainor Masinaigan.

* * *

ILLINOIS: FLYING TRIANGLE SIGHTINGS.

PARK FOREST -- On October 6, 2001, the witness reports seeing a flying triangle with circle lights in each corner. There was a light in the middle that was reddish orange blinking and going in slow motion at 10:00 PM.

* * *

MT. VERNON -- We had pulled into the driveway of the house on October 8, 2001, and decided to sit out in the car and talk for a bit. While sitting there talking, I had noticed 3 very bright lights, shaped as a triangle, hovering over the neighbor's house. The lights were entirely too bright and close to be stars. I immediately asked my friends what it was. We knew that the lights were too low to be any airplane.

As we watched the lights, they began to slowly fade away, leaving no trace of existence. We had decided to call my two friend's Mom and she told us to come over there.

From the stories we heard tonight, this isn't the first sighting that people have seen around this area.

* * *

MISSOURI: FLYING TRIANGLE.

COLUMBIA -- On October 10, 2001, I was driving in my car, way out in the country, when I saw, to my right, three white lights formed in a triangle shape. At first I thought it was just an airplane. The "craft" was moving south, very slowly. So slow that I had to stop the car to see if it was moving at all, which it was! I stopped the car at 11:32 PM, and noticed that it was getting close and still wasn't making any noise of any kind. I got back in the car and started the engine. There were some trees in the way so I couldn't see the "craft" now, so I turned around and headed east.

I looked to my right and the triangle had changed direction, almost like it knew I was trying to follow. Now it headed east as well and, as it started to really pick up some speed, I now could no longer follow.

The white lights started to turn red and blue. They didn't change like a light going on, more like a transition.

(The case is under investigation by the Missouri Investigator Group.)

* * *

MINNESOTA: FLYING TRIANGLE.

DULUTH -- A large flying triangle craft, about four times the size of a stealth jet, was seen while two men were driving north on Highway 53 through the northern suburb of Hermantown on March 5, 2001. The flying triangle was dark, but the color seemed to be a gray/silver color with a light on each corner and one in the center from 9:30 to 10:00 PM.

The craft crossed the highway from the left side, moving to the right. It was moving very slowly, almost hanging over the highway for a while. One of the men thought that it should be moving faster and be out of site when compared to commercial planes. It was a little higher than treetop level, about a block high. They pulled the car over to the side and stopped to listen. There was no sound coming from it. It continued drifting slowly until it went past a bunch of trees and then it suddenly either took off extremely fast or just disappeared.

It was angling in the direction of the Duluth Air Force Base, which has been officially closed for quite some time. I think there are Air National Guard fighter jet operations there now, since the September 11, attack. The unidentified craft was triangular-shaped, except in the back. It wasn't a straight line like a true triangle but was indented some.

Thanks to Fire2@cpinternet.com (Bonnie).

* * *

OHIO: TRIANGLE HOVERING NEAR FREEWAY CHRISTMAS EVE.

COLUMBUS -- The witness was driving east on I-70 late on December 24, 2001, when he saw a bright light hovering over the highway at 11:00 PM. As he drove closer, there were two lights 1500 to 2000 feet up and just sitting still.

The witness states, "While going past it, I lowered my window and heard no sound but I could barely see the shape of a triangle. The front, two lights were noticeable, one at one corner, and one at another. A third light was observed at the back (apex) that was much dimmer. It was not a helicopter, as I am an EMT. I had my CB radio on and didn't hear anyone else saying they saw it. Visibility was good and sky clear. It was about the size of my thumbnail."

* * *

INDIANA: ORANGE, HOVERING FLYING TRIANGLE.

MIDDLETOWN -- We noticed an orange colored light in the sky straight ahead on April 19, 2001, so we watched it for about twenty minutes at 4:30 AM. The light appeared to be in a triangular formation. A plane flew underneath the UFO and, as it went under, the red lights appeared on the UFO as if it were giving a warning. The UFO started moving slowly at first gaining speed toward the right and then it came to a stop and hovered for about five minutes. Then a small star-shaped object branched off of it and started flying straight up and around, as if it were in orbit with the earth but still in the atmosphere. The star-shaped light disappeared but we continued to watch the other object as it started moving further away and disappeared.

It was neither a plane nor a star and I have never seen anything like this before.

* * *

ARIZONA: FLYING TRIANGLE.

FOUNTAIN HILLS -- On January 10, 2002, at precisely 3:00 AM, the witness saw a bright light in his front yard. He looked out his window and saw a triangular craft hovering over the street with red and yellow lights moving around the shape of the craft.

"I watched it for approximately fifteen seconds and went outside to investigate. I walked up the spiral staircase to our roof but it had already left. I stayed on the roof for about ten minutes and saw a little flash as if something was leaving our atmosphere."

* * *

WISCONSIN: FLYING TRIANGLE SPOTTED.

EAU CLAIRE -- On February 16, 2002, at about 9:00 PM, Jerry was standing outside his place of work to take a break. Jerry reports, "I looked to the south and noticed a very bright light in the sky that I thought was Venus or another planet because it was so bright. At that point another worker came outside and I asked him what he thought it might be. He thought it was an airplane. Another worker came out and thought it was a helicopter, because it started to move straight up but there was no noise.

"The light looked circular and it had two lights that flashed red on either side of it. When it moved closer, the object changed from a circle to a triangle shape. The flashing red lights were on either side of the points at the base of the triangle and they were flashing in unison.

"Then the triangle started to rotate right and it seemed to divide in half and become two separate pieces. At about a 45 degree angle, it came back together and reformed into a wedge shape that resembled an F-16 shape with swept wing. The red lights were at the tips of the wing.

"At this point, I realized that this was not the whole object. A darker, black object surrounded the bright light. It was ringed by faint, flashing, white lights that gave it its shape, which was very large, maybe two times as big as a commercial airliner. The object approached, stopped, rotated clockwise ninety degrees and headed southwest.

"This craft did not display normal flying characteristics in the five minutes we observed it."

Thanks to John Hoppe, Director@ufowisconsin.com, Wisconsin's UFO Reporting Center,
http://www.ufowisconsin.com/county/reports/r2002_0216_eauclaire.html

* * *

OKLAHOMA: LARGE, LOW FLYING TRIANGLE.

CAMERON, LEFLORE COUNTY -- The witness reports, "We were driving through Cameron on May 31, 2002, at about 11:00 PM, and I saw slow, flashing lights reflected on the upper part of the windshield. I looked up through the windshield but didn't see anything and just absently thought, 'well, that's a reflection', but realized that there was nothing I'd seen that there could be a reflection from. So I looked upwards through the windshield again and was jolted by what I saw. It was a very large, low flying object. The lights on the front of the object looked like large windows.

"My companion had put his head outside the window and asked if I was seeing what he was seeing. He was driving and almost ran off the road, so he told me to look through the rear window to see if I could see it. I saw it seeming to follow the side of the highway, then veered off, crossing the highway and was out of sight over an area of dense trees.

"My companion had seen the lights approaching us while driving but thought they were stationary. I did not see them until the craft was overhead. He was looking up underneath it and saw the triangular outline of very soft solid lights. The flashing lights were on top of the object. I did not see the lights on top or the triangular shape of the object from the front view. It was a low, slow-moving object and, despite its size, there was no sound coming from it whatsoever."

* * *

GEORGIA: ELONGATED FLYING TRIANGLE.

FLOWERY BRANCH -- The observer was fishing off the bow of his boat, looking at the stars, and noticed one of the brighter stars did a U turn and took off and disappeared on June 6, 2002.

"I know this wasn't a satellite as it moved way too quickly. It moved across the sky, maybe two hand lengths and then started to distance itself, till I could no longer see it."

* * *

TIFTON -- MUFONGA's Dr. Joye Pugh, a MUFON Consultant, contacted State Director, Tom Sheets, on Saturday, June 8,

2002, at about 10:30 PM. The witness and her husband were traveling northeast on Highway 319 toward Ocilla.

About four miles out of Tifton, her cell phone rang and a female apologized for a wrong number. Dr. Pugh thought this unusual, as it had never happened before. Shortly thereafter, she noticed some specific lights low above the trees, off to the left. The sky was overcast but the glow of the city lights from Tifton lit up this section of cloud cover. They considered these particular lights to be unusual because they were so low.

Proceeding on, they approached closer and she observed an aircraft shaped like an elongated triangle. She further noted there was a white light at each corner and a red light in the bottom center.

She was close enough that she could clearly see the dark triangle shape against the glow of the overcast. Traffic prevented her from pulling over, so she drove on a short distance and turned into a water tower area. Quickly looking back, she saw the lights slowly move across the road. She turned around and drove back to get a closer look but could not locate it. She drove back toward Tifton and turned off onto another road in her search, then encountered two additional but indistinct craft with lights to her front but they were opposite the glowing overcast and against a black sky. They could hear the sound of roaring jet engines apparently coming from the lights/craft, as they seemed to fly along very slowly.

These lights went back to the area where first observed and as Dr. Pugh got turned around and drove to the tower. Once again she observed the hovering lights. Headlights from passing traffic blinded her momentarily. The lights then crossed the road again and disappeared as she continued to negotiate traffic.

This, in my opinion, is a classic triangle encounter made even more unusual by what Dr. Pugh described as secondary indistinct slow moving craft ("things") with lights, accompanied by a sound like roaring jet engines. Dr. Pugh made a valiant effort to close with these unknown craft.

John Bodin, MUFONGA's Deputy Director for South Georgia, and Dr. Pugh will investigate further.

Thanks to Tom Sheets, SD MUFONGA.

* * *

WISCONSIN: ORANGE LIGHTS.

MADISON -- UFOWisconsin reports that on July 2, 2002, at 10:30 PM, the witness caught a brief glimpse of three, bright yellow/orange lights, in a perfect triangle, streak south across the clear sky almost straight overhead.

The witness says, "It took, less than two seconds for these lights to move the entire length of the sky. I dismissed that it was a shooting star because there were three lights moving in perfect triangular formation.   Ten minutes later, I saw the exact same formation of triangular lights streak across the sky at the same speed and direction."

Thanks to UFOWisconsin
http://www.ufowisconsin.com/county/reports/r2002_0702_dane.html

* * *

CALIFORNIA: FLYING TRIANGLE WITH TWENTY LIGHTS,

HAWTHORNE CITY -- A large black flying triangle was sighted on July 22, 2002, traveling along the California coastline at around 10:15 PM. The following night, the witness stated, "I walked out unto my patio at 10:21 PM, and saw a string of lights, ran inside my house, grabbed my camcorder and recorded this spectacle for a few seconds. There were about twenty lights, all flashing a cherry red color and all of them were flashing heading southeast.

"They started off in a triangular pattern and started forming a crescent shape. Some objects were further away and not part of the configuration. I was with two friends and we were outside talking. Some red lights, approaching from the north (going south), caught our attention. We saw a very huge boomerang or V-shaped object with a bright white light at the "nose" and red, blinking lights around its perimeter (maybe four or five on either side of the white light). We were all pretty impressed with its massive size and we kept the object in sight as it traveled along the coastline.

"We kept sight of it until it was too far away to see. It was totally silent and seemed to glide slowly across the sky. I am totally shocked it did not make the news since it flew right over the LAX flight path."

* * *

PALOS VERDES -- A flying triangle was reported coming from the Redondo Beach direction along the coast, moving slowly, just before 11:00 PM, on Tuesday.

Thanks to Bill Hamilton Executive Director Skywatch International, Inc. Website: http://www.skywatch-research.org

* * *

NEW YORK: FLYING TRIANGLE AND DISK.

CHEEKTOWAGA -- A triangular shaped object with flames and green lights floated over while friends were sitting talking around the bonfire on July 28, 2002, at 1:00 AM. The witness says, "I was looking up at the sky, looking at the stars, when, to my left, a triangular shape appeared. I first thought it was a plane and then realized that I never seen a plane like that before.

"I was able to point out three corners of the craft which did indeed look like a flying triangle. The front had two green lights at two points and what looked like a red flame in between them. It was moving a bit slow for a few seconds and then picked up speed.

"We stood up and ran to the front of the house because the house next door was in the way of our view. When we made our way there it had disappeared. It wasn't a cloudy night so us not being able to see it anymore was a bit strange."

* * *

GEORGIA SIGHTINGS FLAP.

DULUTH -- At 10:55 PM, on July 17, 2002, I was traveling south on Highway 141 when, off to my left, 125 feet above the tree line, I witnessed two bright lights less then a quarter mile away. It was a long triangle shape with bright round lights at each corner as well as on each side of the craft with a rotating blue light in the center of the craft. Ground lights reflected off the solid black craft, with a thin strip of dim lights going around the side of the ship.

As it made a complete 180-degree turn, it slowly descended to just feet above the trees just behind a small car dealership. I pulled into the dealer's lot and my clock still read 10:55 PM, and walked towards the object 175 feet away. I could clearly see the triangle craft 4 to-5 car lengths (100 feet long) and about 15 to 20 feet tall. As I got closer it started to move away. At this point I remembered I had a camera in my car so I ran back to get it. I noticed other motorists slowing down to look and I grabbed my camera but the craft just disappeared.

* * *

CALIFORNIA: FLYING TRIANGLES SPOTTED BY MANY WITNESSES.

SEQUOIA NATIONAL PARK --About 9:45 PM, a family was camping when one member pointed out a huge craft in the form of a V with red lights flying slowly over. They were able to see the object for about two minutes and it made a humming sound but nothing like an airplane. Numerous campers saw the craft.

* * *

CATALINA ISLAND -- At 10:30 PM, I was at a summer camp at Toyon Bay near Avalon and was walking away from the beach in a crowd of forty people when we saw a triangle formation of lights, moving very slowly in formation. There was a very bright white light in front with red lights trailing it. The entire formation was several times larger than the full moon. The lights did not flash. A very low, quiet engine sound was audible. I thought it could be a formation of military jets but the lights did not blink or flash and they stayed in perfect formation. It was flying from the northwest towards Avalon.

* * *

PENNSYLVANIA: FLYING TRIANGLE.

SUSQUEHANNA COUNTY -- On August 3, 2002, about 11 PM, a witness reported seeing a triangular shaped object appear in the east and move west at a high rate of speed across the entire sky. The high altitude object was faintly lighted and larger than a nickel at arm's length.

* * *

NEVADA: VERY LARGE FLYING TRIANGLE.

FALLON -- Cosmo reports, "I saw a dark substance that dimly lit a very large craft that flew by at about 1000 feet on September 5, 2002. At first I thought 'B 52.' This craft traveled west down Reno Hwy 50 with no running lights at 11:13 PM, but dimly lit light nodes were seen but they were NOT lit. The nodes were in the shape of the whole triangular craft and 7 to 9 nodes were seen. It flew at 20 mph or faster without noise. I was surprised by this event and said 'why me?'

"I have hosted a UFO Television talk show for ten years in Portland. I believe this was a true and real triangle craft that was so close and so large! I did not see a leading edge or rear of the craft. I just saw a triangle from the side and bottom of the ship.

"The sky was clear and about 70 degrees. Total event time 8 seconds. I still can't believe what I saw but it was there."

Thanks to Cosmo, Cosmic Connection Television & Radio Show.

* * *

UTAH: ORANGE UFOS IN HUGE 'V' FORMATION.

TAYLORSVILLE -- The witness reports, "On September 26, 2002, we were traveling home when several objects in a 'V' formation were seen. The lights were slowly moving and hovering into straight lines. At 9:15 PM, a triangle shaped object flew over our heads, making a low humming sound. Then, one shot straight up like something going into space but it didn't. One flew right over our heads at 300 feet and looked like a triangle and immediately changed directions moving at 1000 to 3000 mph.

"Nothing that I know of can go at that speed and move from right to left so quickly. The other lights were still there, they had an orange glow to them. We stayed for an hour and watched these strange objects. It was not of this world, or maybe it was the government testing something, very large and strange.

"There wasn't a logical explanation of what I saw. Now there is no doubt in my mind that we are not alone in the universe."

Thanks to Dave Rosenfeld.

aliendave@earthlink.net Utah UFO Hunters,
http://www.aliendave.com

* * *

FLORIDA: FLOATING TRIANGLE.

WELLINGTON -- The witness writes, "My teenage son and I were leaving Wellington High School on January 21, 2003, at 7:30 PM, after a JV basketball game, when we noticed a floating triangle with three lights on each corner just hovering about 200 meters above the ground.

It was north of Forest Hill Boulevard, about one mile west of Route 441. I lowered my window and turned off the radio to listen for any sound (to see if it was a helicopter) but I couldn't hear any ascertainable aircraft engine noise. I tried to slow down and study the craft but had to move on as we were in traffic.

"Previously, I've seen a traveling 'ball of light', with my wife, flying 500 meters above the ground at 70 MPH for two miles in Boca, which then hovered over the Boca West development for 30 minutes this past summer."

Thanks to Guy in Boca.

* * *

ILLINOIS.

BREMERTON -- On February 25, 2003, about 7:30 PM, my husband, going to his vehicle after work, looked up and noticed a strange looking aircraft flying directly over the Puget Sound Naval Shipyard. The craft had a triangle/chevron shape with one light at each point of the three points, which did not blink as most aircraft running lights do. The craft was at an altitude of only 900 feet without sound and was moving slowly north. There is a strict no-fly zone in effect over the shipyard and naval base.

* * *

WISCONSIN: FLYING TRIANGLE.

MADISON -- Joel N. was visiting a friend who was using his 16X70 binoculars for stargazing and was checking out Jupiter at 10:30 PM. "I was talking about how I could see Saturn earlier in the evening when I suddenly saw six, dim, reddish lights in a "V" formation moving slowly from the south – three on one side and three on the other.

"I said to my friend 'What the hell is that?' He started to say 'That's an airplane,' when he realized there was absolutely no sound, the lights were not flashing and it was way too close and large to be an airplane. At arm's length it was just smaller than my hand.

"It disappeared suddenly. He must have gotten a slightly better look at it than I did. He said it never changed pace or direction. At first we both decided that it must have been a flock of birds reflecting red light from the city. We agreed that the speed and formation of the dim, reddish lights were perfect the whole time and most likely rectangular-shaped.

"I found an article about the possibility of a secret Military 'Stealth Blimp' that could match the description. I looked at a drawing taken from Popular Mechanics Magazine of what this secret aircraft could look like and it's amazingly close to what we saw. There is a military airbase nearby, so perhaps it is a secret aircraft."

Thanks to UFO Wisconsin, http://www.ufowisconsin.com/

* * *

WASHINGTON.

EDMONDS -- A pilot reports that he was returning from the beach with his Golden Retriever when he saw two bright landing lights coming towards him at 7:30 PM, on March 16, 2003. "The craft was flying northwest at a very low level, only 200 to 300 feet above ground level (AGL). They were about one mile away traveling just above the tree level about 20 MPH. I saw three bright lights and they were on the bottom corners of a black triangle (about 100-150' to each side). I was standing in the middle of a park with the craft heading straight for me.

"At that moment, I decided that I would not want to become an abductee statistic and said out loud 'I'm not ready for this!' So I quickly made my way to the closest trees for some cover. I looked back and it was gone. It was as close as 250 yards and traveling at about 20 MPH with no sound. This happened about 5 miles south of Paine Field - my home airport – within their Class D airspace.

"I have contacted Paine Field Airport Management and they are researching their radar tapes and talking to the tower personnel for that time period."

* * *

CALIFORNIA: UFO SIGHTINGS.

SACRAMENTO -- Hi, my name is Spencer and I had a UFO sighting on January 14, 2002, at 7:01 PM, on the Garden Highway going to a King's game. The shape of the ship was an acute triangle moving about 20 MPH. It had four lights, one on each corner and one big blue one in the center

Thanks to Spencer.

* * *

WASHINGTON: AIRCRAFT CARRIER SIZE FLYING TRIANGLE.

STANWOOD -- At 8:30 PM, the onlooker saw a huge triangle-shaped craft going from north to south from his living room window on March 30, 2003. The witness stated, "The flying triangle was the size of an aircraft carrier and looked to be traveling in and out of the cloud cover at about 12,000 feet! There were three white lights that each looked the size of the moon. It was moving very slow with no noise. I was looking to see if it was going to appear from around my tree but it vanished in thin air. My dog did not bark and even the frogs kept up their noise."

* * *

Texas: Triangle Craft Observed by TUX Nuclear Power Plant.

GLEN ROSE -- On December 17, 2003, at 11:50 PM, the observer was going to work on the night shift and off in the distance was a very low flying plane near the TXU Nuclear Power Plant, about five miles away. "We don't often see low flying craft because of it." The observer noticed three dim lights with a green light on the left and a red light on the right. In the middle, slightly higher, was another red light that was noticeably smaller than the two on either side of it. "These lights were not blinking like aircraft lights. It was flying very low and there was no sound."

"When the object passed overhead it was a perfect triangle and looked mostly black or a dark gray. I jumped in my truck and tried to follow the flying triangle but lost sight of it behind nearby houses and trees. I estimate the size to be about that of a private jet moving at about 50 mph and only 125 feet altitude."

Thanks to Brian Vike, Director CANADA HBCC.
* * *

Mississippi: Flying Triangle.

MERIDIAN -- Chris Shelton, a teacher, writes, "The last encounter was on Thursday, February 19, 2004, when I was heading home to Toomsuba. I live on a country road called Smith Spur. I was coming to the end of Will Garret Rd., when I noticed, up in the sky, there was this mysterious triangular-shaped vessel hovering at tree top level. I pulled over on the side of the road and watched for five minutes as the vessel just sat there taking no notice as I watched through the windshield of my car. It was a solid, black, flying triangle and it stood out against the bright night sky with three white lights underneath near each point. In the center of this triangle of lights was a red flashing light.

"The vessel was hovering over a small pond at 6:45 PM. I didn't think much else of it, so I started the car and left as I wanted to get home."

Thanks to Chris Shelton.
* * *

California.

LOS ANGELES – The witness saw a flying triangle with unfamiliar red, green and blue light patterns. The object had an abnormal flight path at 8 PM on March 8, 2004 and flew low, then high over the area. The lights changed from white to colored lights. We've been seeing this thing for a couple of weeks. It was very strange and didn't look like a police helicopter because it flew too high for that.

R. David Anderson writes, "I have been seeing these UFO's while working on a sunroom addition on our house. I noticed one twice last week while I was working and on March 22, 2004. I finished up around 4 PM. and rested with my new 4.3 digital camera nearby. After about 35 minutes, I saw the UFO to the north flying at about 30 mph and was probably about at least 250 feet high. Its direction of travel was toward the Southeast. I picked up the camera and began to take pictures, following its movement as it went from the northern sky to the eastern sky in about 45 seconds. It went behind a large tree. When it came back into my view it had climbed much higher and began to dim as it moved farther away. My seven year old daughter also saw this UFO."

Thanks to R. David Anderson.

94

* * *

Georgia – Flying Triangle Investigation,

DULUTH --David Brown SSD Field Investigator reports, he interviewed a lady who had seen a large flying triangle glide by on January 7, 2004, at 7:30 PM.

While returning home she noticed an extremely bright, white light originating in the northwest, directly under the bright moon. As the object approached, the witness saw that the craft was not a conventional aircraft as it glided by the driver's side of the vehicle. The object was a huge triangular object the size of one to one and a half football fields in length (450 feet). The sighting lasted about five minutes and, when she returned home, she called the Gwinnett and Duluth Georgia Police Departments. She also contacted the Channel 11 local news and MUFON.

The object was flying at 130 feet, just above the treetops, and moving at 40 mph. The speed was determined as the object kept pace with her vehicle and she had looked at her speedometer that was reading 40 mph.

The large wing was sharp gray/silver and had four extremely large, white protruding lights, similar to fluorescent tubes, surrounded by what appeared as suction cups. She followed the object and noticed it began to ascend to the northeast and banked sharply back to the northwest and she could see the underside more clearly. Her radio was playing and the craft did not affect electrical parts of the vehicle or her radio.

Dobbins Air Reserve Base is 25 miles to the northwest. Dobbins Information Offices were contacted but they provided no information. There are no known military craft that match this description, although experimental lighter-than-air craft may perform as described by the witness. The craft is labeled as an unknown.

I wish to thank Tom Sheets GAMUFON State Director and David Brown SSD for their excellent work.

* * *

Georgia: Flying Triangle.

CALHOUN - On April 5, 2004, at about 10:30 PM, a 30 year old male reported that he was outside with his astronomy telescope and had a strange tingling sensation and then looked up and observed a large triangular-shaped object just above the tree tops. His first impression was a helicopter but he heard no sound.

This craft was moving slowly towards Calhoun proper, projecting a bright, blue searchlight-like beam. It continued on, south to north, until it went over to the other side of an adjacent mountain and vanished from sight.

* * *

MANCHESTER – April 16, 2004, at 10:20 PM, a female, 47 year old, along with her 16-year-old daughter, reported they were driving home from Columbus when they thought they saw a helicopter from nearby Ft. Benning. Upon getting closer, she felt it resembled a Stealth Bomber with a triangle-like shape. Their closer observation found the witnesses slowing and letting down the vehicle windows, which revealed NO sound.

Near Ellerslie, in Harris County, the witnesses then observed the craft to be a dark triangle hovering at relatively low altitude. The triangle was blinking red and green lights at the rear, plus projecting a spotlight-like beam with an adjacent blue light under each "wing."

The daughter became a little concerned, stating they needed to get out of there, continue on home and tell her Dad. The primary witness stated that she had observed similar triangular craft before, along with her older daughter, but had never reported it.

MUFONGA's Dan Worsham of Columbus has agreed to further investigate this incident. These are preliminary reports in nature.

Thanks to Tom Sheets, SD MUFONGA.

* * *

Upstate: New York.

MILTON -- Two witnesses were sitting on their front porch talking at 10:40 PM, on June 5, 2004, and observed two shooting stars and then another star moving slowly in the sky. The neighbor noticed two more lights behind it and these formed a flying triangle. There were no clouds this night and the object was traveling slowly east and remained in the triangle position for five minutes, then each light blinked off one after another. No aircraft was noted in the area and it was moving ever so slow.

Thanks to Brian Vike, Director HBCC UFO Research.

* * *

Utah: Transparent Triangles.

SANDY --At 11 PM, on June 13, 2004, a couple and their two cousins saw a transparent triangle-shaped object fly over. "It was kind of fuzzy on the edges as the transparency did not go all the way to the edge. There was no sound and there was no emitted light. The sighting lasted all of about two seconds before it disappeared from view behind some trees. We all said, 'What the hell is that?'

"One cousin missed the craft and ran out and pointed up. A smaller triangle had appeared in the sky and was headed southeast. It looked like two shaded triangles that may have been linked by a transparent piece. This one had more speed and disappeared into the night sky. We all agreed on the shape and transparency of the triangles. We also all agreed that they appeared to be paper-thin. They made no noise at all, and also made no apparent air disturbance.

"I will post drawings on my web page. http://www.undergroundvine.net/ufo."

* * *

96

North Atlantic – Boomerang.

350 NM EAST OF NORTHERN FLORIDA -- I was delivering a sailing yacht to Ft. Lauderdale, FL from Boston, via Bermuda, standing the twelve to four deck watch in October 1990. It was a beautiful night, very warm and clear at 1 AM, when the boomerang object flew directly over us. Its approach had been hidden by the very large mainsail of the Schooner. The object was huge, twice the size of Ursa Major. It glowed with a pale, luminescent gold or yellow with a pale blue triangle at leading edge or apex of the arch. The sharp tips at the trailing edges also were blue. It was climbing and following an easterly course. It was totally silent and left a wake of gold "glitter" behind. Soon it seemed to almost explode into several small bright lights, then re-condense into a very bright single light and disappear into space.

I saw the exact same thing three years later in 1993 and, once again, it seemed to be heading east to climb up over the Atlantic from the Southeast U.S. The second craft came from the SW horizon and I could see its trajectory clearly and also its very distinct shape and color. Both sightings occurred in the middle of the Bermuda Triangle, 30N 70W. Many mariners have seen these craft but don't report them for fear of ridicule.

Whatever this vehicle is, whether extraterrestrial or government; it is astonishingly huge, incredibly fast and absolutely silent. The fact that I've seen it twice in a three-year period makes me think that this is some kind of routine, late night departure to some other planet. I watched the thing punch through the atmosphere twice with my own eyes.

Cape Canaveral is located to the west of that position but I seriously doubt we have anything this wild flying under the stars and stripes. I've always felt that if a UFO wanted to hideout, where better but under the sea. Noah's flood has not yet receded: Two thirds of the earth is still underwater. The southern edge of the Bermuda Triangle is where the Puerto Rico Trench is, the deepest water in the Atlantic hemisphere, 28,000 ft deep I believe.

Thanks to Brian Vike, Director HBCC UFO Research.

* * *

South Carolina: Teardrop and Hovering Triangle.

GREENVILLE – At 11:15 PM, the witness was heading east on I-185 on August 23, 2004, when he saw four white lights, about 1.5 the brightness of Venus, in a line that was a distance of about 1.5 the diameter of a full moon. A fifth light was in back of the four lights. About half way between the single light and the middle of the four lights there was one red light, slightly brighter than the white ones. He exited onto I-85 south and turned around and went back to try and find a place where he could stop his car. The object was moving very slowly south, parallel to I-85, about 65 degrees up. From this angle, there were two white lights the same distance apart as the farthest of the line of four and there was a red light, about 1/4 the diameter of the moon, above the middle of the white lights.

"I watched it for about a minute and looked back and it was gone. It is possible that it flew into a cloud." He turned around again but it had disappeared.

www.hbccufo.com

* * *

Illinois: Flying Triangles.

LAKE IN THE HILLS – A network Computer Engineer for twenty years and his chemist wife witnessed a triangular-shaped object moving across the sky on August 20, 2004, from 10:25 to 10:27 PM. At first glance, it looked like three lights heading south. Then the flying triangle flew right over their heads at a low altitude and its length was longer than three large commercial aircraft.

The witness looked at the flying triangle through Tasco mini binoculars. The object had three lights with one located on each corner. The object tilted toward the west and then leveled off. The witness states, "I grew up in Elk Grove Village with a commercial flight path over the top of my parents' home since I was two years old. This was something that I have never seen before and my wife agrees that this was the strangest object we have ever seen. The object only stayed in sight for three minutes and completely vanished right in front of us in the partly cloudy sky."

Thanks to Brian Vike. www.hbccufo.com

* * *

Pennsylvania: Rounded Triangle.

MOUNT COBB -- On September 10, 2004, about 10:10 PM, the witness saw a bright moving object in the crystal-clear sky and called to his Mother and his two sons to view the light. It was moving near the Big Dipper and was changing colors from green to red to dark orange to white, as though it was spinning.

The witness reports, "As we looked at it through binoculars we were able to see the colors clearly. On the top of the object, above the rotating colors, was a very bright, white light. The object was hovering, and then it moved to the left and then to the right. It hovered there for a few minutes and then it started to move northwest and climbed higher in the sky. The main color of the object was yellow.

"My older son told me it was a rounded triangle shape and we all saw the same thing. A military aircraft was flying northwest, while the object flew southeast. The strange object was much brighter, much bigger and much higher than the military planes."

Thanks to Brian Vike, Director HBCC UFO Research.

* * *

Washington: Huge Triangle of Lights.

REMOTE CAMPGROUND – Cliff Mickelson writes, "A group of highly credible witnesses are reporting the sighting of a huge triangle of lights that passed over a remote campground on the eastern edge of Washington State on September 12, 2004. The sighting occurred several hours after dusk. The phenomenon was described as being a 'huge' triangle of lights that moved with an eerie exactitude across the night sky.

"Although campers were not certain as to whether it was one object with three lights or three different objects, there was consensus that the lights moved in faultless unison across the heavens. Several campers report that the stars appeared to be occluded in the space between the lights. All witnesses agree that the object (or objects) were located at a great altitude, perhaps bordering on the edge of space. The object(s) remained in plain view for several minuets despite the narrow confines of the heavily wooded canyon campground location, ten miles west of Tampico. The triangle seemed to be in no big hurry.

"This latest sighting has taken place in an area enclosed by Mt. Rainier, Mt. Adams and the upper and lower Yakima Valleys. It is an area unsurpassed for the number of documented UFO sightings. The Yakima Indian Tribal Police, as well as individual tribal members often report these and other such sightings during routine patrols in the more inaccessible parts of the Yakima Reservation."

Visit James Gilliland's web site:
http://www.eceti.org/index1.html http://www.rumormillnews.com/

Thanks to Cliff Mickelson of Surfing the Apocalypse Network http://www.surfingtheapocalypse.com.

* * *

Washington: Close-up Sighting of Black Triangle.

SEATTLE -- Gary Val Tenuta writes, "In November 1993, on a Sunday night about 9:30 PM, I was driving next to the main Boeing Aircraft facility, northbound, and noticed three unblinking red lights low in the sky. They were moving in unison, very slowly across my field of vision from east to west. In all that time, I'd seen plenty of airplanes and helicopters flying low in this area. Then, only about two blocks away from being, directly under the flight path of these lights, I still could not make out what they were attached to. However, from their slow, steady movement in unison, I was pretty sure all three of them were attached to a single object. They were about to enter the airspace above Boeing Field to my immediate left. At this point I was convinced it was a single, low-flying craft of some kind and I knew there was something very odd here.

"I pulled my car off to the side of the road and rolled down the window to get a better look. But the craft was now directly overhead so I had to get out of the car to see it. I opened the car door and stepped out as the craft passed slowly and directly over my head at an estimated altitude of less than 500 feet and perhaps only 150 feet above me. I could see it was a gigantic black triangle. It was just one big, three-sided, cookie-cutter straight-edged, black, geometric shape; a triangle with one large, round unblinking red light at each of its three corners, flat up against the underside of the craft. I could clearly see a huge, dense, black silhouette against this gray cloud cover ceiling.

"It flew past me and was now over Boeing field about seventy-five to a hundred feet above one of the main Boeing hangars, flying at five miles per hour. Its heading was west. It appears to be about the size of a football field.

"The object didn't make a sound! Not even a hum, a rumble or anything. It had just passed a few miles to the east, directly over hundreds of cars on the freeway. I watched it until I couldn't see it anymore. All the way home I just kept asking myself, 'What the hell was that?' I'm still wondering.

"That weekend, I told my ex-wife about it. She is a cocktail waitress and has conversations with customers. She was told by a Boeing employee that there is an underground manufacturing facility where they build a huge triangular craft. Boeing made big news in 2002 when a story hit the press that they were experimenting with anti-gravity propulsion. So, just what did I see? Was it an alien craft or a secret military craft? I don't know."

Thanks to Gary Val Tenuta Everett, WA.

* * *

California: UFO Wave.

PALMDALE -- While out photographing a meteor shower, "Mike" (22) and "Lance" (22), sighted three triangles in a circle, spinning at fantastic speeds, then stop and disappear on the evening of August 16, 2004 at about 1:30 AM. While they sighted this event, "Mike" called his girlfriend on his cell phone and, while talking, the cell phone died. Then the camera they had, which was fully charged, died and would not work. The camera noted "Battery Dead". When both returned home, the cell phone worked and the camera, as it was placed in its charger, stated. It had a full charge.

Their location was 47th and "S" streets. The craft were flying at the height of high altitude jet flight patterns, an estimated 20,000 feet. At arm's length, holding a quarter, the craft were the size of a quarter. No noise was associated with this event. The triangles had a half sphere shape to them. The men saw high definition shapes in the crafts bodies.

Thanks to Cosmic Connection http://tvufo.tripod.com

* * *

SAN DIEGO-- Melvin Podell of MUFON is investigating a case. The witness stated, "After fifty years of looking at the sky in the hope of seeing a UFO, I now have! On Saturday, October 30, 2004, at 9:44 PM, I was standing near the corner of Poway Road and Gate Lane at the eastern end of Poway, a northern suburb of San Diego. I was looking almost exactly overhead in a cloudless sky with a light haze that was illuminated by the city lights and the almost full moon about 15 degrees above the eastern horizon.

"I was stunned to see a black triangle moving at tremendous speed directly south toward the hills that are the southern boundary of Poway Valley. The distance between my location and the crest of the hills is 5.5 miles and 5 miles NE from MCAS (Marine Corps Air Station). The speed of the triangle was not less than that of many meteors! The craft was in sight for about 1.5 seconds. It was an entirely black, equilateral (or close to equilateral) triangle having seven, bright, yellowish-white lights, rather like the color of incandescent lamps, except much larger and brighter. There was one light at each apex and two equally spaced between the leading apex and the apex on each side. There were no lights on the trailing flat edge. It was because of these lights and the reflection from the ground light that I could see the object clearly.

"It was completely silent, probably even in the ultrasonic range as none of the many dogs in the area seemed disturbed. Although it was below the line-of-sight radar at the MCAS as long as it was in Poway Valley, it clearly would have entered its view as soon as it rose above the southern hills, because the MCAS is just a mile or two directly south of the hills.

"The triangle did not maneuver, except for one slight dip of the right wing which was quickly corrected. The angular width was that of my thumb at arm's length. What impressed me was the incredible speed of the object. Its speed was literally, not figuratively, meteoric. It increased its altitude to clear the hills."

Submitted by Mel Podell, MUFON-San Diego, mpodell@juno.com

* * *

Indiana: Flying Triangle.

BLOOMINGTON -- Lynn Taylor reports, "At 7:10 PM, the witness was southbound on Walnut Street on November 13, 2004, approaching the intersection of State Highway 45 when she observed a large triangle-shaped object. The object was traveling southeast, toward the busy intersection ahead. As the object approached, the witness could see two red lights, one on the tip of each trailing edge. She also described the center of the craft as having an amber-colored light or lights that constantly changed shape.

"As the object crossed the intersection, the witness momentarily looked away to check the traffic conditions. When she looked up again to observe the craft, only a single red light was visible.

"She was insistent that the object was triangle-shaped and was not an advertising blimp. The witness indicated her confidence in the object's shape because its lighting partially illuminated the underside.

She further offered that the object was much too fast and low to be a blimp anyway. From her conversation and description of the sighting and my familiarity with the area, I would estimate the object was flying approximately 120 feet above the ground."

Thanks to Lynn Taylor, Sentinel Files,
http://sentinelfiles.tripod.com/sfiles.htm
* * *

California: Huge Triangle With Red Lights.

LOS ANGELES -- While walking in West Hollywood, the witness noticed two red lights in the sky at 7:45 PM, on December 3, 2004. They were an arm's length away from each other. He noticed a third light up ahead of the other two, forming a perfect triangle, all moving in unison, heading north.

"The three lights would pulse at the same moment. At that point, I realized there was the vague outline of a mass connecting these three red lights. Then I watched as four or five other lights pulsed along the outer edge of the triangle with more lights being on the western edge of the object. I could not detect any pattern to the flashing of these other lights. A couple of times, all seven or eight were on at the same time.

"This thing was huge! If it was just up a few thousand feet, you could fit dozens of commercial jets within its base outline. If it were really high up – well, it would be beyond massive.

"One of those sweeping, movie premiere spotlights swept under the object and didn't touch it, so it was at least higher than those things can project light. It seemed to glide across the sky without a sound and was near the 405 Highway."
* * *

New Hampshire.

TRIANGLE -- Brian Vike received a telephone call from two witnesses who were driving towards home when they spotted a black triangular craft on November 26, 2004, at 2:15 AM. They saw a bright, elongated light coming towards them at low altitude heading south and descending. The driver pulled off the road as the light flew close. One of the ladies got very frightened as this object was rather close and just sitting in the sky over the power-lines, moving slightly from side to side. They could see lights on each of the points of a triangle, which pulsated rather quickly. They were also able to see the silhouette of the craft against the clear night sky just above the trees.

The passenger told the driver to get the car going as the passenger was terrified at what they were watching. The object had now moved to the opposite side and the ladies guessed it was only 500 feet away from them at this point.

The object was estimated to be the size of a normal sized car. The sighting lasted for four minutes. There was no sound.

Thanks to Brian Vike www.hbccufo.com

* * *

Pennsylvania: Flying Triangle Follows Lady.

MARTIN'S CORNER – Mary E. Spitz, a former Captain in the Army, reports she was driving to her Mother's house on Mother's Day of 2004, at 10:10 PM, when she saw a triangular UFO with flashing red and white lights. It had no sound. It flew in very low and started to follow her car.

She states, "I was alone and very scared after I sited it in the town of Martin's Corner and it followed me to my Mother's house, which is Wagontown. I traveled eastbound on Highway 340 and then on some country roads ending at Red Mill Road in Wagontown.

"The craft followed me at only 100 yards above my car until I got to my Mother's house and I ran inside the house very frightened. The craft hovered and seem to land in the field across the road. It seemed as though it wanted to take me but did not force me to go. I kept on telling it to leave.

"After ten minutes hovering above the open field, it flew away towards the east. It was about 50 feet on each of the three sides. There were three blinking lights; probably the red one was in the center.

"What I really want to know is who flies in triangular space craft?"

Thanks to Mary Spitz and John Schuessler, MUFON International Director.

Chapter 7

Worldwide Nocturnal Triangular-shaped UFOs

AUSTRALIA: FLYING TRIANGLE.

SALT ASH, NSW -- Darryyll Jones writes that he holds an ultra light pilots license and is a yachtsman, so he is more aware of the sky. "On April 26, 2001, 15 miles north of Newcastle, I was looking at the sky with a friend at 8:00 PM when a huge, triangular outlined shape, formed by white lights, mostly on the leading edge but enough on the trailing edge to define this boomerang outline, flew directly over head.

"It had to be massive! My first impression was that it was between 10,000 to 30,000 feet high. It was 5 degrees wide, silent and flew straight with no ionization trail. Suddenly it was gone like the lights went out.

"Only minute's later, single lights began scribing perfect arc's between 40 to 80 degrees south, first in one direction then the other in exactly the same circuit, and then they too were gone. They were making a crescent shape as they too were fading out in the western portion of their arc.

"I have wracked my brain for an explanation such birds, aircraft or asteroids. My friend and I sat down and made notes that were near identical. We concluded the most likely explanation was a mother ship and the single orbs somehow came from it.

"I am still far from satisfied with that explanation though. As the military aircraft from a nearby RAAF base were out in larger than normal numbers. The three helicopters and possibly five F18's might have been a laser type focused display. The triangle was flying in the direction of the base. My friend was looking the other way when I spotted the triangle approaching. He got two and a half seconds to observe it, while I got five.

"We agreed on what we saw. The orbs were around for 13 passes for three minutes at very high speed. They dimmed out as they headed west for the sun, now over the horizon, suggesting again 'deep space objects'. The main group and then fractured and returned to earth much like fighter pilots peel off. There was a small storm in the distance with heavy lightning that continued all night.

"Others claim to regularly see the big triangle inland at Bathurs."

Thanks to Darryyll Jones, vital.earth@hunterlink.net.au.

(Editor's Note): Two well qualified witnesses observed a UFO. The craft may be stationed at the nearby air base or they may be pulling into our atmosphere for protection from unusually heavy solar flares emanating from our sun.

George Filer.

* * *

AUSTRALIA: FLYING TRIANGLE.

The witness reports, "We were sitting outside having a game in the back yard on July, 2, 2001. We all quickly glanced up as something reflected into our eyes and almost stopping our vision for a bit.

"There was a triangular (flat equilateral triangle) craft moving across the sky at 11:30 PM. We live next to an airfield but we didn't know what to make of it. Therefore, we carried on playing our game. Fourteen minutes later it came back again but going the other way. It would occasionally float across and then vanish again. But this time it was closer.

"We rung the airfield and they said that there was only something reflecting and they couldn't make out what it was. We started to get very nervous and scared, so we went inside and observed outside while watching TV.

"Nothing happened until about 17 minutes later when the TV went off, the phone started ringing and the fax came through with all types of weird stuff. I have the fax to prove it. Our cell phones went dead and we saw it again but this time it was hovering right over our house. It slowly picked up speed, flew over some trees and we never saw it again.

"We live in the country so there are a few valleys where it could have gone down and hidden. We saw a group of jets fly over the valley just as the craft vanished."

* * *

CANADA: FOUR FLYING TRIANGLES.

REGINA, SASKATCHEWAN -- Bridget reports that four UFOs were sighted on Monday, July 22, 2001, at 12:30 AM. Four objects were seen heading south from the Regina area. They were triangular with an orange haze discharging from the base. They approached traveling approximately 55 K.P.H (30 MPH) prior to stopping. They paused and hovered for several seconds and departed out of sight, moving toward the south-southwest in less than a second.

Thanks to Bridget, briquette4000@yahoo.com

* * *

BELORUSSIAN: FLYING TRIANGLE.

MINSK (BELARUS') -- On July 19, 2001, at 11:20 PM, Michael Goldencov, a journalist, and his girlfriend Olga Korotkina, a student of Minsk State University, noticed a triangular object high in the night sky of Minsk, Belorussian capital. They walked opposite the Lithuanian Embassy when Michael saw strange sparkling lights that he first considered to be an aircraft's signal lights. The object flew making square turns. The shape of it was triangle with like a police car sparkling big lights in each corner.

Michael and Olga watched the sparkling lights for two minutes. Michael Goldencov said, "I think that it was scanning the city and filming it. I am sure that somebody else had to see it because the object was pretty slow and stayed above the city. No doubt the police and militaries saw this object."

Thanks to Vadim Deruzhinsky, Editor-in-Chief of the Secret Researches Analytic Journal vd@gtp.by

* * *

ENGLAND: UFO SIGHTING.

BRIDGEWATER, SOMERSET -- On or about August 19, 2001, a flying triangle-shape object pointing towards earth and a circle-shape on top with alternating red, blue and green lights was seen at 11:45 PM. "It was silent and rotated in front of my car, then flew off and hovered for roughly an hour above a small village called Brent Knowle. It is here that 3 witnesses, including myself, observed the UFO with binoculars. Broken clouds started to form in the distance and gradually our vision was limited until, after the last bit of cloud passed, we looked back to see that it wasn't there."

* * *

CANADA DISK: AND FLYING TRIANGLE.

VANCOUVER, BC -- The witness was heading west on Barnet Highway while returning from Christmas dinner on December 25, 2001. At 7:30 PM, the witness noticed an object in the northeast. His wife confirmed seeing a triangular-shaped flying object with green and white lights. It was not moving and was just hovering perfectly still. It was flying above the mountains but they could not stop on the highway.

The witness said, "We lost sight of the triangle through the trees in just under a minute."

* * *

ARGENTINA POLICEMAN SEES GIANT UFO.

CHAJ'N -- Guillermo Arias was on patrol at 11 PM, on July 21, 2002, when a radio call alerted him that police in Achiras were seeing lights heading toward them. As he drove the police patrol van, he saw a formation of seven lights and followed them ten kilometers along a rural dirt road when his engine died. The van's dashboard lights began turning on and off, the police radio went haywire and its dial displayed random frequencies while the van was filled with an acrid odor like burnt wiring. The interior lights came on and off.

Seized by fear, Arias jumped out of the van and lost his cell-phone. Suddenly an immense light emerged from an adjacent field. A triangular object rose majestically. He described it as a real "floating city", 200 meters long with a long row of about 100 windows.

Arias saw something move behind him that he defined as "non-human." Numerous beams of light came out of the giant triangle, aimed at the ground for several seconds. The object suddenly rose and sped away lighting up the area like daylight.

Recovering from his nervous condition, he returned to the vehicle and notified his comrades of the experience, receiving radio instruction that reinforcements were being set out. Patrolman Barrios from Achiras was trying to keep him calm over the radio, while Sgt. Medina, who was the first to arrive on the scene, and Sgt. Cordoba were among the officers who reached the area to lend aid to their comrade in distress.

Thanks to Scott Corrales Translation (C) 2002, and C.O.R. (Circulo Ovnilógico Riocuartense).

* * *

CANADA: SIGHTING.

PARRY SOUND, ONTARIO -- The object was observed by three adults while they were boating in Georgian Bay on September 1, 2002, fifteen minutes after midnight. The actual latitude and longitude can be retrieved from data stored in my GPS. We were anchored overnight near Port Rawlston in Parry Sound and the sky was clear and, given our remote northern location, there was no interference from rural lighting.

The object, compared to commercial aircraft observed earlier, appeared to be at a higher altitude and was extremely large. It consisted of three lights in a triangular shape. Not a perfect triangle but with one side shorter than the other. It traveled west with no sound. As it went further west, the lights suddenly dimmed out and it was no longer visible.

* * *

MERCIER -- My husband, myself and our two children were driving home from our country place near Huntington on September 15, 2002. I saw what appeared to be really bright stars and asked my husband, "Are those airplanes?" He said "helicopters."

After five minutes, the two lights ahead changed position. Around 8 PM, we got closer and what I saw gave me shivers. The object was triangular with lights at all three corners and unlike any aircraft. We saw them for ten minutes as two flew overhead and my husband said he could "see through it". We all saw the distinct low flying triangle shape, larger than a 747.

There have been other sightings along the St. Laurence River in Quebec.

Thanks to Brian Vike, HBCC investigator.
http://www.geocities.com/hbccufo/home.html

* * *

LEDUC, ALBERTA -- On September 15, 2002, at 2:45 AM, Denny Unger decided to step outside on a clear and windless night and saw three points of light forming a flying triangle. "My first thought was that I was having a dizzy spell so I refocused, and the lights were there.

"Thirty seconds later the flying triangle of lights changed direction from north to east. The object was either very large or very low and appeared to blot out passing stars without a sound. The lights on each tip were solid white but of very low intensity. There was a distinct impression that the corner lights were used to camouflage the object and it was doing its best not to be seen. It was completely silent.

"I entered the house and grabbed my digital video camera, and began filming the object but soon lost sight of it as it flew behind a neighbor's home. I attempted to follow but lost it. This was all captured on video but the triangular formation of lights could not be resolved on film."

* * *

CALGARY, ALBERTA -- On January 10, 2003, two brothers report sighting a flying triangle at 9:30 PM. Reports of these flying triangles are becoming very numerous and may indicate a base in Northern Canada.

* * *

COQUITLAM, BRITISH COLUMBIA -- The witness had just stepped outside, on March 25, 2003, to have a cigarette and said he noticed this "thing" out of the corner of his eye at 8:55 PM. He said, "The craft was just above the clouds after it broke into a clearing in the night sky. It was a very large, black, flying triangle with three points of light on each of the object's tips. It moved very fast and was totally silent. The craft was flying roughly east to west just above the cloud cover."

He checked with the weather channel and was told it (cloud cover) was about 11,000 feet. He was located around the shadow of Burnaby Mountain and the object was seen close or flying over the 401 Freeway. It was bigger than three jumbo jets that could have fit into the object easily. The object was witnessed for approximately 3 to 4 seconds and freaked him right out!

Thanks to Brian Vike HBCC UFO Research.

* * *

EAST OF HOUSTON - A 56-year-old man and his mother, on their farm, sighted a flying triangle on April 21, 2003. Brian reports a lady and her husband also witnessed a large triangular-shaped object on

April 21, 2003. The interesting thing is they watched the craft just before the son and Mom had their sighting. The lady and her husband were just west of Houston at 11:30 PM. So the timing of the two sightings works out great.

* * *

HOUSTON, BRITISH COLUMBIA - Investigator Brian Vike reports the sighting of a triangular-shaped object around March 15, 2003, is being seen by a number of people over a two month stretch and just recently. The family, who reported this sighting, said they were caught off guard by what they witnessed. A low and slow flying triangular-shaped craft cruised from the east to the west from the direction of Mount Harry Davis and continued on its flight path over the mountains towards Grouse Mountain and the Smithers area. The triangular-shaped object was longer than wide and very large. Also there were a number of lights, which ran along the underside of it and close to the outer edge but rather dim. It was completely silent and dark in color.

From the witnesses' vantage point from their home, they guessed it took the object 15 to 20 seconds before it went out of their line of sight.

(HBCC UFO Note): I visited this family on the same day I met with the other folks who witnessed and reported their sighting, which was of a flying "C". Both the C-shaped object and this triangle sighting come from the same area west of town. Once again we have some very credible older folks who never saw anything like this before. Many residents claim there were a large number of sightings in the last two years.

* * *

ENGLAND: FLYING TRIANGLE SPOTTED.

SALFORD, - Warren Knocerman states, "The last sighting was June 19, 2002, at 12:35 AM, when I saw a big triangle-shaped object in the sky change shape into a circle and disappear over Irlam in Salford. I've seen it 13 times now. I'm getting sick of it!"

Thanks to Warren Knocerman

kay@maxieshouse73.freeserve.co.uk

* * *

BELGIUM: FLYING TRIANGLES RETURN.

ANTWERP -- A 19 year old resident from Edegem spotted a triangular-shaped object on May 14, around 1 o'clock at night, while driving home on his motorcycle. On June 20, 2003, he sighted the triangle again, with flashing lights, hovering 125 meters above a house. He drove to the object and the UFO gradually departed and accelerated. The biker had to speed up to 20 km/h to keep up.

Somewhat farther, the object halted again above a house. The witness put his motorcycle aside and waved to it but there was no reaction and no sound. From beneath, it looked like a triangle but

110

without sharp edges. Besides the flashing lights, the object had blue and red lights. From behind, the object looked like a "flattened pyramid-shape."

He tried to make "contact" with a laser pointer but didn't succeed. After a minute, the object began accelerating again; first jerkily and then fast. The biker got on his bike and followed it to the next town at high speeds. Near a bridge, the UFO accelerated and disappeared.

Thanks to Toine Trust, http://www.ufoplaza.nl/

* * *

Northern Ireland: Triangular UFO Sighted.

CLOGHER, COUNTY TYRONE -- On Thursday, December 11, 2003, Milton Clarke was outdoors in his hometown when a UFO approached from the north.

"It seemed like a glowing triangle, a really bright glow," Milton reported. "I couldn't see any markings. It was very close to the ground; at one point only 20 meters (66 feet) off the ground. It came in very fast, slowed down to a stop, then flew away very fast towards the west.

"I took some pictures but it's hard to know if it will come out. It was very dark and I didn't have the right type of film for this kind of thing."

Thanks to UFO ROUNDUP Volume 8, Number 48 December 17, 2003 Editor: Joseph Trainor E-mail: Masinaigan@aol.com Website: http://www.ufoinfo.com/roundup/up/

* * *

Northern England: Flying Triangles.

WEST CUMBRIA - Three UFOs were spotted during the festive season over Workington and Whitehaven. Shining balls and spooky triangles were seen in the night sky. Daley Rogers, of Hensingham, was left spellbound by a red object hovering overhead. He said: "We were coming home and we could see something in the sky that dropped something white and bright that exploded. Then, it took off." Daley, 23, admits that, although he wasn't frightened by the ball-shaped object, he found it hard to get it out of his mind.

At least six other people witnessed strange goings-on in the West Cumbrian skies over Christmas. UFO expert Sharon Larkin, of Broughton Cross, near Cockermouth, said: "We have had sightings of a triangular-shaped craft and an orange ball over the Workington area. The triangle was going over the Stainburn bypass at around 10.30 PM. on a Sunday at the end of December. Before that it was sitting over Clifton. The orange ball was spotted over Broughton Moor last week. The area has a higher than average number of unexplained sightings. The night sky in Cumbria is particularly alive. From September onwards, the skies are full of lights. With it getting darker earlier, people are more aware of what is going on over their heads."

111

Thanks to Emma McGordon and Fiona MacRae, The News and Star. 05/01/2004.

* * *

Netherlands: Massive Flying Triangle.

ALMELO, Overijssel -- A 47-year old witness was walking a dog outside on Sunday, January 11, 2004, around 8:15 PM, when he saw a huge, massive triangle-shaped object. At the moment of the sighting, the sky was very clear and the stars were very clearly visible.

The witness states, "The triangle, with red lights on each of the three corners, was huge! In the middle of the object, there were five lights in a small triangle. There were three indigo blue-colored lights in the middle and two red lights on each side. The wind blew suddenly very hard from another direction, possibly caused by the craft. There were no engine sounds.

"The craft moved slowly from the east to the west with two bright white sphere lights on top. The object was very big – much bigger than a jet – and was 250 meters distance with a height of also 250 meters."

It was moving slowly at a constant speed of 30 km/h as it passed overhead of the witness. When the object had passed the witness, he noticed that above the object it had a "hilly shape" and on top of that, 2 sphere-shaped bright lights.

The sighting caused some psychological side effects: "I came home nervously and stayed in that condition for a couple of hours. I had a strange, restless feeling. During the sighting I was, for a moment, frightened – a kind of panic almost." He also reported the sighting to the Air Force Base but they said they don't do anything with the report. However, even though it was Sunday, a half hour later he could hear fighter jets fly over!

Thanks to Toine Trust, Site Admin UFOPlaza – UFOPortal. Editor UFOPlaza Nieuwsbrief site, www.UFOPlaza.nl mail: ganzEgal@UFOPlaza.nl: UFOPlaza@hotmail.com

* * *

Newfoundland.

ST JOHN – There was an over flight of the City on January 17-18, 2004, near midnight, of a very large flying triangle craft. The craft was observed with large lights on each of three corners and a dimmer light was in the center of the craft.

Thanks to Bob Toutman.

* * *

Canada: Heavy UFO Activity.

SURREY, BC – On April 7, 2004, at 9:45 PM, the witness, a pilot, saw three lights rapidly approaching from the west in a triangle formation at 2 o'clock low.

"The object between the lights was solid and triangular and, when the object banked north, the angular relationship between the lights was consistent with the banking of an aircraft. However, this was no ordinary aircraft. It moved completely silently and covered half the horizon that is from Surrey to the North Shore Mountains in about four seconds. I am guessing the altitude at 2000 - 3000 feet and the brightness of the lights of the object, relative to the brightness of passing aircraft lights, at within 7000 feet. I felt it could not be man-made. The flight path of the object was directly over the approach path to YVR."

* * *

Kelowna, B.C. - A glowing flying triangle was spotted on April 26, 2004, at 9:45 PM, by a husband and wife who were outside smoking. The triangle was visible for 20 to 30 seconds before it left the couples line of sight. It was glowing white in color. No lights were seen on the craft. The man guessed the object was flying at 20,000 feet. They explained that it was extremely bright but went on to say, "you couldn't miss it either."

There was no aura or glowing light surrounding it. There was no trail or tail following behind. The witness said he saw no aircraft before or during the sighting but said, right after the object passed by, a helicopter was seen flying at a low level shinning its spotlight down towards the ground.

The craft flew in a straight line towards the northeast over Okanagan Lake. At arm's length, the witness guessed the object would have been 1 to 2 centimeters in length, looking from his location. No sound was heard. The man said the craft was solid in color and not just points of light in a triangular shape. The witness also said he tried to contact the Kelowna, B.C. airport tower but they were closed.

Thanks to Brian Vike, Director HBCC UFO Research Home.

* * *

Mexico: Flying Triangle Over the Ocean.

CANCUN – A couple was looking at the Gulf of Mexico from their balcony at the Hotel Riu Cancun at 2 AM, on April 20, 2004, and saw a flying triangle hovering and illuminating the night sky.

"The distance was hard to determine but I could hear the sound of it breaking the wind. We stood there in amazement as the object darted into the clouds and then it faded away."

They ran to tell their friends across the hallway and they all ran out to their balcony to see if it could be seen again. "After a couple of minutes we spotted it again but not as close as the initial sighting. Now it appeared as an illuminating circular object. It seemed more energetic then before because it was speeding left to right, zigzagging in and out of the clouds. It maneuvered in the sky for a good hour."

* * *

South Africa: Flying Triangle.

CITRUSDAL – As the two witnesses were walking home, the grandmother pointed to the sky and said she saw a flying triangle that moved very slowly on April 12, 2004, at 9:30 PM, about 170 km from Cape Town.

"At each of the three points of the triangle there was a yellow light and in the middle of the craft was a blue and red light that went on and off and circled each other. My grandmother and I stood there for about 4 minutes watching the craft and then I went home. I told my father about it and he went outside with me, about 6 minutes after my grandmother and I first spotted it but we could only make out a faint light. My grandmother had seen a similar craft several nights ago."

Thanks to: Brian Vike, Director: http://www.hbccufo.com

* * *

France: Observation d'un Triangle Volant.

TOWER N'ÉMETTAIT -- J. Boutin writes in French, "I translated to the best of my capability.

"About one year ago, in the evening while walking my dog towards the ancient medieval tower called Tower N'émettait at 11:15 PM. (23:15 Hours), I raised my head to look 30 meters above the top when on the left I saw a black triangle. On the sides were small red lights – six I believe, along the side of the dimension and in intensity comparable with a star. The object was flying at low altitude towards the northeast and appeared larger than the Tower N'émettait. It did not make any noise as it flew slowly. The sky was clear without the moon.

"I do not know which is this type of d'appareil j'ai. I thought of a secret military plane but I do not find any reports of this type. If you have an idea or if others observed the same thing, please return an answer to me, because I remain intrigued without really believing in the small, green men."

Thanks to: J.boutin4@tiscali.fr

* * *

Canada: Triangular Shaped Objects.

MONTREAL, QUEBEC -- It was quite early in the morning of Sunday, January 2, 2005, at about 2:30 AM, when my girlfriend and I were looking out our downtown window and noticed an extremely bright, flickering light in the sky.

The sky was slightly overcast and no other lights were visible. The object was lighting up the clouds and moved closer to us, which is when I got my binoculars. After focusing my binoculars, the object looked triangular-shaped with red lights surrounding it on the bottom. After remaining relatively stationary for some time, it began to move horizontally and vertically so quickly that I couldn't keep the binoculars steady because I started shaking. It appeared to emit a colored beam from the bottom of the triangle.

It stayed in the sky for about an hour or so and then eventually traveled.

Thanks to Brian Vike www.hbccufo.com
* * *

WHITBY, ONTARIO -- On February 24, 2005, at 6:50 PM, the witness was driving home on Highway 401 and noticed the full moon and three white lights with a single red light in the center of a craft. "It was hovering over a spot slightly northeast of my position; I'm going to guess it was triangular. This hovering craft was definitely over Whitby, as I watched it while driving east toward it.

"My distance from the object was about 4 miles at an altitude of 2500 feet. As I drew closer to it, it started to move toward Oshawa, Ontario. It was definitely not a helicopter, it was way too long, not to mention the lighting sequence. The red light seemed to be rotating. I flashed my headlights on and off twice while driving. It appeared to flash back but not brightly. There was a difference in its lighting tone. After that happened, as I drew closer to it, that's when it started to move off."

Thanks to Brian Vike.
* * *

SYLVAN LAKE --The object moved fast in a westerly direction. It was low with no sound.

As I walked home from a friend's, I looked up into the sky to look at the constellations. I saw an object move swiftly over, low, no sounds and it was a Triangle V formation. It moved in a westerly direction. The object passed overhead for roughly 30 seconds before I lost site. It was almost like a U-2 spy plane but they can't travel that fast and that low.

Chapter 8
Cigar-Shaped UFOs

This entry from Filer's Files # 14 2001:

MOTHERSHIPS MAY BE BACK -- Reports of large cigar or cylinder shaped UFOs are coming in from Georgia, Colorado, California, Texas, and Washington. NASA reports that our sun is in the middle of powerful coronal mass ejections that send huge geomagnetic storms into space. The solar flare activity has been picking up for the last several months. Sky watchers as far south as Mexico have seen the Northern Lights (aurora borealis). The most recent strongly magnetized storm began March 30th when a coronal mass ejection (CME) struck our Earth's magnetosphere.

These intense storms may be tied to recent sightings of the motherships in our atmosphere. Earth is a relatively safe port in a solar storm. The most powerful flare of the current solar cycle is an X17-class event that erupted near sunspot 9393 on April 2, 2001. This CME is more powerful than the March 1989 event that led to the collapse of a power grid in Quebec. This is the second most powerful CME in 25 years. The increased activity may be the reason for increased mothership sightings.

Reports of large, cigar-shaped, aircraft carrier sized UFOs, also known as "motherships", appear to have started as early as 1896-'97 with sightings throughout the Midwest United States. During World War I hardly a night would go by without numerous reports of German Zeppelin activity over England. But the Germans only had one Naval Zeppelin and five Army airships in service when war was declared.

Historian Dr. David Clarke claims that, within a few months, most of the Zeppelins had been destroyed or wrecked. German records reveal Zeppelin activity was very limited anywhere near the UK. Yet pilots and other military personnel reported thousands of sightings of airships.

Captain Stansfield of the trawler SS Ape and many of his crew, on December 15, 1914, reported sighting a black airship. After the war, airship records were read and all German airships were in their hangars due to bad weather.

On September 6, 1914, Flight Commander C. E. Rathborne of the Felixstowe Naval Air Station, Suffolk, returned from an early morning patrol in his seaplane to make perhaps the first report of a UFO by a military officer: "At 5:35 AM, whilst on patrol, I sighted an airship steering south-southeast with a silver-colored envelope on the horizon, while flying at 1,300 feet, 27 miles south of Orfordness." Scottish Command Intelligence estimated the total number of reports of "enemy signaling" to be as high as 2,000 during 1914 alone.

By January 31, 1916, nine Naval Zeppelins had been built and were ordered to bomb central England. The Zeppelin scares and rumors generated thousands of reports of phantom airships that, based on their records, seldom ever flew near England. It appears that many of the reports may have been UFOs.

Commander Graham Bethune just returned from the Nevada UFO Conference where British author Nick Redfern spoke regarding World War II documents that were just released by the Public Records Office in the United Kingdom. The records revealed that a fleet of flying discs called "Foo Fighters" was launched from huge cigar-shaped mothercraft during B-17 daylight raids over Germany in 1943. The huge aircraft carrier sized mothership cut through a flight of B-17 bombers, launching its discs in front of the B-17 amazed aircrews. Another report by two RAF fighter pilots saw a similar "mothercraft" sitting on the ground.

* * *

CALIFORNIA: TWO CYLINDERS STOP CAR ENGINE.

ANAHIEM - The witness was driving home from his job at noon on May 13, 2003, when his new car suddenly stopped, as did the cars following him. The witness states, "Some of the people behind me got out of their cars and asked me if I knew what was going on? I said, 'I have no idea. This car is new, so I'm kind of mad.'

"I heard a humming sound, so I look around and I saw two cylinder shapes just sitting there above us. They then landed then took off into the air and vanished. When the cylinders were gone, my car and the one's behind me started up."

* * *

CALIFORNIA: CIGAR-SHAPED SILENT OBJECTS.

T.B. reports seeing a huge, cigar-shaped craft while driving on the freeway on January 29, 2001. "A group of people and I decided to chase this object at 9:00 P.M. I heard neighborhood dogs barking outside my kitchen window and I noticed a bright light in the western sky, southeast of the crescent moon. It was in the shape of a diamond.

"The light was not blinking nor did it have any color distortion and I gauged it next to a tree limb to verify if it was a star or if it had actual movement and indeed it did. It moved up and down slightly.

"I jumped into my car, driving from Kirby and Westpark at 35 mph, and I chased it going west at Newcastle & Westpark. It was larger. Then I noticed, from the South, a helicopter going north. The light dimmed as the helicopter passed it. I pulled into a parking lot at Rice Street and Westpark. After the helicopter passed it, the light stayed dim and then completely went out. This is less than 1/2 mile from my home.

"I tried to observe the object through the trees at my home ten minutes later but it had gone."

* * *

CALIFORNIA: CIGAR-SHAPED UFOs.

DUBLIN - The witness reports he sees these craft almost every morning at 7:40 AM, while waiting for the BART train. On March 31, 2001, he made his second report of this cigar-shaped object. "It flies over every morning. In my first report the object was flying much lower and much slower. I called the FAA office at the Livermore Airport.

"Is it coincidental that the object now passes overhead at a much higher altitude so that it will go largely unobserved. It appears to be white, cigar-shaped with no wings, no sound, no windows, nor anything that would make it resemble a known object. It flies from the southwest to the Northeast or East."

* * *

Ohio: Cylindrical Object.

CLEVELAND -- At 7:30 PM, a long, silver, cylindrical object without visible wingspan was first sighted on May 12, 2001, at an elevation of 45 degrees moving slowly west. The sighting was verified by two other witnesses who saw the UFO move horizontally, just above the power lines. The lack of visible wings and lack of any vapor trail behind the object was most notable.

One observer speculated it may be a rocket of some sort but no exhaust was seen and no sounds were heard. The object passed behind broad vapor trails created by passenger aircraft moving in the opposite direction. The object slowly faded into the haze in the southwestern sky. No wings or rudder structures or emanations were noted. The object moved much faster than the Goodyear Blimp, often seen in this area, and any lighter-than-air craft we've seen shaped like a fat cigar with markings and running lights, which this shiny object never displayed.

* * *

LAKEWOOD – The witness was a passenger on his way to work and driving past houses. He saw a UFO for a couple of seconds at 5:50 PM, on December 3, 2004. The object was cigar or cylinder-shaped and was going towards the northwest fairly high in the sky. There were no contrails, even though it was high enough. Many military jets were observed flying around the area shortly after.

"An hour before my sighting, the Mike Trivisanno Show on WTAM 1100 AM, reported a caller had also seen a cigar-shaped UFO. During the show there was another caller that said he saw some fighter jets coming towards Cleveland form Wright Patterson Air Force Base. I would like to receive your weekly newsletter, since I have been having lots of UFO sightings around Akron. We have been to Fostoria Ohio to look; we believe there was a crash there. Great site! I have taken some interesting photos too. Now I have somewhere to go to see the recent sightings and compare notes."

Thanks to Amy.

* * *

ILLINOIS: CIGAR-SHAPED UFO.

PALATINE -- At 2:17 PM on Saturday, May 19, 2001, two people saw a cigar-shaped, metallic object extremely high above the scattered clouds. The witness reports, "My friend first sited it but we didn't know what it was. It flew directly over us and gleamed in the sun, as it was moving at a very high speed. The shape was an elongated oval. From our perspective, it looked somewhat like a missile or something that we could not identify.

"We watched this object for approximately two or three minutes."

* * *

NASHVILLE, IL -- On August 28, 2001, in the early afternoon, the witness was fishing on the lake at Washington County Conservation Center. "I heard what I thought was jet noise and looked up and saw a long narrow object, silver in color. The craft had no wings or tail and had a long cigar shape, longer than most jet liner fuselages. If this is not a UFO, is it possible that the wings of a jet may blend against the sky or clouds and not be seen under some circumstances?

"There were some high clouds and sky was visible behind the object. If the lighting had somehow obscured the wings, I would have seen the engines. In addition, the 'windows' were on the bottom and visible to me. Airline windows are on the side!

"The area is near several airports so jet noise is common. I am now listing this as one of my UFO sightings, bringing the total up to four since 1958."

(Editor's Note): Based on your description it is difficult to determine if you saw an aircraft or a UFO. Most likely the color of the wings, engines and tail blended with the background since they are often painted white or gray while the rest of the aircraft is a more prominent color. However, there are no aircraft with windows on the bottom and we *do* get UFO reports of silver, cigar or cylinder-shaped craft

120

frequently. These have included near misses where the pilots ducked down in the cockpit. The jet noise would indicate the craft had jet engines but we will probably never know the true answer.

George Filer.

* * *

NEW ZEALAND: FLAMING CIGAR-SHAPED, ORANGE COMET.

WAIHEKE ISLAND, AUCKLAND -- Joe Trainor received this report from Anthony Milas and his girlfriend who saw a gray cigar-shaped craft surrounded by trailing flame on July 13, 2001.

"The sun was setting at 5:30 PM and the object was two-thirds its size. The flaming trail moved very slowly downward and arcing to the north. It was moving with the head of the trail leading. After five minutes, it broke into two trails - a larger and a smaller. The smaller one appeared to hover. The larger one was observed for five minutes before it disappeared behind clouds, close to the horizon. The object slowed its descent, moving to the west."

Anthony states, "Using my binoculars, it was now maintaining a steadier altitude and I clearly saw a gray cigar shape and the flaming orange/yellow was surrounding this and trailing off it.

"The object disappeared behind a cloud near Rangitoto Island, several kilometers away. My girl friend saw something similar several weeks ago but assumed it was an artifact of the sunset. The sun had set and this cannot be explained by natural phenomena.

"The object was observed for ten minutes close to the horizon and I assume it was very large, far away and traveling very fast."

Thanks to Joe Trainor, Editor of UFO Roundup reports@ufoinfo.com and (Anthony Milas anthonym@internet.co.nz)

* * *

WISCONSIN: UFOs HELP LAUNCH UFO REPORTING CENTER.

APPLETON COUNTY: CALUMET -- John B. reports, "We saw three flashing lights on August 30, 2001, at 8:30 PM, that were lined up in a row. They were flashing in sequence. Two flashes, pause, three flashes, pause, four flashes, pause, and then repeated. The front light was amber and the others were white.

"At first, it looked like they were all connected. Using binoculars, it looked like only the front light was attached to the next segment and the other segments were separate. The object was cigar-shaped and had some sort of windows in it.

"Suddenly, the rear lights split apart and flew in different directions. Then, as it got further away, it 'realigned' into one cigar-shaped craft that was headed toward Outagamie County Airport. My wife called the airport and the tower had not seen anything as I described on radar.

"I also saw them on August 27th when we saw only two similar lights."

* * *

NEBRASKA: LARGE, CIGAR, METALLIC, HOVERING OBJECT.

OMAHA -- On September 21, 2001, the witness was driving down 84th street and noticed a metallic object in the sky near Offutt Air Force Base, about 8 miles away, at 2000 feet in altitude. At first, he thought it was an "American Airlines" aircraft on approach to Epply Air Field. However, the object was not flying a normal approach.

"At 2:30 PM, the object appeared to be hovering which piqued my attention, so I drove to a higher elevation in town. As I drove closer, the object descended and disappeared from view.

"I don't believe it was a normal jet. Even a Harrier aircraft does not begin a descent from that altitude."

* * *

MISSOURI: SILVER CIGAR UFO.

KANSAS CITY -- On November 10, 2001, James A. Tutt Jr., saw a silver cigar-shaped UFO flying over East 87th Street toward the Kansas City limits near the over and under pass area of I-435. It was 11:00 AM and the sky was clear.

James was using his powered + binoculars and noticed an object standing still east of him at about 25 to 30,000 feet altitude. The object continued hovering over the I-435 until he lost sight of it. The cigar was a silver color and may have had fins on it but it was too high to tell.

This is not the first time that a similar object was seen. On September 27, 2001, there was a sighting of another cigar-shaped craft with several fins on its side. The craft was the size of a small house.

Thanks to James Allen Tutt Jr. Tutt64110@hotmail.com, MUFON Field Investigator and Joe Trainor, Editor of UFO Roundup.

* * *

BRAZIL: ASTONISHING UFOs.

PERNAMBUCO -- Unexplained lights, cigar-shaped, luminous objects, small points crossing space at prodigious speed have been seen along the coast, particularly in the municipality of Brejo da Madre de Deus.

President of the Grupo Ufologico de Guarujá (GUG), Edison Boaventura, took advantage of a transfer to Recife and collected reports from persons who saw UFOs. For example, Attorney Wilson Andrade Souza, a resident of Boa Viagem, claims he has seen UFOs on repeated occasions and speaks delightedly about his experiences. "My wife and I were standing on the porch to our house when we saw an object in the sky resembling a cigar, surrounded by 20 smaller disc-shaped objects, flying in disarray. It was a beautiful sight," he states.

Souza has also seen UFOs over the Guararapes Airport in the municipality of Cupira, 168 kilometers north of Recife. "Some employees on a ranch saw one land and disgorge little men who helped themselves to the guava trees."

Boaventura's investigations also included a complete sweep of Brejo da Madre de Deus, famous for being one of the most important archaeological sites of the Northeast, and will probably wind up being known as a UFO hotspot nationwide.

Thanks to Scott Corrales, Institute of Hispanic UFOlogy. Translation (C) 2002.

* * *

AUSTRALIA: CIGAR FLIES NEXT TO AIRLINER.

SYDNEY -- At 4:30 PM, the witness was waiting for a bus in a residential area on June 4, 2002, when he noticed a strange looking object floating above to the north. He states, "There was a longish object like a cigar or tube, white in color, with red lights glowing around it. I could clearly see the red lights. At this moment, a passenger plane was climbing and flew past and I made some comparisons between the two aircraft. I could clearly see the wings, tail, the markings and even the portholes on the airliner. I could compare them and saw they were about the same size and about the same attitude but the cigar had no wings, no tail and no specific characteristics to tell me that this was something I have seen before.

"I thought that if it was UFO! The people in the passenger plane must have seen it in the brilliant cloudless sky. However, there were no newspaper reports. So, I called New South Wales UFO Investigation Center (phone 02-94844680.)"

* * *

CALIFORNIA: CIGAR.

CLAREMONT – Two, distant, three-sectioned, cigar-shaped, white UFOs were observed on June 23, 2002 around sunset. Two witnesses observed two very distant UFOs about 65 degrees above the northern horizon. They were cigar-shaped to the naked eye but, with binoculars, they could be seen to have three sections. They were white, as seen in reflected sunlight, and were a little smaller than a high-altitude jet and they drifted very slowly east. At one point, a plane approached one of the objects and flew in its vicinity for several minutes. Finally the objects themselves became fainter and disappeared from view.

* * *

CANADA: Cigar-shaped UFO Sightings Continue.

TERRACE BRITISH COLUMBIA -- Brian Vike reports that a 17 year old science oriented youth called to say, "Although I always believed there had to be other life out there, I was never truly convinced until two nights ago when I saw one of the most unbelievable life changing things of my life.

"It was 12:25 AM, on July 27, 2002, when I saw a moving light in the southwest sky fly towards Prince Rupert at high elevation. As the object began moving further east and higher up but closer, I began to realize it was cigar or pancake-shaped with a flickering bright light moving around the side. I still wasn't completely convinced until I noticed how eerily alien its maneuvers were. This was not human technology and was unlike anything I had ever seen before.

"Two minutes later, it moved from a horizontal position to a diagonal position but continued to move slowly with a light still running up the side. I was walking home but, the last minute I saw it, it began moving northwest, losing altitude and trees obstructed my view."

Thanks to Brian Vike (Yogi) Independent UFO Field Investigator/Researcher, HBCC UFO Research Box 1091 Houston, B.C.

* * *

FLYING SAUCERS FOLLOW MICK JAGGER.

PHILADELPHIA -- UFO specialist Mike Luckman says, "UFOs seem to follow Mick Jagger," who is in concert this week with the Rolling Stones. Mick and his friend, Marianne Faithful, saw a rare, cigar-shaped mother ship while camping at Glastonbury Tor in England in 1968. "Mick kept setting off a UFO alarm whenever he left one of his estates in England," the author of "Close Encounters of a Musical Kind," (Pocket Books) said.

At the Rolling Stones' notorious 1969 concert in Altamont, California, one UFO was even caught on tape. "You can see the crowd turning away from the stage and looking up at the sky. I have quite a few reports of UFOs showing up at other concerts. The music seems to attract them,"

Luckman is trying to cash in on music and aliens by producing a "Signal to Space: Countdown to Contact" concert next year at a yet-to-be-named outdoor amphitheater. "It is not inconceivable that we may get a message that will prove once and for all that we are not alone in the universe," he said.

Thanks to Page Six, and the UFO Data Exchange at http://wakeup.to/ufos.

* * *

SCOTLAND: CIGAR.

DUNDEE -- Whilst at work, I looked out of the main door on October 27, 2002 and saw what looked like a cloud in the shape of a cigar, which was white in color. The object was, at first, stationery at 5 PM and then began to move from the south heading north quite slowly for about 30 seconds then stopped. Then a few seconds later, it moved again in the same direction as mentioned above. The object stopped again then appeared to move off to the west and eventually faded away. The above-mentioned object was around ten miles away from where I was standing.

BRAZIL: CIGAR-SHAPED UFO SIGHTED.

RIO GRANDE DO SUL -- A silvery cigar-shaped UFO was sighted in several cities near the border with Uruguay on November 1, 2002. Hundreds of people saw a silver UFO flying rapidly over the cities of Gravatai, Cachoeirinha and Canoas. The same day, at 4:35 PM, a silver UFO was spotted in Praia do Cassino, a town on the South Atlantic shore.

Eyewitness, Eduardo Enderle Oliveira reported, "I was playing ball on the beach with my son and his friend when the boys sighted something unusual in the sky and saw it was a metallic fuselage in the form of a cigar. There were no wings. I called the attention of several beachgoers to this object, which flew at a very high altitude overhead. There was a brilliant gleam in the sky (most likely a reflection of the sun) and, as it departed, it resembled a brilliant sphere which gradually diminished in size."

On November 18th, dozens saw a UFO over Casimiro de Abreu. The object was videotaped by Sergio Chapelin. On November 22nd, at 8:50 PM, witnesses observed the over-flight of a ring-shaped object over port city Santos with rapidly alternating yellow, white and blue lights around the rim. The object flew southeast and was seen by hundreds of people.

Thanks to the Brazilian newspaper O Globo 11/19/02, Eduardo Enderle Oliveira, Rodrigo Branco of Ufologia Brasileira, and UFO ROUNDUP Vol.7, #48, 11/26/02 Editor: Joseph Trainor http://www.ufoinfo.com/roundup/

* * *

LOUISIANA: REPORTERS SEE UFO.

ALEXANDRIA -- I wanted to let you know that I had a strange sighting on December 6, 2002, just about 15 minutes ago at 2:10 PM, on Interstate 49 and Pineville Expressway interchange in a crystal clear blue sky.

A photographer, Douglas Collier and I were returning from an assignment. I am a reporter for the Alexandria Daily Town Talk. Just as we were approaching our exit into downtown Alexandria, I happened to look up and I noticed an armada of about 12 military helicopters flying west in formation, most likely heading to nearby Fort Polk. This in itself was an unusual sight, but then, something else caught my eye, a cylindrical white-colored object hanging motionless beyond the group of helicopters. I immediately informed Douglas about the object and I told him to pull over, which he did once we got onto the exit ramp and found a safe place to pull over. Unfortunately, he could not get a visual on the object, although I kept pointing at it. I watched it for about three minutes before it began picking up speed and disappearing in the northeastern sky.

We put in a call to the Rapides Parish Sheriff's Office, but there have been no reports of unusual aerial activity. The sighting immediately reminded me of that famous videotape from Mexico where the military helicopters are flying in formation and a UFO is spotted in the background. There was a similar report made in January 2002 where a hunter said he saw a cylindrical or cigar-shaped craft fly over him in rural LaSalle Parish.

This area is very wooded and swampy. And in Jan. 2002, I wrote a couple of stories in The Town Talk (www.thetowntalk.com) about strange lights seen in the sky. Just a little background for you.

Thanks Andrew Griffin.

* * *

ILLINOIS: DIGITAL IMAGES OF FOUR UFOs.

NILES -- Walter Lawrence took a digital photo on Thanksgiving at about 3:30 PM, roughly one hour before sunset north/northeast of O'Hare International Airport. The formation of cylindrical or cigar-shaped UFOs lasted approximately 45 seconds.

"I ran into the house and grabbed a small digital camera and snapped off one photo. They made no sound and were virtually motionless. When I returned, they were moving from west to east and, after taking the photograph, three of them shot off to the east so fast that, if I had blinked, I would have missed their departure. The fourth one took off almost due south right past O'Hare airport and was lost in haze."

Thanks to Walter Lawrence. The photo shows four cylinder-like objects flying in formation. See views at: Filer's Files UFO Center Views. http://www.nationalufocenter.com/

* * *

OKLAHOMA: GRAY, CIGAR UFO HOVERING OVER FIELDS.

ENID TO TULSA -- The witness was driving back from Enid on January 2, 2003, when he saw a silver/black cigar-like object far away, past the hills, at 4:30 PM. It rocked slowly back and forth like a leaf falling, but not falling. After two minutes it was gone, leaving no trail, no fast bang or light.

The "falling leaf" pattern is often report in UFO sighting cases, which is untypical of conventional aircraft.

David Twichell.

* * *

COLORADO: VIDEO OF UFO.

SOUTH PARK -- Tim Edwards reports that his daughter, Brandy Edwards, and their cousin, Sashay Rauter, first noticed an object in the western sky about 30 degrees above the horizon that appeared as a very bright tube or cigar of intense white light. Over a dozen vapor trails in the area were also observed and taped entering on November 22, 2002, on Highway 24, and leaving the area and western horizon during the duration of sighting.

"The UFO was 2 to 3 times brighter then illuminated (setting sun) vapor trails in the area and clearly not diffused or exhausting. Object didn't appear to move during the duration of sighting (25 minutes), staying in a fixed horizontal position.

"Object was filmed in the western sky from 2 locations on Highway 24 in South Park; the first about 40 miles east of Buena Vista Colorado and then about 30 miles east of it. The object was filmed with a Canon CCD-TRV43 NTSC Hi 8 Video (20 optical zoom) camera for about two minutes. It appeared very distant from the camera, about 1/4 of an inch long, at arm's length. Buffalo Peaks are in the video, just to the north of object. Other objects were observed around the main object but were not real clear with the naked eye and we didn't have binoculars.

"As close as I could tell, the object was 40 to 50 miles away, which would have put it over Buena Vista Colorado or west of it. In the video it appears that a plasma field or something was surrounding the object and two barbell-shaped objects are with it and stationary in conjunction with it.

"Video did not show the intense, white cigar in it but rather a red and tan colored envelope. Object gradually diminished and disappeared before our eyes as a vapor trail approached the location and passed through it and was not visible after that or after dark."

Thanks to Tim Edwards.

* * *

BRAZIL: CIGAR-SHAPED CRAFT WAS FLASHING WHITE/BLUE LIGHT.

RIO DE JANEIRO -- At 2:40 AM, the sky was clear on March 4, 2003, when the witness saw a craft moving slowly about the speed of a Goodyear balloon and stated, "I estimate the cigar shaped object was two miles from my 22nd floor apartment with a flashing white light on top center, a red light at each end and a red light at the bottom below the white light. Every few seconds there would be a blaze of extremely bright, intense, white/blue light that would stay lit for a few seconds. It covered a very large area of the craft (at least 50%) and, when it switched off, you could see some darker, "yellowish" lights, as if interior lights.

I lost sight of it as it passed beyond my apartment building.

* * *

CRIMEA: UFO HOTSPOT.

In May, the Crimean peninsula confirmed its status as the UFO Hotspot in Europe with UFOs being observed almost daily! Late in the evening on Tuesday, May 13, 2003, a cigar-shaped object was hovering north of the city of Simferopol' (republic and capital of our autonomy). The object was noticed at 10 PM by its bright, front, yellowish light that outlined the cylindrical shape of the craft. The impression was that the object demonstrated itself to the witness, Mrs. Lenura A. Azizova, by activating this light.

Very soon after that, the light was switched off and the craft dissolved into darkness. The craft was 50 to 60 meters long. Mrs. Azizova claims to see UFOs often because of her 360-degrees panorama of the sky.

* * *

WASHINGTON: DAYLIGHT DISK SIGHTING AND PHOTOS.

KINGSTON - Dr. Annamarie Johnstone reports she was photographing chemtrails in the Thriftway Parking Lot on Highway 104 on May 30, 2003. "The town is eleven miles east of Bangor submarine Base and in the general area where I had photographed a cigar-shaped cylinder, angled downward and moving to the west on May 12th.

"I took several 35 mm photos in seconds, facing south, with no craft visible. Upon film development, two sequenced prints displayed two discs joining, followed by two joined discs in juxtaposition with a very distinct atmospheric ionization line fore and aft.

"The craft were moving east over Puget Sound toward Seattle."

Thanks to Dr. Annamarie Johnstone author of "UFO Defense Tactics".

* * *

WISCONSIN: DAYLIGHT CYLINDER SPOTTED.

EAGLE RIVER -- On Saturday, July 5, 2003, the witness was putting the cover on his boat and noticed an extremely shiny (metallic/silver) cigar-shaped object traveling in an east to west direction.

"The object traveled at a very slow rate of speed over the Evergreen Forests of Vilas County." The witness said. "There was no contrail, no wings, no windows, no lights or anything of a discernible nature. The object seemed to reflect the bright sun off its surface but then I noticed that a vertical band of light started to appear from the front of the object and traveled slowly to the back of the object. This band of light appeared every 15 seconds or so and traveled over the surface of the object from front to rear.

"The object did not change speed or direction for two minutes and was the size of a small plane at about 1,000 feet.

"I am truly blown away!"

Thanks to John and Jenny Hoppe of UFO Wisconsin.com/
* * *

California: Cigar Mothership Launching Ten Spheres.

MADELEINE -- Debbie D'Amico writes, "I have a couple of good friends who, between 1992 and 1999, lived in a small town which is close to Likely, California and about a 30 minute Cessna flight's distance from the famed Area 51. One told me folks in this little town have seen grayish, metallic, cigar-shaped craft that are reflective of moonlight and are about the size of a C-51 C-5 Galaxy military aircraft. Using his telescope, he saw a cigar craft after dark when there was a relatively full moon, which emitted a very low whining sound. It was just outside our atmosphere going about its 'business' as our sun reflected on its surface.

"On another occasion with a relatively full moon at about 2:30 AM, as he went to his outhouse, he saw another larger craft that he judged to be about 15 miles away. The cigar was the size of a very small town and, in the darkness, it released ten small sphere type vehicles that would probably accommodate one human sized operator. These vehicles spread out as if they were sent to explore.

"These UFO's do not match most of the generic descriptions and he is unsure as to whether or not they are extraterrestrial in origin or part of US Top Secret operations.

"There's even a rather well known story of an elderly woman who, for years, was known to relate stories of being abducted and who was found, at different times in the years before her death, wandering several more miles than chance would allow without a car to drive!

"One of my friends had several unique UFO sightings during the Vietnam War on an LSD-31, the U.S.S. Point Defiance and in California. One night they were out in the ocean while on their way to Vietnam, silently moving along, when he as the Captain's personal driver, assistant and boson's mate, the Captain and several others were on the top deck with some gazing at the night sky. All of a sudden, there was this dark shadow hanging over and beyond the ship and a bright, all-enveloping, beam of light literally came down as if to observe and then, most strangely, as if light had matter like a curtain, lifted itself back into the large dark mass that then throttled upwards with very little sound.

"All on the top deck were in awe. Some became ill and actually became incontinent from fright. My friend, standing next to Captain Goiter, was more curious than anything and just turned speechless to the Captain along with a few others. The Captain said 'Officially I'm not supposed to tell you boys what that was but I think we all know what we saw was some unknown type of spacecraft.' He related that he had witnessed things like this before and so have many other sailors and that it is nothing to be too alarmed about and probably best just to 'keep it to yourself', since most folks would not believe it.

"Those who start websites such as this one or http://www.disclosureproject.org, which feature volunteers with solid credentials and first hand experience of these things, are the beginnings of the understanding that we are not alone."

Thanks to Debbie D'Amico.

* * *

New York: Witness Takes Photos.

STATEN ISLAND – Tops writes, "I'm 37 years old and, when I was about 14 years old in 1983, it's been a long time, my friend and I were at a nearby pond and we looked up and saw the strangest ship. I will never forget it. It was oval to cigar-shaped with lights around the whole ship. It moved very slowly back and forward, up and down. We both froze and were shocked. I said 'what in the world was that' to my friend. He was shaking and I had goose bumps all over.

"For 2 minutes we were still looking at this ship and then it took off in a blink of an eye. I mean like turn your lights off and on real fast. Sorry, it's hard to explain but there's no way in my mind that ship was from this planet."

Thanks to Topthat97.

* * *

UK/England: Cigar-Shaped UFO.

CHELMSFORD -- The 5 craft hovered in a triangle shape and then seemed to freeze and then the craft sped off without a trace on February 13, 2004, at 3 PM. The craft were fully visible and were quite low. The bottom side of the craft each had a black circle on the bottom. They sounded like a cross between a lawn mower and a vacuum cleaner. Inside the house, all radios had a strange chatter on them, which stopped when the craft went away. When the craft left there was a light red trail, which hung around for about 10 minutes. Before the craft left little black dots (like spores) fell to earth.

* * *

BRIGHTON – A UFO buzzed my back garden by Brendan Montague. A UFO, captured on film, hovering above Brighton, is the latest in a spate of mysterious sightings across the world. Theatre technician Ben Losh spotted the strange cylindrical object hanging in the air above his home and rushed to grab his video camera. He managed to snatch footage of the large, gray object as it drifted towards the golf course near Hollingbury. It is the second UFO sighting in Brighton in two months - a glowing globe was spotted near Shoreham airport last month. Ben was alone in his back garden, having a break from decorating, when he saw the object. The 32-year-old lives in Woodbourne Avenue with his wife, Vanessa, and two-year-old son, Lucas. He filmed the sighting as evidence to show his skeptical wife.

Ben said. "There was a long cylindrical object just hanging in the sky. I was watching it for about 10 to 15 minutes, as it appeared to float away and come back. It looked like a huge floating cigar and was a couple of hundred feet up. It didn't do any quick turns or have flashing lights and there were no 'green men' but it was certainly unidentified.

"My wife came home and I was quite excited - this is the first time I have ever seen a UFO. I'm a great fan of science fiction but I do have my feet firmly on the ground. I have always wanted to see a UFO but never thought I would. I am sure this is something we can explain but I hope not."

Vanessa, 32, who works for American Express in Brighton, said, "Ben has never claimed to have seen a UFO before and he's not a crackpot. I don't know if it was a UFO but I have seen the video and it does look a bit odd."

A spokeswoman for the Ministry of Defence said, "We do not investigate UFOs so I am not aware of what Mr. Losh could have seen. We used to investigate UFOs many years ago in the interests of national security and never found anything that could not be explained."

The sighting comes weeks after alien enthusiast Brian Barnes spotted a UFO from his Bevendean home. The 62-year-old filmed the object as it hung in the sky above Shoreham airport and reported the incident to the police and Coastguard.

Ben's claims come as increasing numbers of UFO sightings are reported across the world. Video footage recorded by the Mexican air force, showing 11 shining objects picked up by radar, was released on Tuesday last week. A number of sightings were reported in the Iranian capital Tehran during the last few days of April. State television broadcast video images of a sparkling white disk and other UFOs have been reported in cities to the north.

Ben, who has been joking with friends about his experience, said, "The fact there have been so many sightings around the world makes me look slightly less mad."

Thanks to the Skywatch International Inc. Website, http://www.skywatch-international.org

* * *

Canada: Rash of Sightings.

TORBAY, South Devon -- Colleen Smith and Paul James of the Herald Express report the switchboard was swamped with calls on 27 May 2004, from readers who said they spotted mysterious objects over Torbay. Some reckoned what they saw was a Jumbo jet-sized party balloon while others accepted it as a UFO. There was a suspicion the cigar-shaped craft was nothing more harmless than an "8 Meter Airship" sold for £12.95. Chef Nick Borne from Paignton, who took the main picture using his mobile phone to snap panoramic views from the Berry Head Hotel when the craft suddenly appeared in shot.

A bemused Nick secured a couple of images and continued eating. But the object, which he captured for posterity at 6.30 PM, was witnessed by at least 20 others elsewhere in the Bay at around the same time.

One mystified sky watcher was retired British Aerospace engineer, Roy Dutton. He tracked an object for 20 minutes through a high-powered telescope. He reckoned it was flying at 10,000 feet and was at least the size of a Jumbo jet. After about 15 minutes it stopped.

Then, it just wobbled and ascended to probably double the altitude, drifting away over the Channel. "I lost it eventually at about 5.25 PM, when I had to move the telescope because of the trees," he said. "What concerned me was that it was in the flight path often used by aircraft approaching Exeter airport."

Thanks to Jim Hickman Director Skywatch International.

* * *

VANCOUVER, B. C. – The witness was driving towards Vancouver Airport around 7:45 PM, on June 22, 2004, when he noticed a slow moving white cigarette-shaped object in the sky. He was on his cell phone talking to a friend and told him he was looking at a UFO. It floated around for about a minute before it took off towards the west and then disappeared. He states, "I'm positive that this was NOT an airplane. An airplane makes a lot of noise while the UFO was silent. This is the first time I've been 100% sure of what I saw. I get Goosebumps every time I tell people what I saw."

http://www.hbccufo.com/

* * *

PORT COLBORNE -- On August 1, 2004, the witness, who has twenty years of investigative/security background and served as a military policeman, reports a strange cigar-shaped object with rectangular wings moving slowly at low altitude at 5:45 PM. "The wings were longer than the body of craft (individually longer) and the wings were wider than the width of the craft. It looked much like a satellite with the traditional solar panel. The body of the craft was white with the center appearing darker. Wings also appeared white but difficult to judge because it was reflecting the sun's light as it flew northwest. It flew slower than a Beech craft-type but faster than a blimp."

Thanks to Brian Vike, www.hbccufo.com

* * *

ALDERSHOT -- The sighting of a mystery object in the sky over the weekend has baffled passers-by, air traffic control experts and Army officials. A couple spotted the object on Saturday September 4, 2004, as they played with their sons in Aldershot Park. The cigar-shaped object appeared in the sky at about 2:15 PM, and the family watched it ducking around for around 20 minutes.

"It caught our attention because it didn't move like an aircraft," said the mother. "It was a shiny cylinder-shaped object with random moves and it turned and flew horizontally, vertically and diagonally."

The News received several other calls about sightings. The director of Farnborough International Airport, Ann Bartaby, said the object had nothing to do with them. The Army said, "We were not flying any type of cylinder-shaped aircraft on Saturday afternoon."

Thanks to Jim Hickman and Skywatch-International.

* * *

TELKWA, B C – At 8:45 A.M., on December 11, 2004, the witness had just awakened and looked out his bedroom window, which faces Tyhee Lake. The clouds lit up the different colors of orange and pinks, which gave a spectacular view for him. He saw, underneath the clouds, an extremely bright light, which looked out of the norm, so he called to his wife. The witness grabbed his binoculars and saw an elongated bright light. He was able to watch and film the object for five minutes before it dropped out of sight behind the mountains.

He described the object as "like a long cigar and much brighter than the clouds which had the sun shinning on them." The witness said, "You could clearly see that the object was much lower and underneath the clouds that were present that day."

Thanks to Brian Vike www.hbccufo.com

* * *

CALGARY, ALBERTA -- On January 11, 2005, at 5:08 PM, my mother and I had just come from a clothing store. As I came out with my mother in tow, I noticed there were no clouds around and the sky was an orangey yellow glow. As I scanned the parking lot, I happened to see an odd looking cloud in the SW part of the sky. As I pointed out this grayish cigar to my mother, she was looking in the wrong direction. When she did see what I was pointing out to her, she said, "Oh that's just a cloud." I responded, "That's no ordinary cloud."

I watched as I descended the stairs and how it changed shape and started moving upwards. As I unlocked the van's doors, I still kept a watch on it. As the cloud disappeared, I saw a grayish cigar-like shape going straight up in the sky.

There was no contrail or chemtrail behind them and this was no plane, because it disappeared straight up and out of sight. I have never seen anything shoot straight up like that before.

Thanks to Brian Vike www.hbccufo.com

* * *

Portugal: Military Fires Missile at UFO.

The Portuguese military fired a ground-to-air missile at the luminous UFO that passed over their country during the early morning hours of Monday, June 7, 2004.

Portuguese UFOlogist, Gregorio Sao Xavier, reported "the cigar-shaped UFO was tracked on radar. It moved in a south-to-north direction. It was reported in the Portuguese newspapers that 'a target on radar was found at three separate military bases.'

"These included Beja, south of Evora and north of the Algarve region, Montijo, near Lisboa and Oporto, the second largest city in Portugal. The news was released by a colonel in the Portuguese Army. That same day, only one report came from a civilian identifying the trajectory of the unknown object as coming from north to south, and a 'cigar' form was described.

"Some days later, it was reported on Spanish and German TV that an official of the Portuguese Army confirmed that a missile had been launched. What most people saw was trailing smoke from the missile launched at the UFO. Visual contact with the object was made at the base in Beja."

Gregorio added, "A week later, the photo of a cigar-shaped object appeared in a popular (Portuguese) magazine. And a few days later, the military officials charged with the investigation of the incident closed the case, calling it an 'unknown object.'"

One of the most curious aspects of this case was the multiple sightings of a radar-domed AWACS plane provided by NATO, which was seen flying offshore just west of Cabo de Sines, 120 kilometers south of Lisboa.

(Muito obrigado a Gregorio Sao Xavier por esas informacoes.) Thanks to UFO Roundup.Vol. 9, #26. June 30, 2004, Editor: Joseph Trainor Website: http://www.ufoinfo.com/roundup/

Chapter 9
Anomalous Lights

Arizona: Five Disk-Shaped Ships.

TUCSON – The witness reports, "On February 14, 2004, I lay there enjoying my spa's pulsating water on my back at 7:45 PM, and saw something that I have never seen before. As I looked up into the southern sky I noticed about eight randomly spaced, light flashes that would flash on and off. They looked like miniature fireworks, as they had bright centers and little flashes or beams that emanated from the center. The Tucson Gem and Mineral Show did have fireworks that weekend to celebrate 50 years but, unlike fireworks that usually have embers drifting down, these light flashes had no embers etc.

"At first I figured them to be planes, then helicopters, as Davis Montham Air Force base is in that direction. There was no sound that I could hear. They flashed on then off for about 20 seconds then, one by one, blinked off and did not reappear for the rest of the time I was in my spa. 'Interesting,' I thought to myself."

Email report.

* * *

Oregon: Disk, Brilliant Strobing Lights.

LINTON – "On two evenings, September 3rd and 5th, 2004, about 10 PM, my partner was outside and called to me to come out and take a look in the sky," the witness reports. "We used 10 X 50 binoculars to see brilliant strobing lights hovering in the sky. It was a clear night and I framed it in my sight line with the telephone wires and a tree and it hovered within that space for around half an hour. We were looking across the Willamette River and saw it hover and shift position, tilting from horizontal to a vertical position, then rotating slowly enough to see the underside, then flatten out to horizontal again.

"We distinctly saw four colors of lights; red, white, green and blue, but not all at the same time. They flashed and rotated around the edges. I wondered at the time if this was one of 'ours,' – some advanced technology being tested out here. There were airliners taking off from Portland Airport and they must have seen this object.

"On the second sighting, our two friends joined us outside to see it as well."

Thanks to Brian Vike, Director HBCC UFO Research.

* * *

NEW YORK: FLYING TRIANGLE WITH FLAT EDGES.

NEW YORK CITY -- It was a chrome-like color, as big as a one story building, maybe about 250-500 feet in the air and it glowed reddish black and left a whitish trail when it left on October 15, 2001, at 2:00 PM. During this event, the object changed colors three of four times, between reddish black to a very dark red. It sounded like a whistle at first, but became silent and came on again. It was similar to Morse code. I saw at least a dozen lights on it that were various colors.

I was talking on my cell phone at the time to my wife, telling her about this, and it was coming in kind of fuzzy. Then I heard a noise coming from my cell phone, (Maybe a transmission) and then it went dead a couple of seconds later. The noises I heard from the phone could have been a language but I could not understand a word of it.

After my phone went dead, the UFO left a few seconds later.

* * *

UNITED KINGDOM: UFO ON HALLOWEEN NIGHT.

CROMFORD -- The Matlock Mercury Newspaper reports that a nervous Winster driver was just seconds away from photographing a UFO on Halloween. Derek Holmes (66) was driving home from Lea Croft Road when he spotted a strange bright light in the sky.

Mr. Holmes said: "I thought to myself good God what is that? I could see this very big, bright, white object. I felt nervous; it was a peculiar feeling and I had read before about UFOs, thinking there must be some simple explanation."

Mr. Holmes on Bonsall Moor first spotted the UFO near the Salter's Lane junction at 10:32 PM. As he drove nearer the light, (he could see) it was a round airborne object, with curved edges. Slowing down, Mr. Holmes searched for a safe place to stop on the narrow road to capture the brilliant image on film. But, despite having a camera in the back, he was too slow.

"The size of the light went down. It was as if someone had hit a dimmer switch and it went yellow," added Mr. Holmes. "It started to move into the distance and then disappeared."

Thanks to Matlock Mercury via Matlock Today, 11/8/01, and FarShores UFO News. www.100megsfree4.com/farshores/index.htm

* * *

CALIFORNIA.

HACIENDA HEIGHTS -- The boyfriend was driving his sick girlfriend home who was laying down in the back seat on November 13, 2002. The witness reports, "I looked towards Turnball Canyon at 6:15 PM, and saw a huge, round, strange, orange object with lots of red and white lights around it. It was round like an upside down, charcoal gray bowl with red lights around the rim. I could see some white lights underneath the object like it was searching for something. There were little white lights, just enough to see very dim. I yelled 'Is that a UFO?' My boyfriend freaked as he saw it moving. This thing was huge, maybe as big as an air balloon, when you look at it while it is still on the ground. Out of excitement, terror or amazement, I started tearing. Just as fast as I took that look is how fast it was gone."

* * *

ILLINOIS: FLYING TRIANGLE AND OVAL-SHAPED UFO.

WINFIELD -- Last night at 8 PM, while pulling his car into the parking lot of the Behavioral Health Services Building on March 14, 2003, the witness noticed three flashing entities coming down in front of his car. He noticed more dropping out of the sky until there were several. They were mostly red, flashing, white lights that had no visible wings. They did not make a sound and some had blue and aqua lights.

The witness states, "Some were triangular, some cigar-shaped, and some like a small box with four perpendicular lights. I brought several people out of the building and we all watched this phenomenon until 11:30 PM. Also, during the time I was watching, a bona-fide helicopter with multicolored lights flew over. A few, but not all of these objects, left a contrail.

"I have spent seven years in the air force and I know what aircraft look and sound like. These were not conventional aircraft. I called 911 and a Winfield police officer responded and watched them with me, replying that he could not shoot them down and that this was beyond local jurisdiction. The lighted objects also spat out balls every once in a while that also flew."

* * *

CANADA.

GEORGETOWN - The observer was sitting in the window watching a movie on May 13, 2003, when a distraction of light caught her attention at 8:15 PM. She says, "As I looked up, I saw a beautiful display of rotating lights that slowly hovered, moving no more than 5 km/hr about 100 feet from my roof top. I was paralyzed knowing what I was witnessing and never in my life believing I would ever see or believe such a thing.

"I rushed outside to gaze at the UFO, almost terrified in fear. I got a moment of enjoyment and a real good look at the craft. It was not as big as I thought it would be and very quiet. The outer ends were rotating with a wondrous arrangement of lights and it quickly sped off into the night in an instant. I will never forget that experience! We are not alone!"

* * *

FLORIDA: THREE,   STATIONARY,   ORANGE, RECTANGULAR LIGHTS.

DAYTONA BEACH -- The observers were walking south on the beach on June 13, 2003, around 11:30 PM, and noticed some unusual lights over the ocean. The lights were one-third above the horizon and were an inch to two inches across together.

"The lights were rectangular-shaped and evenly spaced in a parallel line. The stationary lights were orange in color and disappeared like someone had turned off a light switch.

"We observed them for about 15 to 30 seconds on a fairly clear night with a few cirrus clouds over head. It was a full moon and plenty of stars visible. After the lights disappeared nothing could be seen where they once were. I believe it to be one craft, if a UFO."

* * *

Washington State.

SEATTLE -- Cliff Mickelson reports, "Heavy meteor showers on June 20, 2004; that Saturday, was one for the record books. The new summer sky had scarcely darkened when a show of unprecedented magnitude began! I've seen lots of meteors over the years. I live near Mount Adams, Mount Rainier and Yakima Valley. The triangle has produced some of the most spectacular UFO sightings ever recorded. Nothing in the past could have even remotely prepared me for what I, and a small group of friends, saw! What a show!

"It began with a rapid fire overture of meteors. One after another, they blazed and burned with increasing fury across the sky. From out of the southern heavens, a rain of rocks from distant worlds hurtled down. One, two, sometimes even as many as five meteors a minute provided a ceaseless, pyrotechnic display. And then a bright blue-white flash of light stunned us all. From out of the flash emerged a bright, glowing, white, luminescent object. This is the form that UFO's commonly take in these parts.

"The object quickly sped off across the firmament and, behind it, came more! One after the other, we counted the emerging and brilliantly white objects as they dispersed in all directions across a night sky, illuminated by a continuing backdrop of fiery rocks from the stars.

"In all, my group counted 25 UFOs in the space of 10 minutes. They crossed the sky in a leisurely fashion and each seemed to have a singular destination. An impressive moment was beheld when several of the objects moved out in formation, but they soon vectored to different directions – some of them even crossing over each other in the mix.

"My friends, we have visitors. We have LOTS of visitors. I don't know where they are from or what they may look like but they are here! And I wager they are here for a purpose."

Thanks to Cliff Mickelson.

* * *

Washington: Numerous Sightings.

CUMBERLAND -- The witness writes, "When I lived in Maple Valley last summer, my good friends and I would go camping a few miles up some logging roads. We drove up to Kanaskat Palmer State Park on the gravel road winding its way up to a rock quarry where we usually stay. Around sunset a strange, green meteor, heading west, faded out around the Olympic Mountain Range. We couldn't sleep, even though it was 3 AM, so we drove six miles up to Huckleberry Point where there is a great view of the valley and Mt Rainier. We were excited that we had found such a spectacular view and noticed three lights to the lower left side of Rainier. They were fast moving lights that reformed into a straight line that was moving in excess of 400 mph. They were a little brighter than any stars in the sky. The lights traveled all the way across to the right side of the mountain and moved into position to form a triangle. The triangle, as a whole, then shifted to reveal two more lights and a half diamond shape. The light then flared bright red and all the lights separated. The top light turned red and morphed into two lights. They acted fixed like a pair of eyes and they would wander around looking back and forth.

"One eye would disappear before the other, as though they were giant, black heads with glowing eyes. One of the pair of lights disappeared behind a hill about 300 feet away. What appeared over the hill makes me question reality. We all described a jellyfish or octopus the size of a blimp that was clear like glass with small lights running down along the tentacles. I became very frightened but calmed down as it just seemed to wander up and check us out and float away. It sort of bobbed around as though it was propelling itself through water. After that, all the lights pretty much appeared far away, morphing into pairs of 1, 2 and 3 and then combining again.

"We watched them all night until the sun came up. All the lights returned to where the original diamond shape had first appeared and landed on a small hill. They appeared like little white dots in the daytime, occasionally catching the sun and shimmering like a signal mirror. It seemed the UFOs were alive with emotion and curiosity and interacted with us. They would sit and hover for hours rocking back and fourth about a hundred yards away.

"One witness claimed that when the big "jellyfish" peered over the hill, he saw a floating fish with fins. An eel-like object passed right through him and he had trouble breathing, but none of us saw it.

"The next night we came up with cameras and video but none of them seemed to work. We kept going up for many months and we all had many encounters with these entities.

"I now live in California and, at 2 AM, a bright light appeared about a mile away, separated, and they both started wandering around until they disappeared."

Thanks to James Gilliland, www.eceti.org

* * *

New Jersey: Four UFOs.

KEASBEY -- Reverend Barna reports, "I think it was a close encounter of the third kind since I had an understanding of intelligence from the phenomenon.

"On December 17, 2004, at 4:45 PM, on a clear evening during sunset, while standing still in the traffic at the Union Toll Plaza, I noticed four orbs in the sky. They were large, round, luminous balls of white light about 10,000 feet high. At first, the four balls of light were loosely knit and spread apart, then they moved towards each other, then one of them stopped, moving up, while the other three moved to the left and up. One of the three broke off and began moving in a separate motion and direction towards the west. The other two continued their journey southwest, slowly and at a measured pace.

"They came to rest briefly above the one that stopped moving initially. They formed a perfect triangle, the two at the top 'quite level' to the horizon about ten inches above the tree line 1/4 mile away. The three others in the perfect triangle came closer and then stood still for fifteen seconds then began to slowly drift westward toward the setting sun, eventually dipping below the tree line. They stayed in the last position for fifteen seconds while, in the triangle pattern, they gently pulsed brighter each second.

"This was observed by at least 500 people. How many reports do you have about this? What really pains me deep down is the apparent ignorance of our species and can only wonder what other minds comprehended. If the species rejects the visual data that is presented to them, what must we suffer through next?

"Look up! I fear our time is short! God Bless."

Thanks to Reverend L. Damian Barna.

* * *

WASHINGTON LIGHTS.

TROUT LAKE -- Six adult eyewitnesses and five children observed UFOs on April 8, 2001, at 9:42 P.M., Eastern. "After a typically cold winter with snow, rain and cloudy skies, the skywatches have started again on the South side of Mt. Adams. Our first skywatch was spectacular when a large luminous light, turquoise in color, came in from the Southwest. It was a pulsing, green energy field and looked about four times brighter than Venus. The witnesses are writing statements.

"As it crossed directly overhead, it threw off several, very large, pulses of light, which seemed to have a psychological calming effect on the people below.

"The object was filmed as it passed halfway through the sighting and expanded into what looked like infinity, disappearing in the camera but, to the naked eye, it remained.

140

"These anomalies are not uncommon. The UFOs often show they have control over what is being filmed. They can even selectively block their appearance to individuals all standing in a row."

James Gilliland writes, "During our July 1st skywatch last year, a particular guest had a bad attitude. He shot 9 photos of a UFO going directly overhead. He was a professional photographer. The guests and I had no problem filming the UFO, yet not one of his pictures came out that night. Clips of this event from two different camcorders are available on the UFO video we offer through our website.

"This supports our theory that the success of contact and documentation of that contact has everything to do with an open mind, loving heart and pure intent."

Thanks to James Gilliland, Self-Mastery Earth Institute, http://www.cazekiel.org

* * *

ILLINOIS.

ALSIP -- I was walking home from my aunts, looking at the stars on May 19, 2001, and saw some unusual light in the sky. It looked like thunder and lightning but there were too many different colors. I've seen some crazy stuff in the past but nothing like this.

After the lights stopped, a glowing shape just flew off before I could make out the shape. I believe our government is hiding this from us because they probably think humans and aliens won't get along. I believe that ever since the Roswell crash, the UFOs today are trying to find that one ship. If the government is covering up UFOs, I think that mankind should know the truth.

* * *

UFOWISCONSIN REPORTS LIGHTS.

BABCOCK -- My mother and I were driving home, south on Highway 80 towards Babcock around 7:45 PM. And, in the Southern sky, for almost the entire drive to Babcock, which was about a 15-minute drive, we observed a huge light display on November 25, 2002.

At first we thought it was airplanes but the flashing lights remained stationary. Then we thought it might be satellites. It was an amazing display of lights like the Fourth of July. It looked like 15 to 20 lights flashing like strobe lights and they filled the entire front car windshield view of the sky and nowhere else in the side car window views. Amazing!

Then, when we got to Babcock and turned off on Highway 173, our mini van went dead and we coasted to the side of the road! We didn't stop to get out of the van and I got the van started again as quickly as I could. The van stopped mysteriously two more times on the way home.

* * *

DETROIT -- Amy N. (age 30) reports, "I live in the suburbs and, on November 27th, at 6 AM, my sister and I were up. As I let the dog out, I looked into the sky and there was a large, stationary light. We got the binoculars and checked it out. It was a very large, white light. It was at least 20 to 25 times as large as any of the stars located in the sky at that hour of the morning."

Thanks to Amy.

* * *

CALIFORNIA: STRANGE LIGHT RETURNS.

LOS ANGELES -- Dr. Leir writes, "For the 7th Year, the mysterious Camarillo UFO has returned. It has been seen now from two different areas; One in Camarillo and one in Carpenteria, west of L.A. David Anderson with International MUFON is in the process of trying to triangulate the object and get an estimate of its altitude.

"Its behavior is the same as it has been in previous years. It appears high in the Northwestern sky as a very bright star, in about a window from 4:30 to 5:30 PM. It traverses the sky with a southeast heading and lasts for approximately 15 minutes. It is seen to spawn other bright objects, which sometimes return to the original object. When it leaves, it folds up into a straight, bright line and is gone.

"We have no further information to give a clue as to what this object is, since it was filmed through a Celestron 6 telescope some years ago.

"It is just pathetic that there is no interest or money to solve this mystery. I have even called Moorpark College (Local to this area), and they simply did not ever get back to me – even after talking with one of the professors there. I have also contacted the local amateur astronomical society and they also have no interest.

"This is absolutely pathetic and disgusting. Shame on so-called 'organized science.'"

Thanks to Dr. Leir.

* * *

SAN FRANCISCO -- Ken reports, "I feel the need to report a strange sighting on May 29, 2001. My dog woke me up at 3:20 AM whining and he never does that. I got up and let him outside, at which time, I noticed an object in the sky. It was not moving when I first saw it but seemed fairly bright with a white light. Directly underneath, there was intermittent, flashing bright light, which seemed to move to different locations underneath.

"The object was completely silent but began to move slowly north until it passed out of sight over a nearby hill. The object was perhaps a quarter mile away when I first saw it and was relatively low in altitude.

"I have never experienced such a thing. I am an Engineer employed here in the Bay Area and can only assume that what I saw was either an incredible military technology or truly something beyond our abilities. I hope someone else noticed."

Thanks to Ken, KWJ@dolby.com

Connecticut: Maneuvering Lights.

DURHAM – The witness works third shift and goes outside at night on breaks with others who work there. They often see strange flying objects and discuss them since it breaks up the night shift. Two people were outside taking their breaks around 1:00 AM, when they saw a maneuvering light. They called several others outside to watch. It was very bright and dropping down with a red glow at the top. It moved to the left and right, sideways, but mostly down and away behind the tree line.

"It was like looking at the sun, it was that bright. It didn't have a shape as much as a glow all around it. We all agreed that it was not an airplane. At first we thought a plane might be exploding but there was no noise and it wasn't falling from the sky as much as moving around and descending.

"We watched it until it left our view. A short time later, another similar light, but not as bright, flew around like the first and disappeared. None of us had ever seen anything like this and we were all joking about aliens."

Thanks to Zxdragonflyzx.

* * *

TEXAS: LIGHTS HOVER OVER CAR.

CONROE -- ISUR reports a motorist, on March 23, 2001, at about 12:45 AM, was proceeding east on Highway 105 toward Beaumont Texas. The vehicle passengers noticed a group of lights off to the side that seemed to be about 2 miles away. Within three seconds, the lights closed the distance to the vehicle and were overhead and to the left about 125 feet above the ground. The witness indicated that it appeared to be a group of purple and green lights with some mixed white.

While they watched, the lights appeared to depart at an incredible rate of speed; in fact it was described as being so fast that they were unable to determine exactly what direction the formation took. The witness turned his car around to recheck the area but no trace was found.

Thanks to ISUR and Tom Sheets Board. The case has been referred to MUFON of Texas for further investigation.

* * *

FLORIDA: GULF OF MEXICO UFOs.

DESTIN -- This happened a while back when I was shark fishing late one night about two miles off the East jetty, when I saw a small, greenish-colored light on the horizon. At first I thought it was the running light on another boat, but it was coming close in to the shore at a pretty good rate of speed. When it was about a mile out from me, parallel to the shore, it suddenly just stopped and stayed in one spot. After a few minutes, it suddenly shot straight up into the air faster than I have ever seen anything move. It shot up 2000 feet and just stopped again.

I went to get my camera out of the cabin but when I came back I did not see it. I looked all around and saw it again on the opposite side of the boat about a mile away. It was hovering at 50 feet or so.

There is no way a plane can travel that fast and that far in only 15 seconds. I watched for half an hour as it seemed to play leap frog with me. It would shoot up and over me, back and forth, from one side to the other. Sometimes it moved so fast that the light would look like a blur moving across the sky.

I spent a lot of time commercial fishing and some of the things we saw out over the Gulf were downright weird. I asked my father if he knew what they were and all he said was, "I hope that Eglin Air Force Base is testing something."

I saw something similar about 100 miles off the coast one January night at 3:00 AM. I was up in the bridge of my dad's boat when I saw the light. I looked at the radar to see if it was a boat on the horizon. There was a small blip on the screen that disappeared from the radar and reappeared behind us. I looked out the cabin door and there was the light behind us that played leap frog for about 30 minutes before it disappeared.

Numerous times, fishing out there, we saw lights in the sky doing strange things.

Thanks to WalterClwalter1.

* * *

FLORIDA/GEORGIA: SKY LIGHTS UP.

JACKSONVILLE -- James Montgomery wrote: "I don't think anyone has ever seen what we saw that night, 40 miles north of the city. I was in a mortar platoon in the USMC and saw the use of many different armaments and night illumination and nothing comes close. Many of my fellow truckers that deliver our nations freight 365 days a year also saw the strange lights.

"On May 3, 2001, about 2:30 AM, I was heading north on Interstate 95 near the Florida State line. Over Georgia I saw a very intense blue light, as bright as or brighter than lightning in the upper atmosphere. At arm's length, my thumbnail covered up the blue light. This large blue light lasted for only a fraction of a second, followed by an orange, very intense light. The size of the orange light was four times bigger than the blue light.

"The orange light was oblong and the blue light appeared to be round. The blue and orange lights slightly overlapped, appearing to touch, but again the blue light flashed first and the orange light flashed second. It was obvious this was in the outer atmosphere and was not a natural phenomenon. The entire atmosphere, covering the whole southeastern hemisphere, flashed an unnatural sun bright orange. The bright orange light lasted 3 to 4 seconds and was like daytime in my truck and everywhere I looked, but a very strange light – again very orange. I thought it was a nuclear blast.

"Truck traffic was heavy and many of us began to speculate as to what it was over the radio. We speculated it might have been a test of SDI. A second blue light object causing the brilliant flash may have hit the first light above our atmosphere creating the tremendous energy."

Thanks to James Montgomery <monjamf@northstate.net and Frederick M. Fox <telarion@earthlink.net

* * *

NORTH CAROLINA: LIGHTS.

NEW BERN -- Laura called telling me she had awakened at 4:00 AM and looked out her window from her bed early in the morning hours of May 22, 2001. As she looked, she noticed a flying object darting around the sky. It would move quickly from the left to the right, then quickly up and down, then right to left. As she became more awake, she realized that this could not be a normal aircraft since its movements were too quick and too erratic.

She awoke her husband who also saw the darting lights and strange objects in the sky. He pointed out that the there were little white lights flashing near the larger light. They watched until 4:45 AM when the lights suddenly disappeared.

New Bern is on the Neuse River that leads to Pamilico Sound and the Atlantic Ocean. The lights were mostly over the water an estimated thirty miles away. Laura indicated she had checked around and no one else had observed the lights.

Thanks to Laura.

* * *

ENGLAND: STRANGE FLARE.

GRIMSBY, LINCOLNSHIRE -- Mr. D. lives in Northeast Lincolnshire and was amazed to witness an orange colored UFO near his home at about 1.30 AM on April 16, 2001. He was out walking his dog on Milton Road near local school fields. He noticed a signal flare but realized it was too big to be a flare, plus it was giving off a sort of burning coal ember effect.

Mr. D says, "I could make out orange and red moving around like two paint colors mixing together about a half mile up in the sky." As he watched, the object dropped at least half its height then catapulted straight up and out of view. Mr. D was upset and thought it was a serious weapon and expected it to explode on impact, but it didn't.

He got in touch with the British Ministry of Defence who responded that there was no defense significance to the object.

Thanks to Chris Evers, chrishufos@yahoo.co.uk. Faster Than Light, http://www.hufos1.karoo.net

* * *

MAINE: FLYING STREET LIGHT.

OXFORD - Ruth sent an email saying, "In the first week of October 2000, I was driving on a dirt road east of Route 26 and I was looking in the eastern sky. At 9:00 PM, I was in a clearing that allowed me to see a heavily wooded hill. I knew that beyond that hill was a small side road where there should not be lights. I saw a white glow, reminiscent of a streetlight.

"My first thought was, 'Wow, they put a street light there on that road.' But I stared in wonder as this 'streetlight' was slowly rising! The light was not even a half-mile away. It was completely silent and did not flicker.

"I stared as it rose maybe 200 feet in the air, climbing above the tree line. I panicked and headed for my truck, still keeping an eye on it. The object flew toward the Mechanic Falls and speeded off so fast that I knew I had just seen a UFO.

"I have kept silent and tried to see if others had seen things that night in my area."

Thanks to Ruth.

* * *

NEW YORK LIGHT SPOTTED AT DIFFERENT TIMES AND PLACES.

STATEN ISLAND -- Ray Klopchin while on a picnic at the shore on Monday, June 11, 2001, saw a strange light in the afternoon sky. At 12:21 PM, he happened to be watching planes make their approaches to the three metro airports. He noticed a definite and stationary pinpoint of light way up in the southeast sky. The object moved very slowly and was then obscured by clouds.

He alerted at least two other people who saw this light. Looking around the sky, they noticed similar pinpoints of light in the distant sky, now due east of them. They now had more witnesses this time that saw this singular and very distant pinpoint of light. It moved very slowly and disappeared behind the clouds.

They saw the light again thirty minutes later, again in the southeast. The witnesses claim they have never seen anything like this before. It was not an approaching plane nor was it a star. It was very unusual.

Thanks to Ray Klopchin, www.nymufon.org for this report.

* * *

OREGON: STROBE LIGHT SIGHTING.

PORTLAND -- Brad Hoover and his wife have been watching the skies as they travel around the area and have seen a lot of aircraft taking off and landing at the Portland International Airport.

Brad says, "On the night of June 15, 2001, at 2200 hours, we were returning home when we saw a strange light in the clear night sky. It was traveling southeast, heading over the air space of the Portland

Airport. It was strange because it was strobing a bright white light (not a normally seen flashing light, as on other aircraft). The strobe was intermittent. It was kind of like an inch worm but of course very much faster. It appeared to be higher than an aircraft in the normal approach landing pattern, as it was a flyover.

"The entire sighting lasted about 45 seconds.

"I was in the 82nd Airborne and can recognize aircraft. I also took private pilots training and have done some flying in this area."

Thanks to Brad Hoover of Vancouver.

Chapter 10
Abductions and Missing Time

Canada.

ST-PHILIPPE, QUEBEC -- Two witnesses on May 3, 2004, noticed their cat was reacting to a slight vibration that made them notice a flying triangle near the observer's house. The triangle was very dark in color and silent. Then the garage door started to open and shut on its own. The wife reports, "I fell asleep in our bed but my husband found me later on the sofa in the living room half dressed and I felt drained of my energy, really weak and disoriented, and the patio door was open. My husband had a really difficult time getting out of bed because he was also disoriented. He doesn't remember anything except that something prevented him from getting up.

"I have a vague recollection of getting up, being guided by something, then I felt like I was in some strange dream. Three hours passed by between getting out of bed and waking up on the sofa.

"The day after (still tired and taking a shower), I noticed something on my arm. When I was a child, I had a triangular mark that had disappeared since then. Now it was back again and it looked like 3 dark stains and my arm was itching. My husband felt weak the following days. Like me, he felt like he was under observation – spied on. Then the sensation went away.

"I don't know what happened that night but nothing felt normal. I had the same experience when I was 5 and living in Texas. It happened a second time when I was 15. Now I am 29 and it happened again. I don't know what it is but it's not of this world."

Translated from French into English.

* * *

WASHINGTON STATE.

SEATTLE -- A crime investigation specialist was on his way to a crime scene outside of Seattle on February 13, 2003, at 2:30 AM. He had to be at the crime scene by 3:00 AM so he rushed a little.

The witness states, "It was beginning to rain and my car started making these weird noises. The radio turned on automatically and started tuning to numerous stations. The lights inside and outside the car were flashing when I looked up and saw this huge triangle shaped thing above the car. In a few seconds a blue, blinding light distracted me. Suddenly, it all stopped and my car was parked on the side of the road with everything switched off and I looked at my watch and it read 03:03 AM.

"I then realized I lost 33 minutes. I turned on my car and drove to work with a lot of confusion on my mind."

* * *

Canada: Possible Abduction.

QUEBEC -- The Witness reports, "Something happened again during the night of July 2, 2004. I must confess that I am getting really tired of this and scared. Mostly I don't understand what's happening. I am sending you two pictures that I took with my digital camera. Zoom on the lower part and you'll see a triangle almost identical to the mark I find on my arm from time to time. The other picture shows two unidentified objects, greenish in color and facing each other. I took these pictures around 4 o'clock in the morning. I was mesmerized by the sky on that night, at that time. I was glued to the window without knowing exactly why. I fell asleep suddenly in the living room after taking the pictures and again I felt something abnormal happened to me."

Brian Vike writes, "This person has had ongoing close encounters on previous occasions."

Thanks to Brian Vike, www.hbccufo.com

* * *

Canada: Abductions.

PRAIRIE, ALBERTA – The witness reports, "On September 5, 2004, at 11:30 PM, my husband and I were sitting on our roof, star gazing, when I spotted a star moving west. It traveled across the sky and entered a cloud formation and then, in seconds, came out where it entered after reversing direction and traveled east. The whole event lasted about five minutes. We could only explain it as being a UFO.

"A couple of nights later, we had some friends visiting us and were telling them about our experience. They had been camping just outside Dawson Creek when they too had seen a similar event at around the same time.

"I really do believe we have seen alien spacecraft, especially since my daughter has started talking about strangers visiting her in her room. She is turning 4 in October but is very perceptive and has always intrigued me with her abilities to 'know and see' things that she shouldn't. I wonder if she is in fact being visited by aliens.

"A year ago I had a vivid dream and saw a saucer hovering over my neighbor's house and ran for my kids to hide them because I felt we were in danger. About a week later, my daughter came to me and looked deep into my eyes and said 'Mom, you didn't hide in the right place and they found you. I was under the table and they didn't see me.' She walked away leaving me shocked and scared. I followed her and asked her questions about what she was talking about and she wouldn't tell me anything else.

"My daughter has strange marks on her body and unexplained bruising that often appears on her arms and legs in oblong shapes, like finger print shapes. Also, very recently, she woke up with sore genitals. I believe her. She has developed various allergies in the past eight months but never stays allergic to the same thing. I have had all these things checked by a doctor and no answers.

"I am a very concerned parent because she often has bad dreams about bad guys and bad animals. I have a feeling that there is more to all this then I've been told."

Thanks to Brian Vike, Director HBCC.

* * *

Tennessee: Giant Flying Triangle.

MUFON's Kim Shaffer writes, "On October 3rd, I received a report from a man who related the following story:

"He was driving home from work on a rural road at 05:30 on Saturday, October 2, 2004, when he saw what he thought was a fire in the distance. As he drove, he saw the 'fire' several other times and when he arrived at an intersection near his home, he stopped and exited his car to see if he could determine what he was now also hearing.

"A deep throbbing hum preceded the giant triangular object as it rose from behind trees and moved toward the witness. He started to run but realized there was nowhere to run. As he stood in the road, a massive craft, 300 feet long, moved closer and he saw three large domes filled with a turbulent, reddish orange, fiery light.

"Each dome was larger than his car and he could have easily thrown a stone and hit the craft. The witness also reported that the craft was slightly reflective and metallic, also having rib-like structures running the width of the craft, being most defined along the center of the craft.

"This witness also described the sound as passing throughout his body, seeming to burn, tingle and give him a sensory overload. He was unable to adequately describe the feelings. The hair on his head and arms stood straight up as the craft passed over him. It turned 90 degrees to the west, without banking and moved quickly behind trees and hills.

"The witness awoke the next morning with a nosebleed and a metallic taste in his mouth. He also had some abnormal hair loss, felt sick and weak, had a skin irritation on his face and back, not unlike sunburn. We have documented his physiological condition, which has improved since last Saturday.

"After several interviews, we have determined that this witness has a loss of 15 minutes on his watch that had not malfunctioned before the sighting or since. He has agreed to follow-up consultations with my ASD, Dr. Melvin Redfern DCH, and I so that we may help him resolve issues of anxiety and find answers to the possible missing time.

"It should also be noted that the sincerity of the witness is without question."

Further updates can be found as they become available on the Tennessee MUFON web site at http://www.mufontennessee.org/

Thanks to Kim Shaffer, MUFON Tennessee State Director (Eastern).

* * *

WEST VIRGINIA: MISSING TIME.

MARTINSBURG -- Bobby Darren (synonym name) writes: "I really enjoy reading your files and experienced some missing time early this morning on January 24, 2003, before I got up for my newspaper route. Also, when I was leaving my house I was startled by a very large dark colored flying triangle hovering 50 feet above our roof where my bedroom is located.

"When I left the house, the flying triangle tilted slightly and flew off to the east with a really deep sound. The next morning, around 4:00 AM, as I drove through Eastern West Virginia, I saw six, glowing orbs along my route changing from solid colors to a fast pulse. They hovered over houses at tree top level, moving very slow from the north to the east. There was also a very big, round object with a very bright light out there. This object came up from the ground northeast from my location and was very big. It seemed to follow my movements through my whole route.

"I've shown friends and family these objects and we are all left wondering what is going on in our skies. I have tried taking pictures of them before with 400 and 800 speed film but the local Wal Mart would either lose the film or nothing came out. I was thinking of getting binoculars with a digital camera built in, Radio Shack sells them for $99.00. But I would like to talk to somebody that owns a pair first.

"I didn't see anything Sunday but this morning I saw a few more orange orbs and the real big, bright object came up from the ground from the south today."

Thanks to Bobby Darren.

* * *

NEW YORK: ABDUCTION.

RUSSELL PARK -- Paul M. Davis writes, "We had seen several UFOs in the park and experienced twenty minutes of missing time. Several weeks later, I began having awful demonic alien nightmares. I became a nervous fearful person soon after. I have been put on medication to keep me calm.

"I was able to recall the incident fully. The alien craft came down. It was noiseless. I assume it had landing gear because it was not resting on its belly. I saw a ramp open as if inviting me in. I went up the ramp ducking. As I went in, the floor of the ramp felt strange on the bottom of my feet. Almost like a skin more then a metal ramp. I went inside where I noticed it was somewhat dimly lit. I did not see my cousin Israel anywhere.

"Before me were huge, octagonal, metallic walls or doors, about 9 feet high. The inside of the craft appeared to be larger then the outside of the craft. Each wall had a large symbol that looked like a different complex pattern burned into it. I began to receive messages in my head and turned to see three, gray aliens with large heads and child like bodies sitting around some sort of biological hi-tech computer device wearing tight diver-like suits. They did not look up at me.

"I asked questions with my mind. I got answers quickly. I asked, 'What are you and where are you from?' I was informed that these creatures were advanced bipedal animals with the soul or spirit of demons with great scientific knowledge that we on earth could not begin to understand. Their physics seems to have no limits. I was very shocked by all this and prayed to God for help.

"I began fighting heart palpitations, shallow breathing and tunnel vision. I fought to keep my senses.

"The ship was surprisingly simple and the floor had an interesting structure and design, similar to cutting an orange in half and seeing those lines coming out from the center of a single focus point. There were no windows but I believe they were behind the octagonal doors.

"I was told that each symbol on the doors was of an advanced demonic language. One symbol was the equivalent of a massive database of knowledge. I asked them, 'How do you navigate through space and survive?' I was told that they used their minds for navigational purposes. A biological to digital control as best as they could explain it to me. It took three aliens to properly fly and navigate this craft for interstellar travel.

153

"I could see the top of a cylinder that was like looking at an advanced 3-d computer monitor with images stacked over images, like a hologram. The screen was round like a computer monitor that was laid face up. I saw star charts or lines connecting constellations and it had an alien font or hieroglyphic data on the outer rim of this device.

"The aliens told me that they made it work by placing their hands on what I could only describe as a control panel. The aliens placed their hands into the indentation that matched their hand shape perfectly. They had two fingers with an opposable thumb. It was clearly an advanced computer keyboard."

Thanks to MUFON's Director, John Schuessler, for this sighting report that is under further investigation.

* * *

Mysterious Road Trip.
Thanks to Bill Konkolesky, MIMUFON State Director.
(Witness names below are pseudonyms)

At just after 1:00AM, on the morning of Friday, August 27, 2004, 43 year old John Stephens was driving from Imlay City to his home in Leonard with his 14 year old daughter, Rose, in the passenger seat, after picking her up from a visit to Rose's mother, when something very peculiar occurred. They instantly found themselves more than 6 miles away heading in a different direction, on a road they didn't recognize - still traveling at the same rate of speed.

As Stephens recalls, the two of them were southbound on S. Lake Pleasant Road, just fifteen minutes from their home, discussing the start of Rose's upcoming school year at the onset of their experience. Stephens specifically recalls the time (1:09AM on the dashboard clock) and the thought that they would easily be home before 1:30AM on this very familiar route for them.

Then, suddenly, as they were driving, in the words of Stephens, "the road ahead instantly 'fogged' and then immediately 'pixilated' back into clarity. In an instant, John and Rose had both suddenly stopped their animated discussion, as though they had actually completed it sometime earlier in the evening. They then both looked at each other and commented on the strangeness of what had just happened. Then, a few seconds later, things got much stranger for them as they both realized that there surroundings were now unknown to them. Somehow, impossible as it appeared to them to be, they were no longer on Pleasant Lake Road.

Stephens recalls looking at the dashboard clock at this point and noting the time as 1:14AM. The clock supported their impressions that, even with the caveats of the sudden different environment and their seemingly acausal abrupt stop in conversation, no time had passed for which could not be accounted. Also, the radio was not on for them to notice a skip in a song that might have otherwise been playing or any

154

other like indicator. In addition, there was no noticeable depletion in gas or any adverse effects on their vehicle, a 2003 Ford Explorer Sport-Trac.

And, though this may just be an interesting coincidence, adding to their feeling of disorientation, the witnesses noticed that, at their new location, there was a surprisingly high concentration of deer accompanied by small animals including a skunk and raccoon directly alongside, as well as crossing, the road.

Although Stephens and his daughter were completely unaware of where they were, after the momentary appearance of the fog, they felt it safest to continue on the route on which they found themselves suddenly traveling. All they knew was that, according to the vehicle's compass, they were driving west at this time when they *had been* driving south. Within minutes, they discovered that they were somehow on E. Newark Rd, on a stretch of road unfamiliar to them. As they drove forward, they arrived shortly at M-24, a road they readily recognized. As they got onto M-24 and saw a sign indicating the city of Metamora was just south of them, they realized that they had mysteriously "teleported" several miles northeast of their original location. This would turn out to be a distance of approximately 6 miles, as the crow flies, they immediately, seamlessly and most mysteriously had jumped.

When they arrived home, both of the witnesses began to feel the onset of an unexplained mild tingling sensation throughout their entire bodies with a touch of nausea. This lasted until they fell asleep and (the unpleasant feeling) was not present when they awoke. They were so shaken that Rose didn't get to sleep until 4AM and John not until 9AM! No other seemingly-related adverse or unusual sensations were felt by the witnesses at the time of the event or after.

At this time, there is no speculative cause of what happened to them with any firm degree of evidence to support it, including no direct evidence of UFO involvement.

Interestingly, Mr. Stephens has a history of seemingly unrelated anomalous events, including being visited by balls of light and experiencing astral projection. However, nothing that would seem to tie in directly with what happened in the early morning hours of August 27.

There are some details worth mentioning in support of witness credibility. Mr. Stephens is a test-driver for Ford Motor Company, having a thorough and professional knowledge of driving and vehicle conditions. Both John and Rose have excellent vision and do not wear corrective lenses. According to the witnesses, there were neither any intoxicants nor illicit substances involved.

This investigation is ongoing. Any of you who may know the identity of these individuals are encouraged to please maintain their anonymity.

* * *

A U. S. Army Infantryman's Abduction.
© 1999 by Linda Moulton Howe
Reprinted with permission.

October 24, 1999, Findlay, Ohio.

This week, I interviewed a man who fought in Vietnam from 1966 to 1967 and then came back to California to finish his service, as he said, "in the Combat Developments Experimental Command at Hunter Liggett Military Reservation eighty miles from Fort Ord in the middle of the Mojave Desert."

Editor's Clarification since radio broadcast and posting of this report:

Hunter Liggett Military Reservation is located between Monterey and Paso Robles, California, not in or near the Mojave Desert. This fact was brought to my attention by several earthfiles.com visitors. I confirmed the location now called Fort Hunter Liggett on a map and called George Ritter.

He said, "I came out of Viet Nam and went straight to Fort Ord on the ocean. But for the assignment with that Experimental Command, we were bussed for two hours into a desert that I was told was the Mohave Desert. Coming from Findlay, Ohio, I didn't know anything about California and have always assumed that was the desert we were in. I know we passed Soledad prison and Lockwood on our way to where we had guard duty."

Looking on a map, Soledad is on Route 101 and Lockwood is at the edge of Hunter Liggett Military Reservation, which was first built in 1940 after the U. S. Army, purchased the land from William Randolph Hearst, the newspaper tycoon. Straight east of Lockwood is the Salinas Valley, the Cholame Hills, the Diablo Range hill country and San Joaquin Valley north of Bakersfield. The Mohave Desert is much further south. Mr. Ritter says to the best of his memory his Experimental Command's location was described as in the Mojave Desert, but now does not know why if it was two hours by bus from Ft. Ord. If anyone else has information about the fall 1967 time period in relationship to Hunter Liggett Military operations, please contact me.

On the night of October 24th, 1967, he and three of his Army colleagues were on guard duty at the Experimental Command site. Something happened that convinced him the U. S. government is hiding knowledge about non-humans interacting with earth, but he thinks everyone should know. His name is George W. Ritter now retired in Findlay, Ohio.

Interview:

George W. Ritter, Specialist Four Infantry, U. S. Army, honorably discharged from the Armed Forces on September 25, 1968, speaking about an encounter on October 24, 1967:

"I was on guard duty one night with three other guys. And we were standing there talking and I said, 'Look at that, you guys! What the hell is that?' We watched it and it was about the color of a cigarette ember at night. And it was moving from left to right.

HOW BIG?

It was way far away and small. Kind of looked like the size of a star, only a different color, like an orange, reddish-orange. And it got bigger and brighter and started giving off this like orange fluorescent tail. While it was moving and leaving the tail behind, five little ones dropped out of the bottom of it. And they got in a V formation. And we're standing there and wondering what in the heck we're looking at?

So, the five little ones get in a V formation and head straight for us and the other one just keeps on going. So in no time at all, they are right on top of us. They were right over our heads and we're standing there and I'm looking up. They look like they are red hot. But I couldn't feel any heat.

Drawing of five smaller reddish-orange discs that were dropped out of a larger aerial craft where George Ritter and three other U. S. Army Infantrymen were on guard duty for a Combat Developments Experimental Command in association with Hunter Liggett Military Reservation approximately eighty miles from Fort Ord, California, October 24, 1967. Artwork by John Spears for George Ritter © 1996 by George W. Ritter, Findlay, Ohio.

HOW MANY WERE YOU LOOKING AT?

Five in a V-formation. And the other one had passed off from left to right - it looked like it got bigger and brighter leaving a trail. It was like it had to do something in order to get bigger and brighter when it dropped these little discs off and that's when it opened up a hatch or something that let out the lights.

They're (five discs) right on top of us and I could hear just before they got right to us, I could hear an echoing blip. It was like an electronic beep, echoing.

LIKE A SONAR?

Yeah, kind of like water dripping into a large pool of water with an echo sound. That's exactly what it sounded like. I think that was the beginning of the abduction as far as I'm concerned. Because it froze us in place. We couldn't move.

The next thing I know, I'm lifted up into one of these things, but I don't see my friends anywhere. They are not around. Then I seen this, it was a grey, I guess.

WHAT DID IT LOOK LIKE?

A typical looking grey, big, black eyes, paralyzing eyes, those all-knowing eyes! The first one I saw, I thought to myself, 'Oh, my God, I'm going to die.' And instantly, this voice comes into my head and says, 'You're not going to die. You're going to be all right. We're not going to hurt you. We're going to do some things and then we're going to let you go.

Drawing of grey "boss's head" that seemed to absorb George Ritter's memory and all lifetime experiences © October 20, 1999 by George W. Ritter, Findlay, Ohio.

AND AT THIS POINT, YOU'RE A PART OF THIS COMBAT DEVELOPMENT EXPERIMENTAL COMMAND AT FT. ORD CALIFORNIA. YOU HAD BEEN THERE WATCHING WITH THREE OTHER MEN THESE APPEARANCES OF THE HALF A DOZEN RED-ORANGE GLOWING OBJECTS THAT CAME OVER YOU. DO YOU KNOW WHETHER OR NOT YOU HAVE BEEN PHYSICALLY MOVED SOME WAY? OR YOUR OTHER MILITARY COMRADES HAVE BEEN MOVED AWAY? WHAT HAS HAPPENED THAT YOU ARE ALONE?

I am on the ship. I realized that, but I don't remember how I got on there. And I don't know where the other guys are.

YOU'RE IN THE SHIP AND THE MEN AREN'T AROUND YOU AND YOU HAVE BEEN SCARED BY THIS GREY ENTITY WHO IS NOW SAYING THEY ARE NOT GOING TO HARM YOU. WHAT HAPPENS NEXT?

The first time I really got a good look at this thing, I realized I was laying flat on my back and I was naked. And this grey thing bent over the table and put his head right up to mine and I'm telling you what - everything I'd ever known or experienced or every lesson I had ever learned - all of a sudden, he knew exactly what I knew.

TAKING YOUR MIND OUT...

Borrowing my tapes or something, you know? It was a strange feeling.

DID THIS ENTITY PUT BACK IN YOUR HEAD ANY INFORMATION?

I'm not exactly sure if that entity did. But I was constantly being reassured that I wasn't going to die and I was all right. Nothing was going to happen to me. I was going to be returned. I wouldn't remember any of that.

BUT YOU HAVE REMEMBERED.

Yes, I have remembered. And I found out through some hypnosis with Budd Hopkins that they spent some time looking at my feet, maybe because my feet were callused. But they seemed to be interested in my feet. And they moved up to my right thigh. And I got an injection from the right side in my thigh. I know it was an injection because I knew what an injection felt like and that's what it was. I'm sure of it. I couldn't really look right down and see what they were doing because I couldn't move my head. All I could move was my eyes. But I knew I was flat on my back and I knew I was naked because I was cold. And at one time I saw the tips of my toes.

DID YOU EVER GET ANY TELEPATHIC COMMUNICATION ABOUT WHY THEY WERE GIVING YOU A SHOT?

No. But all the communication was telepathic. All of it. I never opened my mouth and neither did they.

DID ALL THE ENTITIES AROUND YOU LOOK IDENTICAL? OR WERE SOME DIFFERENT AND COULD YOU DESCRIBE THE DIFFERENCES?

There were three other smaller ones, but the one that bent over me was definitely a little bit different. Maybe a little taller. But he seemed like he was the boss. He was running the show or whatever was going on. And there was a weird misty light in there, sort of the orchid color of black light like it was shining through a fog or something.

Drawing of George Ritter laying naked on table during examination by grey-skinned entities, Three smaller than the taller "boss," © 1999 by George W. Ritter, Findlay, Ohio.

159

DID THE TALLER GREY BEING ALSO HAVE THE LARGE BLACK EYES?

Yes.

DID THEY ALL HAVE THE LARGE BLACK EYES?

Yes.

DID YOU EVER HAVE AN IMPRESSION THAT THOSE BLACK EYES MIGHT BE SHIELDS OVER YET A DIFFERENT EYE UNDERNEATH THE SHIELDS?

I couldn't see through it, but I thought about it and sometimes I thought they were almost like sunglasses that weren't connected and didn't have any ear rod pieces on them.

COULD YOU ALSO SEE IF THERE WERE ANY RIDGES OR WRINKLES ON THE GREY ENTITY YOU THOUGHT WAS IN CHARGE? OR WAS THE SKIN ENTIRELY SMOOTH?

It seemed like it was smooth, but it was cold in there, colder than heck.

DID THEY HAVE ANY CLOTHING ON?

No. When Budd showed me a picture of an entity that had on a black turtle neck sweater - that's the guy. That one looks more like the ones I was with than any other pictures I've ever seen. Whitley Strieber's Communion book - that face is too symmetrical - it's not round enough. Their faces are egg shaped or something.

So, anyway they gave me a shot in the thigh near my groin area. I didn't like them messing around like that, but there was nothing I could do about it. And then one of them came up to my left side and put his whole hand, it felt like, inside the upper left side of my chest.

LITERALLY PUT IT INSIDE YOUR CHEST SOME HOW?

Inside my chest cavity, yes.

BUT WITHOUT DOING SURGERY ON YOU?

Yes. It was just like he reached in there and did something and withdrew. I wasn't freaking out, but I was trying to figure out what the hell they were doing. Anyway, after they messed around with my feet, gave me a shot and did something in my groin area, they got me dressed. The reason I knew I was naked, I saw my toes and I couldn't figure out how they got my boots off so fast because they were laced up and tied tight. But then, the more I realized that I figured there must have been some sort of time dilation involved here.

Otherwise, I couldn't have lost three hours in what seemed like three minutes. When they were all done, they took me to another room and there was - I'm going to say it was an angel. That's the only thing I know how to say it was because I've never seen an angel before. Always been told that angels would come as a light source or as a light being. That's exactly what this thing was. It was the source of its own energy.

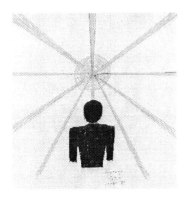

Drawing of ball of light that emanated energy and love to George Ritter and communicated telepathically © 1999 by George W. Ritter, Findlay, Ohio.

CAN YOU DESCRIBE IT IN MORE DETAIL FROM HEAD TO TOE?

It didn't have a form. It was just a ball of light energy that was so bright and so loving and caring, I just knew it was an angel. Unless I was completely fooled. But it told me some things. It told me that in the near future - God only knows what that is to them - that something wonderful was going to happen. This light being told me that I had had syphilis, that I was cured now, and I argued with it and I said, 'No, that's impossible because I got checked before I left Vietnam. And I didn't have it or I would never have left the country.' And the thing seemed to think my arguing with it was amusing.

IT WAS COMMUNICATING WITH YOU IN YOUR MIND?

That's the way they all do. They all did it.

WHEN IT WAS COMMUNICATING WITH YOU IN YOUR MIND, DID YOU ALSO HAVE IMAGES GOING THROUGH YOUR MIND AT THE SAME TIME?

Not that I can remember. But I'm sure there could have been screen memories put in there. They thought they could do just about anything they wanted to.

WHEN THEY WERE TALKING ABOUT SOMETHING WONDERFUL WOULD HAPPEN, DO YOU HAVE THE IMPRESSION THAT THAT RELATED TO THE ENTIRE WORLD OR TO YOU ONLY?

To the entire world. But they wouldn't tell me what it was. And they told me that this was a reminder that I had to keep my end of our arrangement that was made long ago.

YOU UNDERSTAND THAT TO BE WHAT?

That some time, somewhere, I cut some kind of deal with them or made to believe that. And they were just checking on me and reminding me that I would keep my end of the arrangement and that was that. The next thing I know, I'm standing on the ground again right where I was before right next to my friends and they are not there. I am

161

still looking up. The objects are gone. And we're just standing there bewildered.

YOUR MILITARY COLLEAGUES ARE THERE?

Yeah. They had to have seen all of this because when I told them, 'Hey, we're on guard duty and under our general orders and the oath we took, we have to turn this into the Sergeant of the Guard. Our general orders say we have to report everything strange and unusual. And this is strange and unusual.

So, we went to my Sergeant, Sergeant Palmer, who was at the time a Platoon Sergeant and I told him exactly what happened. And he looked me straight in the eye and he said, 'Ritter, keep your mouth shut about this. Do not tell anyone anything about it. Everything will be just fine.' And I said, 'No, Sergeant Palmer, I can't keep my mouth shut.' I reminded him of my oath, my general orders. He said, 'Look, I see these things out here and other people have seen them out here and if you don't keep your mouth shut, you're going to the psycho ward.' So I said, 'Fine, so be it. Send me to the psycho ward.' And they did!

THEY PUT YOU IN THE PSYCHO WARD?

Yes. I was in the psycho ward for two months.

ON WHAT GROUNDS?

That I had reported a UFO I guess. It's OK to see them, but not to report them. At least in the military.

THAT WAS IN OCTOBER OF 1967.

Yes, ma'am.

YOU WERE IN FOR TWO MONTHS.

And basically, in order to get out of there I had to convince them that I saw something but didn't know what I saw. And Jesus, I didn't tell them I was on the thing!

YOU NEVER TOLD ANYONE ABOUT THE EXPERIENCE WITH THE GREY ENTITIES ON SOME SORT OF CRAFT?

Oh, yeah, I told my Sergeant, but I didn't tell them in the psycho ward because I didn't want to be in there forever.

THEY WERE KEEPING YOU IN THE PSYCHO WARD ONLY ON THE GROUNDS OF HAVING REPORTED THE RED-ORANGE LIGHTS?

UFOs and the abduction because they wanted to find out what I knew or remembered, if anything.

YOU DECIDED NOT TO TELL THEM?

I decided to clam up. I figured if I could convince them I didn't know what I saw or what happened, I could get out of here. Well, I did. But I didn't drop the ball. As soon as they got me back to the desert again, I'm out there and I'm investigating some things, turning over every rock I can, and they warned me again and I told them to go to hell. I said, 'This is not right. You guys are covering something up.' And bang!

I'm right back in the psycho ward. They kept me there from January 1968 until my April 1968 ETF.

BUT THAT HAD CONVINCED YOU THAT THEY WERE ACTUALLY USING PSYCHO WARDS AS PUNISHMENT FOR ANYONE REPORTING A UFO ENCOUNTER?

Not only that, but when people in there found out what I was in there for, I got reports from other people!

YOU GOT REPORTS FROM OTHER PEOPLE IN THERE THAT THEY HAD SEEN THINGS AND THEY WERE ALSO IN THERE BECAUSE THEY HAD REPORTED THEM?

Yes, and their family members. This one kid told me that his mother out in California had seen a UFO come up out of the reservoir and take off. After what I'd been through, I didn't doubt the kid.

WHAT HAPPENED TO YOUR THREE MILITARY COLLEAGUES WHEN THE RED-ORANGE THINGS CAME OVER YOU AND YOU WERE ABDUCTED?

Absolutely nothing. They kept their mouths shut.

DID YOU TALK WITH THEM PRIVATELY OFF THE RECORD AND ASK WHAT THEY HAD SEEN HAPPEN TO YOU?

I told them, 'What the hell is wrong with you people? Don't you realize what happened out there? And what's going on here? That we're dealing with something that's not even from this planet, probably.' And they would start to remember different things about seeing it and as soon as I would wait for an answer, they totally forgot about it again. And I wondered, 'what the hell is going on?!' They went to sleep that night and I couldn't sleep for a week. I broke out with a rash in my groin area.

When they let me out after the first two months was up, I went back to the desert and I kept digging, nosing around. And they sent the CID out there, the Criminal Investigation Division.

FOR THE ARMY?

Like I was some kind of criminal. I saw him talking to my Sergeant and they were pointing at me and this guy was writing stuff on a clipboard.

DID YOU GET AN HONORABLE DISCHARGE?

Yes, I got an Honorable Discharge like everything was normal.

Close up George Walter Ritter's name and date of Honorable Discharge.

WHEN DID THAT OCCUR?

September 25, 1968. I went back to Findlay, Ohio to work in the factory where I had worked before the Army, but the Army wouldn't allow me to get back to work and held up my formal discharge for six months.

WHAT WAS THE ARMY'S REASON FOR HOLDING IT UP?

'For the convenience of the government,' I was told.

WHEN YOU ASKED SUPERIORS WHY, WHAT ANSWERS DID THEY GIVE?

They don't answer and you don't ask questions.

TODAY, YOU'RE SPEAKING OUT BECAUSE...

I've been speaking out for a long time. I've been telling this truth to anybody who will listen to it. I was raised always to tell the truth. I took my military training seriously and my orders seriously. And that was all I was doing, following orders. And I was in fact told by my superior officer to forget about the orders and to keep my mouth shut.

BECAUSE?

I just couldn't believe it. Why didn't they want anybody to know what is going on? Or that we were actually being visited by somebody from somewhere else that had craft like I'd never seen before that defied all laws that I ever knew. How did they get me from the ground up there without landing?

YOU ARE UPSET BY GOVERNMENT KNOWLEDGE AND COVER-UP?

Yes, absolutely."

(Editor's Note): Ms. Howe is an Emmy Award-winning TV and documentary producer, investigative reporter, and Reporter and Editor of the science and environment news website, Earthfiles.com. She is noted for her investigative work in the areas of crop formations and cattle mutilations. A wellspring of information may be found at Ms. Howe's web site, http://www.earthfiles.com

David Twichell.

* * *

In recent years, George Ritter has been videotaping a series of blurred UFOs behind a farm in Fostoria, Ohio. Noted artist and Webmaster, James Neff, has written that blurs on videotape are not UFOs but most likely insects. I drove from New Jersey to Ohio to meet with George Ritter to investigate his images and found him to honest and forthright. I believe he is honest and forthright in his attempts to obtain video of Unidentified Flying Objects and regularly captures remarkable images.

George Ritter places his camera on a tripod in his backyard and shoots video for several hours without touching the camcorder except to set up and remove the tape. I was present while he videotaped some remarkable images of UFOs. I did not see the UFOs captured on the video, since they appear to move at very high speeds of over a thousand miles per hour. This was determined by measuring their progression from frame to frame and the distance covered above the farm.

The camcorder generally used by George Ritter is his RCA VHS video camera Model cc 4251. While videotaping UFOs, the camera also videotapes birds, bees and other insects, as the camera automatically changes focus on the object in the center of the video screen almost instantly. On wide-angle position, the camera focuses from an inch from the lens to infinity. The camera is capable of taking images at very close range, as is apparent by the image of the bird that is only a few feet away from the lens, while a bee will fly only a few inches from lens. The following image does not appear to be an insect and we believe the Unidentified Flying Objects that appear over the farm at a distance of approximately 265 yards or more are genuine UFOs.

George Ritter has always been open to have qualified experts attempt to repeat his results with high-speed film. Efforts have been made to obtain help from Ohio State and Bowling Green University to evaluate the images on site.

George Filer.

Below are two examples of stills from videotape by George Ritter, which clearly demonstrates the difference between a bird and an anomalous object.

A plethora of George Ritter's anomalous images may be viewed at George Filer's website by going to www.nationalufocenter.com

Chapter 11
U.S. Astronauts and Presidents

Shuttle Captures Video of Disk UFO.

NASA TV Channel video downloads were recently reviewed Dr. Oren Swearingen who noticed a disk-shaped UFO flying formation with SST 112 Atlantis shuttle. The actual flight took place on October 10, 2002, (003 days: 03 hours: 43: seconds) while the shuttle was flying over the Canadian and Midwest US border.

A disk-shaped UFO is videotaped from the SST Shuttle's Bay video camera. The disk, at first, appears to be some part of the Shuttle Arm because it is barely moving in relationship to the Shuttle. Jeffrey S. Ashby was commander and astronaut Pamela A. Melroy, pilot, and astronaut David A. Wolf was the mission specialist.

The video cuts away to the Mission Control Center repeatedly but half of the white UFO is visible. As the video continues, the UFO gradually moves off screen to the right of the image. The UFO is white and about the same color as the shuttle. It is a typical disk shape and is estimated to be about thirty feet in diameter with a cockpit on top.

The object may be some type of object designed to fit inside the Shuttle's Bay, particularly if its wings fold. Of course it might be a visitor similar to those reported by Russian Cosmonauts.

Thanks to Dr. Oren Swearingen who sent me the complete tape.
* * *

Astronaut Gordon Cooper stated, "Yes, several days in a row we sighted groups of metallic, saucer-shaped vehicles at great altitudes over the base, and we tried to get close to them but they were able to change direction faster than our fighters. I do believe UFOs exists and that the truly unexplained ones are from some other technologically advanced civilization. From my association with aircraft and spacecraft, I think I have a pretty good idea of what everyone on this planet has and their performance capabilities, and I'm sure some of the UFOs, at least, are *not* from anywhere on Earth."

On May 15, 1963, Gordon Cooper launched into space in a Mercury capsule for a 22 orbit journey around the world. During the final orbit, he told the tracking station at Muchea (near Perth Australia) that he could see a glowing, greenish object ahead of him, quickly approaching his capsule. The UFO was real and solid, because it was picked up by Muchea's tracking radar.

Cooper's sighting was reported by the National Broadcast Company, which was covering the flight step by step. But when Cooper landed, reporters were told that they would not be allowed to question him about the UFO sighting.

According to a taped interview by J. L. Ferrando, Major Cooper said, "For many years I have lived with a secret, in a secrecy imposed on all specialists in astronautics. I can now reveal that every day in the USA, our radar instruments capture objects of form and composition unknown to us. And there are thousands of witness reports and a quantity of documents to prove this, but nobody wants to make them public. Why? Because authority is afraid that people may think of God knows what kind of horrible invaders. So the password still is, 'we have to avoid panic by all means.'"

In an address to a UN panel on UFOs in New York, 1985, Cooper said, "I believe that these extraterrestrial vehicles and their crews are visiting this planet from other planets, which obviously are a little more technically advanced than we are here on Earth. I feel that we need to have a top level, coordinated program to scientifically collect and analyze data from all over the earth concerning any type of encounter, and to determine how best to interface with these visitors in a friendly fashion. We may first have to show them that we have learned to resolve our problems by peaceful means, rather than warfare, before we are accepted as fully qualified universal team members. This acceptance would have tremendous possibilities of advancing our world in all areas. Certainly then, it would seem that the UN has a vested interest in handling this subject properly and expeditiously.

"As far as I am concerned, there have been too many unexplained examples of UFO sightings around this earth for us to rule out the possibilities that some form of life exists out there beyond our own world.

"I know other astronauts share my feelings and we know the government is sitting on hard evidence of UFOs!"

Cooper first encountered UFOs as a military pilot in Germany in 1950:

"We thought they could have been Russian. We regularly had MiG-15s over-flying our base. We scrambled our Sabre jets to intercept and got to our ceiling of 45,000 feet . . . and they were still way above us traveling faster than we were. These vehicles were in formation like a fighter group, but they were metallic, silver and saucer-shaped. Believe me; they weren't like any MiGs I'd seen before! They had to be UFOs.

"I had a camera crew filming the installation when they spotted a saucer. They filmed it as it flew overhead, then hovered, extended three legs as landing gear and slowly came down to land on a dry lakebed! These guys were all pro cameramen, so the picture quality was very good. The camera crew managed to get within 20 or 30 yards of it, filming all the time. It was a classic saucer, shiny silver and smooth, about 30 feet across. It was pretty clear it was an alien craft. As they approached closer, it took off."

Cooper, following standard procedure, contacted Washington to report the UFO. Then, according to Cooper, "all heck broke loose! After a while, a high-ranking officer said, when the film was developed, I was to put it in a pouch and send it to Washington. He didn't say anything about me not looking at the film. That's what I did when it came back from the lab and it was all there just like the camera crew reported."

When the Air Force later started Operation Blue Book to collate UFO evidence and reports, Cooper says he mentioned the film evidence. "But the film was never found – supposedly. Blue Book was strictly a cover-up anyway," Cooper said.

On the subject of the Roswell crash, Cooper had this to say: "I had a good friend at Roswell, a fellow officer. He had to be careful about what he said. But it sure wasn't a weather balloon like the Air Force cover story. He made it clear to me what crashed was a craft of alien origin and members of the crew were recovered."

Cooper, in his book, "A Leap of Faith", tells the reader his strong views on the existence of extraterrestrial intelligence and even the distinct possibility that we have "already had contact."

His photographic team at Edwards Air Force Base photographed the landing of a disc craft. In of his book, he states, "During my final years with NASA, I became involved in a different kind of adventure: undersea treasure hunting in Mexico. One day, accompanied by a National Geographic photographer, we landed in a small plane on an island in the Gulf of Mexico. Local residents pointed out to them pyramid-shaped mounds, where they found ruins, artifacts and bones. On examination, back in Texas, the artifacts were determined to be 5,000 years old!

"When we learned of the age of the artifacts," Cooper writes, "we realized that what we'd found had nothing to do with seventeenth-century Spain. I contacted the Mexican government and was put in touch with the head of the National Archaeology Department, Pablo Bush Romero." Together with Mexican archeologists the two went back to the site.

After some excavating, Cooper writes, "The age of the ruins was confirmed at 3000 B.C. Compared with other advanced civilizations, relatively little was known about the Olmecs, who made large statues of their faces that appear they came from the Black Africa race." Gordon Cooper writes, "Engineers, farmers, artisans and traders, the Olmecs had a remarkable civilization. But it is still not known where they originated.

"Among the findings that intrigued me most: that, when translated, turned out to be mathematical formulas used to this day for navigation and accurate drawings of constellations, some of which would not be officially 'discovered' until the age of modern telescopes."

It was this, rather than his experiences as an astronaut that triggered Gordon Cooper's "Leap of faith". "This left me wondering: Why have celestial navigation signs if they weren't navigating celestially?" And he asks, "If 'someone' had helped the Olmecs with this knowledge, from whom did they get it?"

Thanks to Gordon Cooper Chapter 11 "A Leap of Faith"

* * *

In June of 1965, Ed White, the first American to walk in space, and James McDivitt were over Hawaii while orbiting the Earth in a Gemini spacecraft, when they spotted a disk-shaped UFO with long arms protruding from it. McDivitt took some pictures of the object with a cine-camera. Needless to say, those photographs have never been released.

* * *

In December of 1965, James Lovell and Frank Borman, on their second orbit of a fourteen-day flight, observed several UFOs some distance from their capsule. Gemini control at Cape Kennedy suggested that they were seeing the final stage of their own Titan booster rocket. Borman advised control that they could see the booster rocket - that this was something completely different. The following is an excerpt from the taped conversation between Lovell and Gemini control:

Lovell: Bogey at ten o'clock high.
Control: This is Houston. Say again, 7.
Lovell: Said we have a bogey at ten o'clock high.
Control: Gemini 7, is that the booster or an actual sighting?
Lovell: We have several . . . actual sightings.
Control: Estimated distance or size?
Lovell: We also have the booster in sight . . .

* * *

Commander Eugene Cernan of the Apollo 17 mission, stated in a 1973 article in the Los Angeles Times, "I've been asked about UFOs and I've said publicly I thought they were somebody else . . . some other civilization."

* * *

Pilot Walter Schirra, of the Mercury 8 flight, is credited with coining the code word "Santa Claus" to indicate the sighting of a flying saucer near a space capsule. It was probably Schirra's attempt to draw a correlation between two presumably nonexistent entities. It seemed to work well at first. No one seemed to notice when a "Santa Claus" was reported. However, by the flight of Apollo 8, when James Lovell came out from behind the moon and reported to the world, "Please be informed that there is a Santa Claus," many people, who had heard that term from astronauts in the past, began to suspect a hidden meaning.

* * *

UFOs or Dinosaurs on ISS Space Walk?

Jeff Challender, Director of Project Prove reports, "The two crewmen of ISS Expedition 8 prepared and trained for the February 25, 2004, EVA for years. No aspect of the mission to be performed, no piece of equipment, no part to be installed should come as any surprise. Yet, in his own words, to Cosmonaut Kaleri these "Dinosaurs" came as a great and unwelcome surprise.

Kaleri: So, dinosaurs are needed here. You can't do . . . can't do anything without them.

Korelyev: Say it again?

Kaleri: I say when the dinosaur is here. Yes! I have them here! (Pause for several seconds.) Uh . . .these are with me now!

Korelyev: Yes. Let them be with you. Understood. (Several Minutes Later),

Foale: (garbled) Sasha is attaching the dinosaurs now.

UPDATE: A well-known debunker has made claim that Cosmonaut Kaleri was referring to a snipping tool used in space walks. Personally, I don't see the connection. If one takes the word "Dinosaur" by itself out of context, perhaps such a case can be made. But when one takes the entire conversation Kaleri had with Russian controllers in Korelyev, the tool explanation simply does not fit. Both Kaleri and Russian Mission Control spoke of "Dinosaurs" in plural. Astronaut Michael Foale stated that Sasha was "attaching" the dinosaurs. Regardless if this is true or not, the tool claim isn't the answer. There was never any talk about cutting or snipping, any bundles or tie downs.

Thanks to Jeff Challender,
http://projectprove.com/SashasDinosaurs.html

* * *

On that historic day, July 21, 1969, shortly after man first set foot on the moon, the entire world listened in on a live transmission between **Neil Armstrong, and Edwin "Buzz" Aldrin** (on the lunar surface) and Mission Control. Armstrong had seen a strong light coming from the ridge of a crater and went to investigate. Forgetting (or not caring) that the transmission was being broadcast live globally, he began describing what appeared to be two brightly illuminated UFOs on the moon watching the astronauts. The written transcript of the interchange does not reflect the excitement and disbelief of the astronauts nor the panicked earthbound controller trying, frantically, to get Armstrong to shut up, break transmission and go to a secure frequency.

The following is the transcript of the conversation between Armstrong, Aldrin and Houston Control, heard globally, before public transmission went black:

Armstrong: Ha! What is it?

Aldrin: We have some explanation for that?

Houston: We have not. Don't worry. Continue your program!

Armstrong: Oh boy! It's a . . . it's . . . it . . . it is really something . . . similar to . . . fantastic here! You . . . you could never imagine this!

Houston: Roger. We know about that. Could you go the other way? Go back the other way!

Armstrong: Well, it's kind of rigged! Ha! Pretty spectacular! God, what is that there? It's hollow! What the hell is that?!

Houston: Go Tango! Tango!

Armstrong: Ha! There's kind of a light there now!

Houston: Roger, we got it! We watched it! Lose communication! Bravo Tango! Bravo Tango! Select Jezebel! Jezebel!

Armstrong: Ya' . . . ha! But this is unbelievable!

Houston: We call you up Bravo Tango! Bravo Tango!

Even though worldwide communication ceased at this point, unnamed radio hams, using VHF receiving facilities, were able to bypass NASA's broadcasting outlets, and recorded the following transmission:

Houston: What's there? Mission control calling Apollo 11 . . .

Armstrong: These babies are huge, sir! Enormous! Oh my God! You wouldn't believe it! I'm telling you there are other spacecraft out there, lined up on the far side of the crater edge! They're on the moon watching us!

A former NASA employee, Otto Binder, later confirmed this transmission. Armstrong later confirmed that this story was true and admitted that the CIA was behind the cover-up. He stated that they (the astronauts) were "warned off" by the aliens. When asked what that meant, he replied, "I can't go into details, except to say that their ships were far superior to ours both in size and technology. Boy, were they big! And menacing! No, there is no question of a space station."

When challenged with the fact that NASA had other missions after Apollo 11, Armstrong replied, "Naturally - NASA was committed at that time and couldn't risk panic on Earth. But it really was a scoop and then back again."

* * *

Senator John H. Glen Jr., former astronaut and US Representative: "I believe certain reports of flying saucers to be legitimate."

* * *

Edgar D. Mitchell was an Apollo 14 Astronaut and the sixth man on the moon.

Mitchell gave this statement in 1971: "We all know that UFOs are real. All we need to ask is where do they come from?"

Then, in an interview with MSN in 1998, he said, "I've talked with people of stature-of military and government credentials and position-and heard their stories and their desire to tell their stories openly to the public. And that got my attention very, very rapidly. The first hand experiences of these credible witnesses that are now in advanced years are anxious to tell their story. We can't deny that. And the evidence points to the fact that Roswell was a *real* incident and that indeed an alien craft *did* crash and that material was recovered from that crash site.

"The U.S. Government *hasn't* maintained secrecy regarding UFOs – It's been leaking out all over the place. But the way it's been handled is by denial, by denying the truth of the documents that have leaked – by attempting to show them as fraudulent, as bogus of some sort. There has been a very large disinformation and misinformation effort around this whole area. And one must wonder, how better to hide something out in the open than just to say, 'It isn't there. You're deceiving yourself if you think this is true.' And yet, there it is right in front of you. So it's a disinformation effort that's concerning here, not the fact that they have kept the secret. They haven't kept it. It's been getting out into the public for fifty years or more.

"I have been, over the years, very skeptical like many others. But in the last ten years or so, I have known the late Dr. Alan Hynek, who I highly admire. I know and currently work with Dr. Jacques Vallee. I've come to realize that the evidence is building up to make this a valid and researchable question. Further, because my personal motivation has always been to understand our universe better, and my own theoretical work has convinced me that life is everywhere in the universe that has been permitted to evolve, I consider this a very timely question. By becoming more involved with the serious research field, I've seen the evidence mount towards the truth of these matters. I rely upon the testimony of contacts that I have had – old timers – who were involved in official positions in government and intelligence and the military over the last 50 years. We cannot say that today's government is

173

really covering it up. I think that most of them don't know what is going on anymore than the public."

* * *

Dr. Brian O'Leary, NASA scientist, astronaut, Assistant Professor of Astronomy at Cornell University alongside Carl Sagan, remarked, "We have contact with alien cultures."

* * *

Donald Slayton was a Mercury astronaut. In a 1951 interview, Slayton stated, "I was testing a P-51 fighter in Minneapolis when I spotted this object. I was at about 10,000 feet on a nice, bright, sunny afternoon. I thought the object was a kite, then I realized that no kite is gonna' fly that high. As I got closer, it looked like a weather balloon, gray and about three feet in diameter. But as soon as I got behind the darn thing it didn't look like a balloon anymore. It looked like a saucer, a disk. About the same time, I realized that it was suddenly going away from me and there I was, running at about 300 miles per hour. I tracked it for a little way and then, all of a sudden, the damn thing just took off. It pulled about a 45 degree climbing turn and accelerated and just flat disappeared!"

* * *

UFO Witness President Ronald Reagan dies at 93.

The history of the world was changed by Ronald Reagan's interest in UFOs. He liked to say, "God has a plan for everything."

He and Nancy were expected at a casual dinner party with friends in Hollywood when they were first married and showed up a half hour later quite upset. They stated that they had seen a UFO coming down the coast.

In 1974, California Governor Ronald Reagan stated, "I was in a plane last week when I looked out the window and saw this white light. It was zigzagging around. I went up to the pilot and said, 'Have you ever seen anything like that?' He was shocked and he said, 'Nope.' And I said to him: 'Let's follow it!' We followed it for several minutes. It was a bright white light. We followed it to Bakersfield and, all of a sudden, to our utter amazement, it went straight up into the heavens."

174

Reagan told reporter Norman C. Millar about the UFO he had seen and that his wife and him had done personal research on UFOs and had uncovered references to UFOs in Egyptian hieroglyphics.

When he became President, he frequently discussed UFOs with his staff, received numerous reports on sightings and made frequent references to UFOs in his speeches.

On September 28, 1981, President Reagan received a letter from Major Ret. Colman VonKeviczky, Director of the International UFO Galactic Spacecraft Research and Analytic Network (ICUFON) that claimed UFOs were an intergalactic task force that will destroy earth unless world leaders band together to end their hostile actions against UFOs. Chief Military Advisor of the White House, Major General Robert Schweitzer replied, "The President is well aware of the threat you document so clearly and is doing all in his power to restore the national defense margin of safety as quickly and prudently as possible."

November 21, 1981. General Douglas MacArthur also spoke of an ultimate conflict between a united human race and the sinister forces of some other planetary galaxy.

On December 4, 1985, Reagan made a speech at Fallston High School in Maryland telling about his meeting in Geneva where, in five hours of private conversations with Soviet Premier Gorbachev, he had brought up the alien scenario:

"I couldn't help but - when you stop to think that we're all God's children, wherever we live in the world – I couldn't help but say to him (Gorbachev) just how easy his task and mine might be if suddenly there was a threat to this world from some other species from another planet outside in the universe. We'd forget all the little local differences that we have between our countries and we would find out, once and for all, that we really are all human beings here on this Earth together. Well I guess we can wait for some alien race to come down and threaten us, but I think that between us we can bring about that realization."

Reagan showed his perception of UFOs at the United Nations General Assembly September 21st, 1987, when he stated, "In our obsession with antagonisms of the moment, we often forget how much unites all the members of humanity. Perhaps we need some outside, universal threat to make us recognize this common bond. I occasionally think how quickly our differences, worldwide, would vanish if we were facing an alien threat from outside this world. And yet, I ask you," he went on, "is not an alien threat already among us? What could be more alien to universal aspirations of our peoples than war and the threat of war?"

President Reagan apparently developed a plan to defeat the USSR, and Communism that he called "the Evil Empire." A key part of the plan was the Strategic Defense Initiative (SDI) announced in 1983, and called it the "Star Wars defense system" that could destroy Soviet missiles and perhaps UFOs. Reagan proposed a complex set of defensive lasers and missiles intended to shoot down Soviet IBCMs. He even offered the system to the Soviets.

Whether inspired through his conversations with President Reagan or through information provided by his own intelligence, Gorbachev had his own interest in UFOs. On February 16, 1987, in an important speech, at a conference at Grand Kremlin Palace in Moscow on the "Survival of Humanity," Gorbachev stated:

"At our meeting in Geneva, the U.S. President said that if the earth faced an invasion by extraterrestrials, the United States and the Soviet Union would join forces to repel such an invasion. I shall not dispute the hypothesis, although I think it's early yet to worry about such an intrusion. It is much more important to think about the problems that have entered in our common home."

In May 1990, shortly before the fall of the Soviet Union, Gorbachev made a second more direct statement about UFOs: "The phenomenon of UFOs *does* exist," he stated, "and it must be treated seriously."

Reports of UFOs destroying key installations were picked up on intercepts and the Soviets were very concerned about the attacks and the new threats. President Reagan's interest in UFO's may have changed the course of history and potentially saved millions of lives. As Margaret Thatcher reminded us, "He (Reagan) won the Cold War without firing a shot."

In his last public announcement Regan revealed, "When the Lord calls me home, whenever that may be, I will leave with the greatest love for this country of ours, and eternal optimism for its future."

* * *

JIMMY CARTER, THE NOBEL PRIZE AND UFOs.

Former President Jimmy Carter is being awarded the prestigious Nobel Peace Prize. He is a former Naval Academy graduate and naval officer who spent many nights on watch looking at the night skies before becoming the governor of Georgia.

Carter was doing some politicking at the Leary Georgia's Lion's Club in January 1969, when suddenly from the sky, a UFO "as bright as the moon" flashed before his eyes. A red and green glowing orb radiated as it hurtled across the southwestern skies. Ten minutes later, it vanished. That was Jimmy Carter's story and he has stuck to it.

Carter became the first major politician to risk achieving "crackpot" status by claiming he had had a close encounter. "I don't laugh at people any more when they say they've seen UFOs," Carter said at a Southern Governor's Conference a few years later. "I've seen one myself."

Yet, while he was on the campaign trail, he tried to use it to his advantage. "A light appeared and disappeared in the sky," he told a

Washington Post reporter in 1975. "It got brighter and brighter. I have no idea what it was. I think it was a light beckoning me to run in the California primary for President," He joked.

Carter, while running for President, said, "What I would do is make information we have about those (UFO) sightings available to the public (three words unclear). I have never tried to identify what I saw. You know, it was a light in the western sky that was very unique. I had never seen it before. There were about twenty of us who saw it. None of us could figure out what it was. I don't think it was anything solid. It was just like a light. It was a curious aberration. So I don't make fun of people who say they've seen unidentified objects in the sky."

As Jimmy Carter receives his Nobel Peace Prize, it might be important to note that other important Peace Prize winners have also taken an interest in the extraterrestrial angle of world peace.

Former Prime Minister of Canada, Lester B. Pearson actually brought up the extraterrestrial possibilities during his acceptance speech for the Nobel Peace Prize in 1957:

"Perhaps there is a hopeful possibility here in the conquest of outer space. Interplanetary activity may well give us planetary peace. Once we discover Martian spaceships hovering over Earth's airspace, we will all come together. 'How dare they threaten us like this!' we shall shout as one at a really United Nations!"

Thanks to Grant Cameron, http://www.presidentialufo.com

* * *

President Dwight D. Eisenhower.

A secret document surfaced, years after President Eisenhower left the Oval Office, which clearly indicated that he was formally advised of the 1947 Roswell crash, the military's possession of alien bodies and the ET presence in our world. The document that would come to be known as "The Eisenhower Briefing" was handed to Eisenhower when he was President elect.

Providing the document is authentic, it proves that President Truman was well aware of the Roswell crash and considered UFOs and their occupants as a highly potential threat to national security. It also proves that a group of high-ranking military men and some of the greatest scientific minds of the era had been assembled as a think-tank to address the ET problem. This group was known as "Majestic 12" or "MJ 12". MJ 12 was answerable only to the President. As such, the incoming President had to be apprised of the situation and be made to understand that it was a matter of utmost secrecy.

Many UFO debunkers have challenged the document's authenticity, the least of which being Philip Klass, a man who has spent his life as a professional naysayer.

Stanton T. Friedman, a nuclear physicist who hails from Canada and was the man credited with reopening the Roswell investigation in the

70s, has been a favorite target of Mr. Klass' rants for years. The reason being that Mr. Friedman meticulously and scientifically investigates documented evidence and refuses to endorse it until he has the proof to back it up. When an investigator is this thorough, they usually come too close to the truth to be ignored by those whose duty it is to perpetuate the cover up.

After visiting nineteen different archives, for comparison to the document in question, Friedman concluded that the document was indeed authentic. It had been typed on the proper onionskin paper and bore the official watermarks of that period. Yet Klass challenged the authenticity of it, arguing that the typeface was of the large pica type when it should have been the small elite type. Klass claimed to be in possession of several official documents from that time frame that were all in the elite typeface. He publicly offered to pay Friedman one hundred dollars each for any genuine document that he could produce in the pica typeface from that time frame – up to ten documents.

Friedman proceeded to dig twenty such documents from his own files. Then he went to the Eisenhower Library and selected fourteen more that exactly matched the Eisenhower Briefing document as to typeface and style from that same time frame. He then sent the package of documents to Mr. Klass with an invoice for one thousand dollars. Good to his word, Mr. Klass sent a check for that amount to the Canadian scientist. According to Friedman, Klass became quite indignant when he published the challenge and a Photostat copy of the check in his final report "Operation Majestic 12."

It had also been argued that the date format was wrong for the time period. Friedman produced documents with as many as seven different date formats. Others have said that the document had been typed on a 1960s typewriter. Dr. Robert M. Wood hired a professional document examiner who concluded that the typeface was that of a typewriter manufactured in 1940.

With the lack of any evidence to the contrary, the document stands as authentic.

Eisenhower was losing control of the UFO situation toward the end of his presidency. U.S. corporations were apprised of the UFO reality and feared the downfall of the entire capitalistic system should the truth be told to the public. Corporate America became the "shadow government", bought and paid for by consumer dollars and our elected officials became the *puppets* at their bidding.

In his Farewell Address to the nation, on January 17, 1961, President Eisenhower alluded to this fact when he said, "In the councils of government, we must guard against the acquisition of unwarranted influence, whether sought or unsought, by the *military-industrial complex* (my emphasis). The potential for the disastrous rise of misplaced power exists and will persist. We must never let the weight of this combination endanger our liberties or democratic processes."

* * *

President Harry S. Truman.

On July 26, 1947, President Truman signed a decree for the creation of the CIA. During World War II, although there were intelligence-gathering measures in place, an *agency* for that specific purpose was not deemed necessary. Two years after the war ended, that agency was hurriedly established – three weeks after the alleged crash at Roswell, New Mexico.

At a press conference in Washington DC, April 4, 1950, Truman stated, "I can assure you, the flying saucers, given that they exist, are not constructed by any power on earth."

* * *

Gerald Ford.

Although Ford was a U.S. Representative at the time he uttered this opinion publicly, he would later be appointed President after Richard M Nixon resigned. As with other presidents after him, he sought to lift the cloak of secrecy surrounding the UFO phenomenon and present the facts to the public while in office. As with other presidents, his efforts were either thwarted and/or he was made to understand the incalculable risks involved in its disclosure.

In March of 1966 Ford said, "I think there may be substance in some of these reports. I believe the American people are entitled to a more thorough explanation than has been given them by the Air Force to date. I think we owe it to the people to establish credibility regarding UFOs and to produce the greatest possible enlightenment of the subject."

* * *

President William Clinton.

Webb Hubble, a Deputy Attorney General in the Clinton administration, claimed in his "tell-all" book, "Friends in High Places", that President Clinton said to him, "Webb, if I put you over at Justice, I want you to find the answers to two questions for me. One, who killed JFK and two, are there UFOs." Hubbell adds, "He was dead serious. I had looked into both but wasn't satisfied with the answers I was getting."

John Podesta was President Clinton's Chief of Staff from 1998 to 2001. He too was asked by Clinton to seek out UFO related documents for declassification. Podesta's efforts were stonewalled at every turn.

The Sci-Fi Channel engaged Mr. Podesta's expertise in the Washington arena in an effort to foster an all out push to declassify UFO related documents. On October 22, Sci-Fi Channel hosted a Washington UFO news conference. Podesta appeared as a member of the public relations firm hired by Sci-Fi to help get the government to open up documents on the subject. CNN.com, reporting on the conference,

179

quoted Podesta as saying "It is time for the government to declassify records that are more than 25 years old and to provide scientists with data that will assist in determining the true nature of the (UFO) phenomena."

The Las Vegas Journal quoted Podesta as stating, "I think it's time to open the books on questions that have remained in the dark on the question of government investigations of UFOs." He referred to the cover-up as "unthinking secrecy."

During Clinton's tenure, he instituted Executive Order #12958, which called for the declassification of documents older than twenty-five years. The order was responsible for moving many government documents into the light of public scrutiny. Eight hundred million pages of documents were declassified between 1995 and 2000.

Be that as it may, investigator Stanton Friedman (mentioned earlier) had to endure a court battle under the Freedom of Information Act to get his hands on FBI and CIA documents relating to UFOs. The agencies claimed that certain documents did not fall under FOIA protection, as they were a matter of "national security". Bear in mind that these are the same agencies that, for years, insisted they had *no* documents related to the UFO problem, they were no longer interested in UFO reports and that UFOs were "*not* a matter of national security."

Friedman finally won a partial victory in that the documents requested were turned over to him with those segments considered to be of national security blacked out. As he began plodding through the reams of documented evidence, there was a line or two blacked out here and there. Then a paragraph or two blacked out. Then, entire pages were completely camouflaged in black ink!

Other investigators, like John Greenewald, Jr., author of "Beyond UFO Secrecy" and webmaster of "The Black Vault" website, have encountered the same frustrating black ink coating the red tape of governmental secrecy. However, enough information remained in the documents to put the puzzle pieces together and form a clear picture of the seriousness in which the American Government views the UFO problem.

The NSA (National Security Agency) is immune from the Freedom of Information Act for obvious reasons. However, under a previous agreement between the United States and Canada, these sensitive documents are shared between these two allied countries. John Greenewald phoned Canada's equivalent to the NSA and found their Freedom of Information Act to be more relaxed than that of the U.S. With the proper forms and a few dollars, he was able to secure many UFO cases documented by credible witnesses in the United States. These documents had been submitted by the U.S Air Force, FBI, CIA and many other agencies from 1969 to present day, proving that America's interest in the UFO phenomenon has never waned.

Chapter 12
UFOs in the News

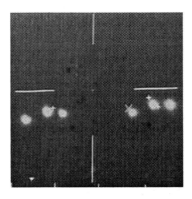

This image, taken from video, shows unidentified flying objects in the skies over southern Campeche State, filmed by Mexican Air Force pilots on March 5, 2004. (AP Photo)

Associated Press. May 12, 2004.

Mexico City — Mexican air force pilots filmed 11 unidentified flying objects in the skies over southern Campeche State, a Defense Department spokesman confirmed Tuesday.

A videotape made widely available to the news media Tuesday shows the bright objects, some sharp points of light and others like large headlights, moving rapidly in what appears to be a late-evening sky.

The lights were filmed March 5 by pilots using infrared equipment. They appeared to be flying at an altitude of about 3,500 metres and allegedly surrounded the air force jet as it conducted routine anti-drug trafficking vigilance in Campeche. Only three of the objects showed up on the plane's radar.

"Was I afraid? Yes," said radar operator Lieutenant German Marin in a taped interview made public Tuesday. "A little afraid because we were facing something that had never happened before.

"I couldn't say what it was . . . but I think they're completely real," added Lt. Mario Adrian Vazquez, the infrared equipment operator. Lt. Vazquez insisted there was no way to alter the recorded images.

The plane's captain, Major Magdaleno Castanon, said the military jets chased the lights "and I believe they could feel we were pursuing them." When the jets stopped following the objects, they disappeared, he said.

A Defense Department spokesman confirmed Tuesday the videotape was filmed by members of the Mexican air force. The spokesman declined to comment further and spoke on customary condition of anonymity.

The video was first aired on national television Monday night then again at a news conference Tuesday by Jaime Maussan, a Mexican investigator who has dedicated the last 10 years to studying UFOs.

"This is historic news," Mr. Maussan said. "Hundreds of videos (of UFOs) exist, but none had the backing of the armed forces of any country. The armed forces don't perpetuate frauds."

Mr. Maussan said Secretary of Defense Gen. Ricardo Vega Garcia gave him the video April 22.

Associated Press: www.globeandmail.ca/servlet/story/RTGAM.20040511.wufos0511/BNS tory/Front/Reuters: www.reuters.com/newsArticle.jhtml?type=scienceNews&storyID=510989 1

This quote from Stephen Bassett of the Paradigm Research, http://www.paradigmclock.com/ on the Mexico sighting:

"Consider this hypothetical: Secretary of Defense, Donald Rumsfeld, releases gun camera footage of very unusual objects encountered on a military mission. He gives this footage to an extraterrestrial phenomena researcher to show on 20/20. Question: Do you think Secretary Rumsfeld does this without approval from the White House? The Mexico footage was released with the approval of President Vicente Fox and was a message to the United States that Mexico, among other nations, is growing impatient with the U. S. dominated disclosure time table."

* * *

Mexican Air Force Sees UFO on FLIR.

Kim Shaffer writes, "In all the conjecture and debunking attempts concerning the Mexican forward looking infra red 'FLIR' that tracked UFO's on March 5 over Campachee. 'FLIR' is a piece of equipment with a lens aperture, which collects thermal images. The 'FL' in FLIR simply means what it says, - 'forward looking'. Everything on this Earth, unless it is frozen at absolute zero degrees, has an 'IR' or thermal signature. The higher the thermal signature (the hotter the object), the brighter the thermal image seen on the IR device – or in this case – seen on film. Humans cannot see infrared, as it is beyond our range of vision.

"The debunkers claim the objects as weather balloons. Helium is what makes weather balloons rise. Helium is not hot. The objects, IF they were weather balloons, would be invisible to the 'FLIR' device, being the same temperature as the rest of the sky.

"One scientist claimed the objects were gas pockets. Gaseous anomalies may well occur in space where there is nothing acting on the gas. Gas would simply dissipate and not form objects that appear as solid in our turbulent atmosphere. Again, gas clouds do not give off a thermal signature, which these objects did. If these anomalies were 'gas' and were obviously hot, why were they not rising, as hot gas would do? They never rose above 11,000 feet.

"Another scientist claimed it was ball lightning. I remember an incident which happened at Fort Stewart Georgia when I participated in war games and was using an infrared night vision device. I was looking through the device at an approaching armored assault, when a lightning strike hit miles away. I was blinded in that eye for maybe an hour and thought I had ruined my eye. This is what lightning will do to an 'IR' or a FLIR device. This lighting heat or thermal energy would be tens of thousands of degrees and would completely wash out the image on such a device. The sighting lasted for over fifteen minutes; ball lightning is usually measured in seconds.

"Lastly, we are discussing a calibrated piece of optical equipment. The FLIR was designed to 'see' aircraft engine thermal energy in the hundreds of degrees Fahrenheit. Why can we not see to it that the designers and manufacturers of this device are given the video which, when analyzed, will give them real "thermal values" from the image. Only they would have this information and no one is asking for it.

"This is the best evidence to have been given to us in some time so why don't we take advantage of it and follow through, contact FLIR and ask for a thermal analysis of the clip?"

Kim A. Shaffer, State Director, MUFON TN (EAST)

(Editor's Note): Another explanation for the 2004 Mexico incident is "oil rigs" off shore in the Gulf of Mexico. Dr. Bruce Maccabee, a civilian physicist for the Navy, a prominent UFO investigator and photographic analyst for MUFON, has done an exhaustive analysis and report on the case that may be downloaded by going to http://brumac.8k.com/MexicanDOD5mar04/

In the report, he acknowledges all of the prosaic explanations proposed to date, to include the "oil rig" hypothesis, and offers scientific and photographic evidence to rebut them.

Maccabee had full access to the data collected by the Mexican military, to include the taped conversations between the pilots and ground control. There were radar returns that showed the objects pacing the planes, although, at one point, the returns were lost but came back. The pilot's conversation indicated that the objects were "above the clouds", moving about seventy-five miles per hour.

In Maccabee's conclusion, he has left the door open for further evidence. But, as you will see from the complete report, the possibility of the objects being "oil wells" is remote at best.

Then again, there are those who would rather believe that we humans have "oil rigs" traveling at 75 miles per hour above the clouds than to concede to the possibility of a more advanced race of beings visiting this little primitive ball of mud.

David Twichell.

* * *

BELGIUM AND FRANCE: NEW UFO WAVE.

On January 1, 2002, Jeff (Rense) told me (George Filer) during his radio show about the considerable upswing in UFO activity in Belgium and France, including the Flying Black Triangles. (I'm a regular guest on the Jeff Rense Radio Show, the first Tuesday of the month.) Jeff Rense reports that the Flying Triangles are back in Europe, particularly in Belgium and France!

In 1989 and 1990, the Flying Triangles were reported almost nightly. In mid-October a young lady reported a UFO in the Avioth area of northern France. The very dark, square-shaped UFO had four lights, one at each corner. Last month, UFO sightings became widely reported on the TV news and in popular newspapers, reporting that "A new wave is hitting Belgium." One of the more popular Belgian papers, "La Derniére Heure" (The Last Hour), on December19th, featured a detailed report by one of its noted writers, Gilbert Dupont, about the return of the triangles with new reports of blue lighting on the underside of the craft, as well as orange and yellow.

Belgian TV interviewed two young men in Namur who reported a very close encounter with a silver, cylindrical-shaped UFO. Triangles are being reported with varying lighting structures: red, green and blue lights, as well as UFOs that are orange in color.

Many of the Belgian UFO organizations believe the Flying Triangles are US military related, considering the presence of SHAPE (Supreme Headquarters Allied Powers Europe), in Brussels, Belgium. The craft cause vibrations that rattle windows and dishes. They are described as huge flying buildings, possibly two triangles stuck together.

Thanks to Jeff Rense who has a detailed report on his web site at www.Rense.Com.

* * *

Article from the Marco Island Sun Times.
UFOs and Aliens in Southwest Florida.

Steven Skelley a minister who writes for the Marcos Island Sun Times.

I was surfing the Web one night when I came across a Web site that offered eyewitness accounts of alien sightings right here in Southwest Florida. The site, UFOinfo.com, also lists alien sightings from across the USA. One such listing is from a Collier County resident who was traveling I75. According to his account, "I noticed an object in the sky. It had three tiny white lights and came closer at a very slow pace. I was able to make out the shape very distinctly as a low flying triangle. It was well below the clouds and its lights were at each apex. The lights did not illuminate any portion of the craft. I pulled over to the side of the road and shut off the engine to listen. It was traveling west and passed by in three minutes. The window was down and the engine off but there was no sound. I turned the ignition to aux to have the radio on. I looked back and the object was gone. I got out of my van and looked around, but there was nothing, not even contrails. I noticed the van's digital clock lost two minutes."

A Web site named UFOs.about.com, lists this Southwest Florida alien encounter. "James W. Flynn was camping in the Everglades when, shortly after midnight, he saw an object that he thought was an airplane in trouble descend about a mile away. He drove his swamp buggy towards the light, which was visible through the trees. About a quarter of a mile from the light, the vegetation became so dense that he could not proceed except on foot. As he got close to the object, he saw it was a large cone-shaped structure hovering close to the ground; it was about 75 feet wide and 25 feet high and had rows of windows with light shining through them. As he neared the object, a beam of light struck him in the forehead, knocking him unconscious and leaving him temporarily blinded. The UFO then vanished, leaving behind burned trees and vegetation. A medical examination showed impairment of muscle and tendon reflexes, which a doctor did not believe could be faked."

Science fiction movies have been using the UFO and alien theme for decades. Do you believe there are aliens among us? I do. Did you know the Bible talks about beings that are "not of this place, not of this world?" And not just anyone in the Bible, but Jesus himself talks about what many people would call "aliens, beings not of this world." If you look up the word "alien" in a dictionary, you'll find definitions like; "someone different, a nonnative, someone from another place." Remember that: someone different and from another place. An alien.

Let's look at what Jesus says in the book of John chapter 17 verses 1, 14-17. Jesus looked toward heaven and prayed: "Father ... I have given them your word and the world rejects them, for they are not of this world any more than I am of this world. My prayer is not that you take them out of the world but that you protect them from the evil one. They are not of this world, even as I am not of it. Set them apart by the truth. Your word is truth."

We could translate the prayer in passage like this; "God, I have given people your word and now other people reject them, other people think they're different. It's true. They are now as alien to this world as I am. Protect them. Continue to set them apart by the truth of your word."

Being a Christian is about allowing God to make us different from what we were and allowing him to make us something alien to the normal way the world works and people are. The Bible says the way to destruction is wide and most people choose to go that way. But the way to righteousness is narrow and few people choose it. The few, the different, the alien.

God's plan is not for us to be the same as most people. Most people are on the wrong path, the wide way. God's plan is not for us to have the same mindset as our peer group. They're probably not living their lives according to God's truth. God's plan is not for us to be tolerant or accepting of things that are wrong, even when most people do.

God's plan is for us to be made into something different. A new person on the inside. Someone in a right relationship with the creator of the universe and everything in it. God's plan is for us to be so filled with his life that we look and think and work in a way that's alien to the rest of the world. God's plan is for us to be so filled with his light and love in this darkened world that we're like Jesus; we just don't fit in anymore.

That is what Jesus was saying: God, they're so filled with your word and your plan and your light and your truth that, just like me, they're alien. They're sanctified. They're set apart. They're not of this world.

There are aliens among us, beings who are not of this world. People who have been set apart, made different on the inside by God himself. This week, let's ask God to mold us into what we were really meant to be, not just what everyone else is. Let's choose to become aliens to this world.

Thanks to Steven Skelley, an ordained minister. ©Marco Island Sun Times 2004

This column reprinted with the permission of the Marco Island Sun Times.

* * *

"UFOs are real!"
By CHARLES SLAT ctslat@monroenews.com
The Monroe News (Monroe, Ohio) May 14, 2005. http://www.monroenews.com/articles/2005/05/14/news/news03.txt

"It might not be an alien spacecraft, but if it's unidentified, it's flying and it's an object, it's a UFO," investigator says.

Jarid Riggs sometimes has seen strange things in the night sky.

"When we've had bonfires in our backyard, I've seen flashing lights move around in a circle," said the 9-year-old Monroe boy. "Some of the lights are red and some are blue."

He can't explain them, and neither can William J. Konkolesky, Michigan director of the Mutual UFO Network (MUFON), a non-profit group of volunteers that investigates reports of unidentified flying objects (UFOs).

"UFOs are real," Mr. Konkolesky said Friday night during the 5th annual Boys Night In program at the Monroe County Library System's Ellis Reference and Information Center. "That's a pretty bold statement to make, but what is a UFO but an unidentified flying object? If you see something up in the sky and you don't know what it is, it's a UFO."

Jarid was among about two-dozen kids who came with dads or friends to learn about UFOs and what they really might be.

Mr. Konkolesky, a Clawson resident, noted that people have been seeing unexplained things in the skies since ancient times. Those sightings have been chronicled in art from as far back as the year 700 and even in cave paintings from before 7000 BC.

He discussed some of the most celebrated cases, from the reported crash of a UFO near Roswell, New Mexico -- first reported to be a flying saucer and then discounted as a weather balloon - to the lights seen near Hillsdale in 1966 that Air Force investigators declared was "swamp gas."

The Michigan MUFON chapter gets about two dozen reports a year, most of them involving "lights streaking across the sky," he said. He said the planet Venus, low on the horizon, also often is reported as a UFO.

One of the latest reports to Michigan MUFON occurred on September 29, 2004 when a Milford man said he saw something "bigger than a football field" moving slowing across the field near his home. Earlier in the morning, many people reported seeing strange lights near Detroit Metropolitan Airport, though airport radar detected no craft.

Later, the same Milford man, whom Mr. Konkolesky described as a credible witness, said he saw a "wedge-shaped object, kind of like a fat horseshoe, flying through the sky." He said it was about the size of a car and it landed in his backyard before then alighting and flying away.

"So far, we're still looking into that and we can't explain it either," Mr. Konkolesky said.

Mr. Konkolesky told The Evening News that he believes extraterrestrials have visited earth "because of what I've seen and haven't been able to explain." When he was 18, he and some friends traveling in a car witnessed a strange light whizzing overhead. After that, he got involved in MUFON, he said.

But he acknowledged that many people report sightings that are common objects that they just haven't seen before or haven't seen under a certain set of circumstances.

He asked his audience why they thought aliens would even want to visit earth.

"Maybe they want to see what we do to have fun, like baseball," said Patrick Mulpas, 11, of Monroe.

"Do you think aliens would attack us?" Jarid asked Mr. Konkolesky.

"I would think that if they wanted to attack us, they would have done it a long time ago," he said. "They probably would have already done it if they had bad intentions."

On the Net: www.mimufon.org

* * *

Australia: UFO Triangle Formation.

MELBOURNE - Phenomena Research Australia reports that on August 23, 2004, two large formations of light were captured on video from a location near Pascoe Vale. The objects were in two groups of three lights and each group was in a triangle formation. The video was taken by Mark and Janine Blease of Melbourne and shown on Channel 7 TV.

A check of Melbourne Air Traffic Control, show no aircraft at that location or in formation at that time and no radar contact was reported. This morning on the Breakfast Show, Radio station 3 AW Melbourne, spoke to the couple who took the video and they said it was quite a surprise and very spectacular, offering no explanation. Other people called the radio station and some did come onto the "talk back" line to support the sighting.

Thanks to John Auchett, Director Phenomena Research Australia [PRA] Mulgrave, Victoria, Australia, 3170 and Skywatch International.

* * *

India: Flying Triangles near Himalayas.

DRANG DRUNG GLACIER -- Lara Mohani of the India Daily reports:

A little girl in Zanskar on the India China border - Indian side of the Himalayas, reported a silent triangular, high-speed, very large air ship in the sky.

Sources say there is a concentration of Asia's largest number of nuke missiles from China and India hidden deep in the earth. Neither Chinese nor Indians allow anyone to go close to these installations. These craft are similar to those seen in the US. Definitely these are frictionless, anti-gravity propelled, flying machines that are UFOs.

The aircraft are said to be either extra-terrestrial or secret advanced US Air Force planes. But when during Chemrey Angchok festival in Ladakh last week, several local villagers gathered to discuss these strange objects, Indian news reporters got curious. According to the villagers these strange triangular objects have been visiting over the last five years and their numbers are increasing. They are silent and can move through the air extremely slowly, so slowly that any conventional aircraft would stall and crash. They can suddenly vanish at tremendous speed, far faster than any known machine built by man could ever possibly move. They are translucent; their flying beacons don't project light, as would a normal earth-made stream of light, and so on.

Are these "extra-terrestrial UFOs" or spy machines of some unknown country? The area is sensitive and it is possible that some countries are watching this area. Also, it is possible that the extra-terrestrials are watching the nuke installations of India and China.

Thanks to India Daily.

http://www.indiadaily.com/editorial/11-25g-04.asp

* * *

UNITED KINGDOM.

YORK -- BBC Radio. York residents reported UFO activity of large flying triangles between June 15 and July 15. Accounts had also appeared in the local press. Journalists have been told there was no RAF or joint NATO exercises that could be responsible for the sighting reports, so everyone is asking the same question: "what could they possibly be?"

An interesting video tape of a red flying wing anomalous object, filmed over London on July 1, 2001, by Christopher Martin, can be observed at the UFO Magazine website.

Thanks to Graham W. Birdsall, Editor of UFO Magazine [UK] http://www.ufomag.co.uk/

* * *

BULGARIA ALSO REPORTS UFOs.

KIRCAALI -- It has been reported that the residents of the Vizrojdentsi district have been witnessing a show by UFOs every night. The "Standart" daily newspaper, published in Sofia, wrote that ongoing visits by UFOs for three days were first reported by 14-year-old youngster, Anton Dimitrov. Anton describes the first UFO as a triangle-shaped bright red object. "Two other UFOs joined the first one making 8 or 10 circles in the sky and then disappeared over Kircaali Dam," he says.

Thanks to Sirius UFO Space Sciences Research Center, Turkey

* * *

UNITED KINGDOM RESEARCH PROJECT.

It is believed some of the UFO sightings in the UK may be do to a secret British research project. A small 30-foot, black triangular craft has been seen by members of the public on the ground at Warton Airfield (British Aerospace). It is believed that it is a prototype UAV, designated Halo and can perform up to 9G turns. It has been seen by numerous people in the UK. Test flights are accompanied by a Tornado fighter aircraft, call sign "Tarnish 3." An official government notice has been served on the BBC warning it not to report on Britain's Stealth program. A larger triangular craft is also in operation over Britain and has been seen landing at Boscome Down. A black triangular "craft", first witnessed by hundreds in the Hudson Valley, NY in '88 and '89 then by thousands in Belgium in '89 and '90 and more recently by thousands more in Britain, has been "heavily D-Noticed" by the government. For this reason the BBC will not be reporting on the triangle craft, because the craft may be part of a new secret military project that must be protected under the secrecy laws.

In an incredible letter obtained by The People' Newspaper, Minister Earl Frederick Howe reveals that all RAF station commanders are under orders to report UFO sightings. And he adds: "So far as the existence of extraterrestrial life forms is concerned we remain open-minded." The letter was sent to Don Valley, Labour Member of Parliament (MP), and Martin Redmond, who is trying to break the MoD's veil of secrecy over flying saucers. He is concerned about a UFO with a red and green rotating light that appeared over East Anglia last month. It was tracked by radar at RAF, Neatishead and RAF Northwood for several hours as it hovered in the sky before flying 50 miles down the coast. It was also spotted by the crews of a tanker and civilian plane, while a video - now in the Ministry of Defense (MoD's) hands - was taken by police. "It's incredible no aircraft were scrambled when a target was picked up so close to the coast," Mr. Redmond told Defense Secretary Michael Portillo.

"This raises questions on the way we guard the UK Air Defense Region." Earl Howe replied that the RAF does not respond unless there is evidence UK airspace has been "compromised". He added: "To date no sighting has provided such evidence. "We do not investigate further or provide an explanation for what might have been observed."

Mr. Redmond is accusing the Government of covering up information on UFOs and says if there is no defense threat, there is no excuse for secrecy either. "The answers I've been given lead me to think there is something more to this," added the Member of Parliament (MP.)

"The only thing I know for sure is this whole issue is shrouded in secrecy." Last week Defense Minister Nicholas Soames refused to reveal how many UFOs RAF pilots have spotted since 1966. He said the information would cost too much to obtain. But he added: "Unidentified contacts penetrating UK airspace are identified by all available means, including interception."

Thanks to Nigel Nelson The People Newspaper, 10th November 1996. uk.ufo.nw and John Burtenshaw. jburtens@bournemouth.ac.uk

* * *

TRANSCRIPT OF EVENING FOX NEWS, July 26, 2002:

SHEPARD SMITH: The nighttime skies over the nation's capital alive with blue and orange lights streaking across the sky, so say a lot of panicked people who called in to a radio station, no joke here. American fighter jets in hot pursuit. NORAD confirmed to FOX News that two F-16s *did* scramble but found nothing!

A mystery in the sky above Andrews Air Force Base . . . that's the one the President uses. Fox reports now from Brian Wilson live in our D.C. newsroom. Brian?

BRIAN WILSON: Fair to say, Shepard, a lot more questions than answers at this point but something strange was going on in the Maryland night sky. Here is what we know; 1:00 AM, the folks at NORAD saw something they couldn't identify in Maryland airspace, not far from the nation's capitol. The track it was taking caused them some concern, so they scrambled two DC Air National Guard jets to check things out.

Now, DC Air National Guard confirms that two F-16s from the 113th Wing were vectored to intercept whatever it was that NORAD was worried about. However, when the pilots got where they were supposed to be, they said they didn't see anything when they arrived on the scene. Now, the folks at NORAD would not provide details about the exact location, direction or speed of the object they were tracking.

Now, independently, a number of folks who live in Waldorf, Maryland, which is not far from Andrews Air Force Base and not far from the nation's capitol, called local radio station WTOP to say that, about the same time, they witnessed a fast moving, bright blue light in the sky. They go on to claim that the light was being chased by military jets. One witness tells the radio station that the jets were right on its tail. Quote: "as the thing would move, a jet was right behind it." End of quote.

An investigation is underway. But National Guard spokesman Captain Sheldon Smith says (and this is another quote), "We don't have any information about funny lights." By the way, this just happens to be the 50th anniversary of a series of still-unexplained sightings over the nation's capitol, a story that made banner-headline news in 1952.

Shepard, we'll continue to watch for this.

SHEPARD SMITH: And now it can be told. Brian Wilson, live in Washington.

Thanks to Kenny Young.

(EDITOR'S NOTE): UFOs were seen from New York to Washington D.C. by multiple witnesses. NORAD was apparently tracking the UFOs on radar and launched two F-16 fighters to intercept but the fighters were unable to locate the UFOs. The incident appears to be a repeat of the 1952, Washington DC over flights.

HISTORY OF WASHINGTON FLYOVER.

Fifty years ago last weekend, FAA controllers had multiple UFOs on their radars and, when these were reported to the Air Force, F-94 interceptors were launched to chase the intruders. Radar Operator, Howard Conklin, says, "The radar operators knew the UFO's location and track so, when they got near, the operators went outside to see the UFO visually as well."

The Air Force decided to deny the reports and claimed they were false radar returns caused by temperature inversions. Rumors persist that there was an unannounced loss of one F-94, but this report has never been confirmed. Conklin also revealed the UFOs came back the next night and were tracked sweeping across the Capital but this time the Air Force was not informed. Once again the UFOs were defeated, not by technology, but by obscuration and denial.

This week's radar track did not look like meteors, satellites or false radar returns or NORAD would not have launched fighters. For weeks, many witnesses have reported UFOs in the area. NORAD stated that the UFO might have been a small plane that disappeared from radar by landing at a small airfield. Based on the New York sighting earlier in the evening, it is likely that the UFOs were spotted on radar for an extended period and moved toward the Washington DC restricted area.

Space Command denies other forms of contact. F-16 pilots at Andrews are on 24-hour alert status. While I was in alert status our requirement was that, once we received the order to launch, we had to be airborne in a maximum of ten minutes. The pilots would need to be ready near their fueled and armed aircraft. Engine start and taxi to the end of the runway takes a few minutes. It appears the response time was good. It is not surprising that the UFOs could not be tracked. They are exceptionally fast and maneuverable and employ a series of tactics to trick the pilots and radar.

I would be happy to provide an intelligence briefing including video to the ANG to help them successfully track the UFOs.

George Filer.

* * *

UKRAINE: UFO AIRSHOW CRASH, BIGGEST UFO STORY OF 2002.

SKNILOV AERODROME -- A stunning video was shown on Ukrainian ICTV and Russian television showing an unidentified flying object skimming a Ukrainian fighter jet moments before it crashed into a crowd of aviation enthusiasts, killing 84 people on July 27, 2002. This is the most tragic air show crash in history. The crashing Su-27 fighter killed 27 children and wounded 199.

The video clearly shows a UFO, which is mentioned by the TV commentator, that passes near the descending Su-27 fighter that killed so many. The UFO is a clearly visible long white cylinder, or cigar-shaped, that quickly flew directly behind the Su-27 for 1.5 seconds. The stunning discovery was made due to the detailed analysis of the videotape by the investigation commission and speculation is circulating it could have been a factor in the crash.

General Evgeniy Marchuk, Head of the state commission on investigation, analysis of the flight recorder indicated that all systems of the aircraft, including engines, were functioning normally and Colonel

Vladimir Toponar and pilot-inspector, Colonel Uriy Egorov safely ejected out of the aircraft. Some other experts conclude that human factor -- bravado of the pilots and insufficient organization by the flight directors of this air show -- caused the tragedy.

According to Colonel Vladimir TOPONAR, the pilot said, "At a certain moment the SU-27 became uncontrollable." He and his copilot were then forced to bail out but stayed with the plane until the last possible moment to avoid even greater loss of life.

The hypothesis that the UFO could have accidentally influenced the aircraft's stability is not totally excluded. The plane appeared to stall and the UFO may have tried to save it or the UFO's momentum may have helped to cause the stall as the object crossed planes course.

High-ranking officials have denied the existence of the UFO despite it being clearly visible on the video.

Thanks to Anton Anfalov, Research Specialist for MUFON. See Filer's Files UFO Center Views. http://www.nationalufocenter.com/

* * *

POPULAR MECHANICS (February 10, 2004) COVER: "WHEN UFOs ARRIVE".

Science Editor Jim Wilson of Popular Mechanics Magazine has written another great article about UFOs. I feel it is an article you should not miss. The cover page of Popular Mechanics headline reads: WHEN UFOs ARRIVE. It goes on to say, on page 64, "Startling Physical Evidence They Can't Explain Away."

At long last, scientists have their hands on the proof skeptics say does not exist. In headlines it says, "Most professional scientists never bother to look at the evidence. Dogmatic dismissals are taken at face value."

(Editor's Note): Jim has data on French government landings and samples of the Ubatuba debris. Thanks Jim for a fair article about UFOs. It's very refreshing to see a major magazine handle the UFO situation fairly. This issue is worth buying to show your friends.

* * *

WASHINGTON DC: F-16S SCRAMBLED TWICE.

CNN announced, "Two Air Force F-16 fighters were scrambled Monday, December 16, 2002, at 10:30 AM, after radar detected a potential violation of the 15-mile restricted flight zone around the nation's capital, said officials with the North American Aerospace Defense Command. Officials speculated either a flock of birds or an anomaly caused by high winds resulted in the radar reading, which indicated a possible flight violation 18 miles northwest of Reagan National Airport. F-16s maintained a combat air patrol over Washington for at least an hour and air traffic was halted briefly.

WBAY ABC Channel 2 News in Wisconsin reports that later that night, two more fighter jets were scrambled on December 17, 2002, to intercept a small plane over the nation's capital. The plane had flown into restricted airspace over Washington but officials determined it posed no threat and called off the intercept. The plane later landed in Martinsville, West Virginia.

Since the nine-eleven attacks, fighters have responded to more than 600 airspace security incidents.

Thanks to Kenny Young.

(Editor's Note): Bill Bean and others are regularly videotaping unknown flying craft over the area that is likely being picked up by radars. Any radar operator knows the difference between a balloon, birds and a UFO intruder.

George Filer.

* * *

The COMETA Report.

On July 16, 1999, French officials published a ninety-page report entitled, "UFOs and Defense: What Must we be Prepared For?" ("Les Ovni Et La Defense: A Quoi Doit-on se Préparer?"). The COMETA (Committee for in-depth studies) Report is the result of several years of study into the UFO phenomenon by top French military officials and scientists. The committee is an independent group of former auditors at the Institute of Advanced Studies for National Defense, or IHEDN. Before it was released publicly, it was sent to French President Jacques Chirac and Prime Minister Lionel Jospin.

The list of committee participants include:

General Bruno Lemoine, of the Air Force (FA of IHEDN), Admiral Marc Merlo, (FA of IHEDN).

Michel Algrin, Doctor in Political Sciences, attorney at law (FA of IHEDN).

General Pierre Bescond, engineer for armaments (FA of IHEDN).

Denis Blancher, Chief National Police Superintendent at the Ministry of the Interior.

Christian Marchal, chief engineer of the National Corps des Mines and Research Director at the National Office of Aeronautical Research (ONERA).

General Alain Orszag, Ph.D. in physics and armaments engineer.

They found that most sighting reports are either misidentifications of conventional objects or natural phenomena. A mere one or two percent were outright hoaxes. However, at least five percent were cases for which a prosaic explanation could not be offered. After citing several of these cases and the method of their investigation, the committee concluded that the phenomenon is real and not imaginary and that they were most likely of extraterrestrial origin.

Their recommendations are:

1.   Inform all decision-makers and persons in positions of responsibility.
2. Reinforce means of investigation and study at SEPRA.
3. Consider whether UFO detection has been taken into account by agencies engaged in surveillance of space.
4. Create a strategic committee at the highest state level.
5.   Undertake diplomatic action with the Unites States for cooperation on this most important question.
6.   Study measures that might be necessary in case of emergencies.

In addition, the COMETA Report criticizes the United States for what it calls an "impressive repressive arsenal" on the subject. It accuses the U.S. of having implemented a disinformation and restrictive military regulation policy that prohibits public disclosure of UFO sightings.

They cited Air Force Regulation 200-2, "Unidentified Flying Objects Reporting," which prohibits public and media release of any information concerning unexplainable aerial phenomena. An even more dramatic example is the Joint Army, Navy, and Air Force Publication 146, which promises to prosecute anyone within its jurisdiction for disclosing reports of UFO sightings that are deemed relevant to U.S. security. This includes pilots, civilian agencies, merchant marine captains and even some fishing vessels.

Edgar Mitchell, former astronaut and the sixth man to walk on the moon, is one of many advocates of UFO disclosure. In commenting on the COMETA Report, he says, "it's significant that individuals of some standing in the government, military and intelligence community in France came forth with this."

Mitchell adds, "People have been digging through the files and investigating for years now. The files are quite convincing. The only thing that's lacking is the official stamp."

* * *

The Disclosure Project.

On May 9, 2001, a group calling themselves "The Disclosure Project" conducted a press conference at the prestigious National Press Club in Washington, DC. The standing-room only gathering of journalists, representing many countries, watched and listened as twenty high-ranking military and government officials, scientists and other insiders, paraded before the microphone. They were there to attest to the fact that there exists a "shadow government" comprising several covert (or black) operations that have reverse-engineered alien technologies from crashed disks of unknown origin. The first (known) crash having taken place in Roswell, New Mexico in July of 1947.

These twenty courageous men and women with impeccable credentials, represented four hundred and fifty like members seeking open congressional hearings where they were prepared to testify, under oath, to their first-hand knowledge of the phenomenon and its cover-up and present unimpeachable physical evidence to support their claims.

The press conference was to be webcast in real time and CNN News had agreed to broadcast it – providing it was a "slow news day". As luck (or the powers-that-be) would have it, Timothy McVey, key conspirator in the Oklahoma City bombing case, who was awaiting his execution on Death Row, was granted a stay. He hadn't sought one; it wasn't the day set for the execution – the stay was simply "proclaimed". Big news day! CNN's coverage of The Disclosure Project's news conference was pre-empted.

But there was still the webcast! Bad luck again. The signal for the conference was over-ridden and scrambled by someone – somewhere. But the web technicians in charge of the broadcast were able to override the firewall and, after an hour of dead air, the balance of the conference went out to millions over the World Wide Web. It was also archived at the project's web site (http://www.disclosureproject.org). VHS videotapes were made available, as well as the book "Disclosure", compiling highlights of the testimonies from sixty-eight of the members, was written and released by Dr. Steven M. Greer, MD, the projects founder and host.

The skeptical media politely began listening to the testimonials and blandly applauded them as they finished and yielded the podium to the next witness. Each member had been allotted five minutes to state their credentials and their involvement with various UFO cases. Each member completed his or her testimony with, "I am prepared to testify before Congress that what I am saying is the truth."

As the press conference progressed, the applause became louder and more sincere. By the time all twenty had stated their case and Dr. Greer summarized the proceedings, the majority of the packed house had seemingly reached the conclusion that this was not a put-on. The Disclosure Project was for real. Its members had nothing to gain and only their hard-earned reputations to lose by attempting to perpetrate a hoax against the public. Not to mention the loss of their very freedom, should they lie under oath before a Congressional Assembly.

(Excerpt from "Global Implications of the UFO Reality", by David E. Twichell. Infinity Publishing. © 2003.)

* * *

THE DISCLOSURE PROJECT CAMPAIGN STARTS NATIONWIDE.

BOULDER, COLORADO -- The Disclosure campaign got off to a great start on June 23, 2001, at the large auditorium at the University of Colorado. A capacity crowd was on hand to listen to Dr. Stephen

Greer and watch the video testimony of twenty government witnesses concerning UFO and extraterrestrial events.

He said he thinks people from outer space are monitoring Earth, in part to monitor nuclear weapons. "We in the Disclosure Project are asking that everyone help by writing or faxing letters to your senators and representatives asking for congressional hearings."

Not everyone agrees with Greer's approach that assumes the Aliens are friendly. Maureen Murphy of the "Allies of Humanity" said, "We don't disagree with Dr. Greer on the disclosure agenda, because the aliens are taking women against their will, they're taking the eggs, they're creating a race that will have an allegiance to the visitors."

(Editor's Note): My point of view is that very little real research is being done to determine what the Aliens are planning. They may be friendly and they may have ulterior motives. First we have to acknowledge they are here and then we have to determine their motives. Dr. David Jacobs of Temple University, in his book, "The Threat", indicates the abduction phenomenon is far more ominous than he had thought.

George Filer.

* * *

EXTRATERRESTRIAL PRESENCE IN OUR WORLD.

It's apparent the Disclosure Project testimonies are breaking new ground. The UFO community owes a debt of gratitude to the Disclosure Project staff for bringing together some of the most knowledgeable people in the UFO community. As a group they are the most well informed personnel I, personally, have met concerning UFOs and alien visitation. Most are firsthand witnesses who either saw UFOs or government documents while on active duty, proving the alien existence.

The testimony of over twenty government employees for the first time provides real evidence of the reality and existence of the phenomenon. I have attended dozens of conferences and most of the speakers had no real evidence and often they had wild stories that made me wonder if they were part of counter intelligence plot to confuse.

If you want to understand what is going on, I suggest www.disclosureproject.org. These persons have indicated they are willing to swear under oath in front of Congress that they are telling the truth. If they perjure themselves, they can go to jail and forfeit all retirement pay and allowances. I wonder if most speakers at conferences are prepared to do likewise.

In almost every field of endeavor, speakers are required to have credentials. But the field of UFOlogy often takes the wildest claims as a reason to give the speaker top billing. I would think the minimum requirement would be to have passed a test as a field investigator or to have worked in a sensitive government position.

I found the testimonies of the Disclosure Project witnesses to mesh and fit smoothly together, giving a much clearer picture of the entire UFO puzzle. The witnesses had a few minutes to talk at the National Press Conference but all could talk for hours about various cases. The witnesses and Dr. Greer have already come under attack and you can expect to see various criticisms of the witnesses.

Remember, in our nation one or two witnesses can convict and send a man to prison or death. Now, twenty witnesses can go into a court of law, or to the court of public opinion, and testify.

These twenty government personnel are backed up by another 400 witnesses waiting to testify, if given immunity. The witnesses include high-ranking personnel ready to appear in Congressional Hearings under oath to prove the existence of UFOs and their intelligent occupants.

* * *

THE FEDERAL AVIATION ADMINISTRATION.

In the US, the FAA controls the skies in peacetime. It seems reasonable to learn the truth about UFOs from representatives of the FAA such as John Callahan, the former head of Accidents and Investigations. He is one of the key witnesses of the Disclosure Project with stacks of government documents, computer printouts and video proving the existence of a UFO over Alaska in 1986. Several civilian and military radars tracked the object while multiple pilots saw the giant craft. It would be very difficult for anyone to dispute his testimony, which is backed by numerous witnesses.

He testified that he provided this information to key government personnel at a briefing at the Reagan White House. The CIA issued instructions that the meeting "never happened" and no information should be released to the public. John admits the FAA generally will not release information about UFOs to anyone – including the pilots.

John Callahan provided more real evidence in five minutes of testimony than I have heard in years of UFO conferences.

I encourage all in the field of UFOlogy to help uncover witnesses of similar stature. There are points of disagreement between Dr. Greer and myself, but he has reached the witnesses that can make a difference. It is time to publicize the testimony of witnesses of the caliber of John Callahan and the other speakers at the Disclosure Project.

George Filer.

Afterward

In the summer of 1962, I was fourteen years old. At about 11:00 P.M., one Saturday evening, I was going off to bed when something caught my attention out of the corner of my eye. I looked out the dark, open window to see a large patch of billowing smoke with seemingly bright, green lights behind it in a cloudless sky. I called to my parents to come and look. A minute later, the whole family was on the front lawn of our Westside Detroit home, gazing skyward.

It was dead quiet. Even the incessant chirping of the grasshoppers was absent. By this time the object was about two hundred feet directly above our house. It was no longer green but multicolored. The thick smoke was illuminated from the other side by huge electric lights. As the smoke began to clear above our heads, we could see giant, round floodlights of yellow, red and white. I don't recall most of what was said between us, other than, "What is it, Dad?" "How should I know?" But I do remember our commenting about the lack of sound.

"Look!" my mother called. Off to our right, a pillar of smoke was descending slowly to the ground. It was as if a jet of air was forcing it down. "It's the Second Coming!" my mother declared, equating this unexplainable scene with her religious upbringing. We looked back up over our heads to find that the lights had receded. The smoke had been so thick that it made the outline of this silent craft impossible to discern. Yet the huge, round, colored lights had still shown through. As bright as those lights were, they never illuminated the ground where we stood directly below.

As we continued to watch in silence, the smoke slowly dissipated, leaving only the cloudless, star-punctured sky. We returned to the safety of our house, unscathed. I do not remember talking at length with my family about the amazing "smoke and light show" we had just witnessed but it was over now and there was church to attend in the morning. We went to bed.

The following morning my father bought a copy of the Sunday morning Detroit Free Press to see if there was anything on this strange event. Sure enough, others had seen it. Some had reported it. We had not. The authorities wasted no time in handing us an explanation. *They were the northern lights!* With all the confusing technical jargon they could muster, a weak case was made for the northern lights making it all the way down to southern Michigan the night before.

"Those weren't the northern lights," I argued. "I've seen them in pictures and in movies. Northern lights are ribbons of different colored lights that streak across the sky. And they don't have smoke with them either!"

"Well," my mother assured me, "if they say they were the northern lights, then that's what we must have seen."

It might be understandable that a fourteen-year-old boy from Detroit couldn't tell the northern lights from a sack of onions. My mother, however, was born and raised in northern Michigan. My father had spent two years in Alaska. They had seen the northern lights on more than one occasion. Yet my father had stared into the night sky in awe and apprehension and my mother was all set for the Judgment Day!

It was at that very instant that I realized that we were being lied to. Not *us* in particular . . . not anyone who had witnessed the event and knew the difference. They were lying to those who had not seen it. Who would those people believe? The United States Government or us? *They* were the experts on the matter. They were the ones sworn to serve and protect . . . the ones who are paid with our tax dollars to tell us the truth about everything – especially what goes on in our air space.

And so the matter was dropped – at least as far as my family was concerned. *I* have never dropped the matter . . . nor will I! This event has set me on a life-long quest for the truth behind the bizarre object that parked slightly above treetop level, for ten to fifteen minutes, over our heads that night.

Throughout the years, I have studied the swelling caseload of documented sightings and abductions with an ever-growing fascination. As the reports become more bizarre, the evidence becomes more compelling.

A skeptical friend of mine once asked, "If these things are real, why is it that only farmers in Idaho see them?" I was so dumbfounded by the question that I don't believe I even offered an answer. I simply wondered where he had been for the past twenty-some years. I hope this book helps to dispel that old myth.

Times have changed since the 1950s and 60s. Although there is still the "fringe" stigma associated with the UFO/abduction phenomenon, the poles consistently indicate that more than fifty percent of Americans believe that Earth is being visited by more advanced civilizations from elsewhere in the cosmos. Admittedly, eighty percent of reported sightings are misidentifications of conventional aircraft or natural phenomena. For this reason, I have tried to select those reports whose descriptions tend to defy a conventional explanation. Surprisingly, only one percent of the reports received by investigative groups, such as the Mutual UFO Network (MUFON), prove to be outright hoaxes.

Despite the hundreds of reports received on a weekly basis, only eleven percent of UFO sightings are formally reported, due to fear of ridicule or a gross mistrust of our government and its denial policy regarding this phenomenon. Taking these statistics into consideration, an estimated 19,000 true unknowns are witnessed each year, worldwide.

As this book has demonstrated, ordinary, credible people, as well as trained observers, such as military and commercial airline pilots, police officers, astronauts and US Presidents, are among the numbers who have risked their career and good reputation to let the world know that we are far from alone in this vast universe.

I consider it a distinct honor to have worked in collaboration with George Filer on this project. Although many of the reports included herein *have* been investigated, most of them are "raw" reports from average citizens who have witnessed something unexplainable in conventional terms. The purpose of this book is *not* to offer the "smoking gun evidence" of the UFO phenomenon but rather to illustrate the volume of reported sightings and the diversity of witnesses universally.

I urge the reader to seek further evidence of the UFO reality by following Mr. Filer's weekly newsletter. Go to "The Filer's Research Institute" on the World Wide Web at http://www.nationalufocenter.com/

I would further urge you to report any anomalous aerial phenomena that you might be witness to in the future (or from your past) to the same URL as above. These reports are compiled and compared in an effort to substantiate previously reported accounts from the same date, time and location. The witness' anonymity is strictly protected upon their request. It is only through the public's concerted cooperation that dedicated investigators have amassed the volume of UFO sighting and abduction data to date. With your continued support, we will, one day, be able to say, unequivocally "We are not alone."

David E. Twichell
http://www.ufoimplications.com

Index

Geographic Locations.

ALASKA: 70, 198, 200
ARGENTINA: 107
ARIZONA: 86, 135
ARKANSAS: 4, 9
AUSTRALIA: 38-39, 45, 51-53, 66-67, 105-106, 123, 168, 188
AZERBAIJAN: 45
BELGIUM: 110, 184, 190
BELORUSSIAN: 107
BRAZIL: 122, 125, 127
BRITAIN: 54, 189-190
BULGARIA: 189
CALIFORNIA: 5-6, 8, 10, 13, 19, 22-23, 26, 28, 30, 58, 62-63, 65, 73, 81, 89-90, 93-94, 100, 102, 117-119, 123-124, 128-129, 136, 139, 142, 156-158, 163, 174, 177
CANADA: 34, 36-37, 39, 42, 44-47, 50-51, 53, 66-67, 94, 106-109, 112, 114, 123, 131, 137, 149-150, 177-180
CHISHOLM: 33
COLOMBIA: 36
COLORADO: 3, 117, 126-127, 196
CONNECTICUT: 7, 143
CRIMEA: 35, 43, 127
CUBA: 39
ENGLAND: 41, 48, 107, 110-111, 117-118, 124, 130, 145
FLORIDA: 17-18, 23, 63, 91, 97, 138, 143-144, 184-185
FRANCE: 114, 184, 195
GEORGIA: 13-15, 62, 73, 87-88, 90, 95, 108, 117, 144, 176, 183
GREECE: 37-38
HUNGARY: 33

IDAHO: 13, 200
ILLINOIS: 70, 74-75, 84, 92, 98, 120, 126, 137, 141
INDIA: 36, 51-52, 188-189
INDIANA: 15, 20, 23, 25-26, 86, 101
IOWA: 75
IRAN: 50, 131
ITALY: 48-49
JAPAN: 40
KANSAS: 4, 6, 60
LOUISIANA: 18, 55, 58, 125
MAINE: 62, 146
MALAYSIA: 45, 50
Maryland: 29, 175, 191
MASSACHUSETTS: 11
MEXICO: 113, 117, 126, 169, 181-183
MICHIGAN: 30, 75, 186-187, 200
MINNESOTA: 33, 85
MISSISSIPPI: 65, 94
MISSOURI: 74, 84-85, 122
NEBRASKA: 122
NETHERLANDS: 112
NEVADA: 8, 91, 118
NEWFOUNDLAND: 112
NEW HAMPSHIRE: 102
NEW JERSEY: 1, 3, 9, 11, 16, 21, 24-27, 72, 78, 80, 82-83, 140, 165
NEW MEXICO: 22, 179, 187, 195
NEW YORK: 2, 4, 7, 19-20, 26, 59, 63, 78-79, 89, 96, 130, 136, 146, 153, 168, 191-192
NEW ZEALAND: 49, 121
NORTH ATLANTIC: 97
NORTH CAROLINA: 8, 12, 14, 28, 145
OHIO: 10, 30, 79, 83, 85, 119-120, 156-157, 164-165, 186

OKLAHOMA: 4, 27, 87, 126
OREGON: 21, 27, 60, 66, 135, 146
PAKISTAN: 67
PENNSYLVANIA: 2, 17, 29, 64, 90, 98, 103
PHILIPPINES: 34
PORTUGAL: 133
RUSSIA: 44, 48-49, 107, 167, 169, 171, 192
SCOTLAND: 38, 124
SOUTH AFRICA: 34, 114
SOUTH CAROLINA: 71, 73, 97
TENNESSEE: 16-17, 28, 59, 151-152
TEXAS: 5, 7, 60, 93, 117, 143, 149, 169
UKRAINE: 35, 43-44, 192
UNITED KINGDOM: 41, 66, 118, 136, 189
UTAH: 64, 91, 96
VIRGINIA: 5, 8, 21, 71-72
WASHINGTON DC: 179, 191-193
WASHINGTON STATE: 3, 12, 16, 22, 28, 65, 78, 93, 99, 117, 120, 128, 138-140, 150
WEST VIRGINIA: 152, 194
WISCONSIN: 6, 25, 61, 64, 76, 80, 82, 86-89, 92, 121, 128, 141, 193

* * *

Proper Names.

Aho, Jim: 76-78, 80
Aldrin, Edwin "Buzz": 172
Anfalov, Anton A: 35, 43, 193
Armstrong, Neil: 172
Ashby, Jeffrey S.: 167
Barna, Reverend L. Damian: 140
Bassett, Stephen: 182
Birdsall, Graham W.: 189

Bishop, Ike: 13
Borman, Frank: 170
Brown, David: 95
Cernan, Eugene: 171
Carter, Jimmy: 176-177
Jeff Challender: 171
Chavez, William: 36
Clark, Larry: 19
Clinton, William: 179-180
Cooper, Gordon: 168-170
Corrales, Scott: 108, 123
Costigan, Conway: 66-67
Deruzhinsky, Vadim: 107
Dongo, Tom: 78
Eisenhower, Dwight D.: 177-178
Farshores, Jerry: 41, 48, 136
Filer, George: 3, 18, 20, 24, 34, 55, 63, 70, 106, 121, 165-166, 184, 192, 194, 197-198, 201
Ford, Gerald: 179
Ginther, Tom: 9
Glen, John: 173
Greer, Dr. Steven M., MD: 60, 196-198
Griffin, Andrew: 58-59, 126
Hamilton, William: 73-74, 89
Hickman, Jim: 27, 74, 132
Hoppe, John and Jenny: 87, 128
Howe, Linda Moulton: 156, 164-165
Huyghe, Patrick: 21
Jagger, Mick: 124
Johnstone, Dr. Annamarie: 128
Klopchin, Ray; 146
Konkolesky, Bill: 154, 186-188
Levengood, W. C.: 75
Lovell, James: 170-171
Maccabee, Dr. Bruce: 18, 183-184
Maussan, Jaime: 182

McDivitt, James: 170
Melroy, Pamela A.: 167
Meyer, Bonnie: 77-78
Mickelson, Cliff: 99, 138
Mitchell, Edgar D.: 173, 195
Novak, John: 78
O'Leary, Dr. Brian: 174
Olson, Mark A.: 64-65
Podell, Melvin: 100-101
Reagan, Ronald: 174-176
Rense, Jeff: 33-34, 38, 66, 184
Ritter, George W.: 156-166
Rosenfeld, Dave: 91
Schirra, Walter: 171
Schuessler, John F: 10, 103, 154
Shaffer, Kim: 7, 16-17, 151-152, 182-183
Sheets, Tom: 10, 13, 33, 62, 73, 87-88, 95-96, 143
Skelley, Steven: 184, 186
Slat Charles: 186
Slayton, Donald: 174
Smith, Shepard: 190-191
Stevens, Wendell C.: 2-3
Strieber, Whitley: 70, 160
Sugden, Roger: 15-16
Swearingen, Dr. Oren: 167
Taylor, Barry: 71
Taylor, Lynn: 24, 101-102
Trainor, Joseph: 11, 34, 37, 66, 84, 111, 121-122, 125, 134
Trout, Beverly: 75
Truman, Harry: 177, 179
Trust, Toine: 111, 112
Tutt, James Allen Jr.: 122
Twichell, David: 11, 25, 69, 126, 165, 184, 196, 201
Vike, Brian: 14, 28-30, 34, 36, 39, 45-46, 50-51, 53, 65-66, 94, 96-98, 102, 109-110, 113-115, 123-124, 132-133, 136, 150-151
Walters, Steve: 51
White, Ed: 170

Wolf, David A. 167
Xavier, Gregorio Sao: 133-134

* * *

Miscellaneous.

Abduction: 2, 75, 149-150, 153, 156, 158, 162, 197, 200-201
Astronaut: 9, 167-174, 195, 201
BBC: 52, 189-190
Boomerang: 62, 89, 97, 105
CNN: 179, 193, 196
COMETA Report: 194-195
Crop circles/formations: 11, 75, 165
Dogfight: 14, 48-49
Disclosure Project: 195-198
Flap: 90
FLIR: 182-183
India Daily: 188-189
ISUR: 10, 33, 73, 143
J-UFO Magazine: 40
Life Boat News: 37
Missing time: 149, 152-153
Mothership: 9, 36, 117-118, 128
MUFON: 3, 7, 9-10, 13, 15-17, 19-20.27, 56, 58-59, 62, 65, 70, 73, 75, 78-79, 87-88, 95-96, 100-101, 103, 122, 142-143, 146, 151-152, 154, 183, 186-188, 193, 201
Mutilation: 165
NASA: 54-55, 117, 167, 169, 172, 174
Popular Mechanics: 92, 193
SAUFOR: 34
SHnSASSY1: 36
Sirius: 37-38, 44, 48, 189
Skywatch: 70, 74, 89, 140-141, 188
Teardrop: 97

Trout Lake: 78, 140
UFO Magazine: 189
UFO Wisconsin: 6, 64, 92, 128
Wheel: 25
Winnipeg Sun: 47